WITHDRAWN

Shelby Foote

Shelby Foote

Novelist and Historian

ROBERT L. PHILLIPS, JR.

University Press of Mississippi
Jackson & London

Copyright © 1992 by the University Press of Mississippi

All rights reserved

Manufactured in the United States of America

The paper in this book meets the guidelines for permanence and durability of the Committee on Production Guidelines for Book Longevity of the Council on Library Resources.

95 94 93 92   4 3 2 1

Library of Congress Cataloging-in-Publication Data

Phillips, Robert L. (Robert LeRoy), 1940–
    Shelby Foote, novelist and historian / Robert L. Phillips, Jr.
        p.   cm.
    Includes bibliographical references and index.
    ISBN 0-87805-531-2
    1. Foote, Shelby—Criticism and interpretation.   2. Historical
fiction, American—History and criticism.   3. United States—
History—Civil War, 1861–1865—Historiography.   4. Southern States—
Historiography.   5. Southern States in literature.   I. Title.
PS3511.0348Z83   1992
813'.54—dc20   91-26636
                                                                  CIP

British Library Cataloging-in-Publication data available

Contents

for

LUCY

Preface

Shelby Foote has received considerable praise for his three-volume history of the Civil War. That is as it should be, for *The Civil War: A Narrative* is a well-researched, authoritative history even though, when the first and second volumes appeared in 1958 and 1963, professional historians questioned the adequacy of documentation. The voice in *The Civil War* is not that of a social scientist reporting the conclusions of his research, and the work is more than a history, an account of events. It is an engaging, well-told narrative; and more, it is a carefully designed and meticulously constructed work of literary art. Foote developed the artistry consciously through hard work, beginning with his first efforts in the high school newspaper in Greenville, Mississippi, continuing with the stories and reviews published in *The Carolina Magazine,* and continuing through the five novels he published before he began work on the history. The basic form of *The Civil War* resulted from years of experimentation, and even though the artistic structure for the history was set from the beginning of his work, the narrative strength of his style continued to develop over the twenty years of his writing.

Language is always a concern for the writer, for, after all, if the writer is an artist, then language is his medium. Art, particularly that made from the written word, is the means by which Western civilization has preserved what is most fundamental to its sense of self. The written word for Shelby Foote has heightened value as the medium for art. For him, to be sure, the word is not to be found in a computer file or on the typed page, or even in the printed book. These are all derivations from the hand-written manuscript crafted in careful calligraphy made with a dip-pen and India ink. His texts are highly crafted artifacts that he has taken pains to shape by hand, and they have the look of medieval manuscripts.

Shelby Foote: Novelist and Historian examines the development of Foote's artistry. The first chapter surveys Foote's biography; it is not an attempt to be exhaustive but rather describes events that in some way contributed significantly to his literary career. The examination of Foote's early stories and the first two novels completed in manuscript—*Tournament* and *Shiloh*—makes up the second chapter. *Tournament* was published in 1949, and *Shiloh*, although completed much earlier, appeared in print in 1952. Between these two came *Follow Me Down* (1950) and *Love in a Dry Season* (1951), and later, after *Shiloh* was published, came *Jordan County* (1954). These three novels, the subject of the third chapter, show Foote's development of form and structure and, in the process, explore the relevance of both to character and action. By 1952 he seems to have found the means that suited him best for shaping his literary artifact, and his sources were many. Early in his life he had found that formal education interfered with his reading—Proust, Faulkner, Joyce, Mann, Ransom, and James, among the many modern authors he read. In the later 1940s he had also developed an interest in music, and the classical form found in Mozart and Beethoven had considerable influence on the overall design, the form, of both the novels and *The Civil War*. The fourth chapter is a consideration of form and the writing of the history. The final chapter examines his latest novel, *September September,* which, like his other writing, explores the significance that narrative design, or plot, gives to action and character.

I have examined Foote's literary career largely in the light of his own comments and have speculated on how these comments reflect on, amplify, and explain his accomplishments, bringing his ideas into clearer focus. And, for essentially the same purpose, I have used the criticism of Allen Tate and John Crowe Ransom whose work Foote holds in high regard. Foote is thoroughly acquainted with literary history and the prevailing critical interest of his generation. My attempt here is to examine Foote's work from this historical perspective and to examine his remarks using, when necessary, the vocabulary of contemporary critical views to amplify or define his language. His texts reflect and enlarge upon the literary sensibilities of his times.

Foote's commentary and anecdotes, which producer Ken Burns included in his video documentary of the Civil War, contributed much to the success of the eleven-part series. It also made a large audience aware of what an engaging figure Foote is and has been over the years. There are three sources that have been particularly useful for this study. First is the collection of his letters in the Southern Historical Collection at the University of North Carolina at Chapel Hill. Foote's letters to his close friend Walker Percy comment on almost every stage of his artistic and intellectual development during the time he was writing his first five novels. Interviewers had discovered Foote long before the large number of television viewers discovered him. The interviews, most of them collected in *Conversations with Shelby Foote,* edited by William C. Carter and published in 1989, have proven a valuable source. Finally there is the series of lectures that Foote gave at Memphis State University in 1967 and that the university had the foresight to record on audio tape. Although he dislikes lecturing and will not write papers to be read in public, these lectures show how successful he could be at making erudition entertaining.

Recent criticism and theory have made us aware of how much we as readers bring to the interpretation of texts. The assumption that has guided this study is that, in investigating these sources, it is possible to make assertions about authorial intention. However, I do not presume to have found *the* way to read and understand Shelby Foote.

The texts of the novels and the history are the primary sources of my study, and I have quoted liberally from them. Foote's interest in the design of narrative has made summary occasionally unavoidable.

Born fifty-one years, seven months, and eight days after the surrender at Appomattox, Foote grew up in Mississippi, where defeat in war and the economic devastation of Reconstruction formed a living memory. At one point Foote wrote Percy that being southern was one of the strengths of his writing. A profound interest in the past and in tradition marks the modern southern writer and, using that as a measure, Foote is most certainly southern, but it would be a serious mistake to think of the past as the antebellum southern past of tradition, as the noblesse of white folk growing out of the history of black slavery. Rather, it is a past and a tradition that incorporate no less than recorded human history and all of the prehistory that is embedded in ritual, language, and the shape of art.

There are many people to whom I am deeply grateful for the contributions they have made to my study of Shelby Foote's career. Louis D. Rubin, Jr., has given me encouragement over the years, and his suggestions for this book have been extremely valuable to me.

The members of the staff of the Southern Historical Collection at the Wilson Library at the University of North Carolina at Chapel Hill were unfailingly helpful, as was the staff of the library at Memphis State University. James E. Kibler very kindly made available to me his correspondence with Foote. Kenneth Haxton followed Foote as editor of the Greenville High School *Pica* and was Foote's close friend in the years after World War II. His interest in music and his knowledge of Greenville history contributed much to my work, as did the comments and suggestions of a number of other Greenvillians, particularly Bern Keating, Clinton Bagley, Josephine Haxton, and LeRoy Percy. A Kellogg Foundation Grant to Mississippi State University afforded me valuable time for research. I must thank, too, those who have helped in the preparation of the typescript— Juanita Guyton, Tammy Bowling, Mary Anne Benoist, Carlene Fields, Janice Dyer, and especially Frances Gamble and Joyce Harris. Their patience has been wonderful.

I am indeed grateful to Shelby Foote for all of his help, especially for his permission to quote from his novels, *The Civil War: A Narrative*, the unpublished correspondence with Walker Percy in the Southern Historical Collection at the University of North Carolina at Chapel Hill, and the taped lectures at Memphis State University.

Portions of my discussion of "Child by Fever" appearing in Chapters III and IV are revisions of "Shelby Foote's Bristol in 'Child by Fever'" originally published in the *Southern Quarterly* 19 (Fall 1980), and reprinted in *Order and Image in the American Small Town,* edited by Peggy W. Prenshaw and Michael Fazio (Jackson: University Press of Mississippi, 1981).

Shelby Foote

Chapter I

The Wilds of the English Language

I n Greenville, Mississippi, in the years just before the United States entered World War II, Shelby Foote wrote a draft of what would turn out to be his first novel—*Tournament*. Foote was as concerned as anyone about the need to win the war against the German armies in Europe, and he had become a private in the National Guard in anticipation of the war. The strength of the military tradition in the South—the heritage of wars with the British, the Indians, and the Mexicans, made fast in the region by the Civil War against the northern invader—demanded soldiering in times of crisis, but amidst the gathering war, Foote found the time to write. "I was thrashing around in the wilds of the English language—happy as a colt in clover, learning how to write, and being pleased with things that I achieved," he said.[1] A love of literature, art forged from language, is the primary reason Foote became a writer; probably the reason most writers become writers. Another reason, one he shares with a number of modern writers is that the novel provided for him a means of searching out answers to "overwhelming questions." "[M]ost people," he told Evans Harrington, "seem to think that a writer is a man who has acquired wisdom and wishes to impart it to a reader. . . . So far as I am concerned, this is totally false. I, for one, write books looking for answers. . . . If I knew the answer I would not be interested in writing the book."[2] Inquisitiveness and his love for language led him to books, but the art of his fiction was shaped as well by the land, the natural world, its geography; by the past, the history of family and region; and by the notion that form and meaning in art lie close together.

The Jordan County and Bristol that Shelby Foote created as a setting for his early stories and for most of his other fiction bear a strong resemblance to Washington County and Greenville, Mississippi, where he was born in room 31 of the Greenville Sanatorium on 17 November 1916, the only child of Shelby Dade and Lillian Rosenstock Foote. "My daddy was working for a gin down in Rolling Fork and came up on a freight train when he heard my mother had gone into labor," he told an interviewer.[3] Greenville, in 1916 a small city of about eighteen thousand inhabitants, set beside the Mississippi River on the western edge of the flat, fertile Delta, was a rather remarkable and unusual place. Settlers of all nationalities had come there during the last three decades of the nineteenth century, from north and south by way of the river and from the east, Faulkner's hill country. There were Scotch-Irish and blacks, of course, like most places in the South, but there were also the Irish, Jews, Italians, Chinese, and even Syrians. "It was a melting pot," Foote often says.[4] This cultural diversity perhaps has something to do with the fact that an unusually large number of gifted writers have had formative connections with the region—Beverly Lowry, Hodding Carter, Walker Percy, Ellen Douglas, Brooks Haxton, Louise Crump, Ben Wasson, Ellen Gilchrist, and others. Foote gives credit to William Alexander Percy for the interest Greenville took in belles lettres.

Although Shelby, Jr., began first grade at the Starling Elementary School in Greenville, he had not lived there for most of the first six years of his life. Morris Rosenstock, Foote's maternal grandfather, had used his considerable influence to secure Shelby, Sr., a position with Armour and Company, the meat-packing firm. The corporation moved the family first to Jackson, then to Vicksburg, and briefly to Pensacola as Shelby, Sr., rose rapidly as an executive in the firm. Late in the summer of 1922, he was transferred to Mobile, but before the family had unpacked its belongings there in September, Shelby, Sr., died of blood poisoning. He had had a wisdom tooth extracted, and before that had healed he entered the hospital for minor surgery on his nose, failing to inform his doctor of the recent dental work. The poisoning could easily have been prevented.

It fell to a friend of the family, a Mr. Watts, to inform Shelby, Jr., of his father's death. "Your father has gone to heaven," Watts told the five-year-old. Shelby, Jr., wanted to be manly and rise to the occasion; "Who will get his money?" he asked. There was not much money. Shelby, Sr., had recently taken out a $10,000 insurance policy, which Lillian divided with her mother-in-law. They buried Foote's father in the family cemetery on Mounds Plantation near Rolling Fork, south of Greenville. Lillian and Shelby, Jr., moved back to Greenville where they lived with Mrs. Foote's older sister and her husband Michael, known as "Mic," Moyse. Shelby began school in Greenville the following September 1922. Lillian opened a gift shop and used what profits there were to purchase a headstone for the family plot at Mounds Plantation. She also began studying shorthand, the Pittman method. Three years later, in 1925, Mrs. Foote accepted a secretarial position with her husband's former employer, Armour and Company, and moved back to Pensacola where Shelby attended public schools, completing fourth and fifth grades there.

The illness of Mrs. Foote's father, Morris Rosenstock, forced her to return to Greenville in July 1927, two months after one of the worst floods in Mississippi history. Again they took up residence with Maude and "Mic" Moyse. From then until the fall of 1935, when he left to enter the University of North Carolina at Chapel Hill, Foote lived with his mother and her family in Greenville. His maternal grandfather, Morris Rosenstock, had immigrated from Vienna by way of New York or possibly New Orleans to Washington County when he was seventeen. He had found work as a bookkeeper at Avon Plantation and then married the daughter of the owner. "How a Jew bookkeeper managed to marry the daughter of a planter, I don't know, but he swung it somehow," Foote says. "He had three daughters by her and she died bearing the third one." Foote's mother was the middle daughter; Maude, the oldest, "had a great influence on me," Foote says, "because I loved her very much and she was very fond of me and we were close."[5] The Moyse-Foote household was not a particularly literary household, and Shelby was often mischievous. There were some very tense days there, but Foote recalls his mother's gentleness. "The best way to describe her attitude toward me," he says, "is that she never once hurt my feelings. It is a very strange thing to be that close to someone and never hurt their feelings."[6]

Shelby spent his summers at the country club, mostly, playing golf and swimming. It was there in 1931 that William Alexander Percy called him aside to explain that three of his cousins, Walker, LeRoy, and Phinizy Percy, were moving to Greenville. Percy thought Shelby might like to meet them and could be of some help showing the new boys around town. In the years that followed the Percy boys were to be Foote's closest and most lasting friends. Shelby spent as much time in the Percy house as he did in his own, maybe more.

Years later, in a letter to Walker Percy responding to an article he had published in the *Saturday Review* about "Uncle Will," Shelby acknowledged the lasting, pervasive influence of William Alexander Percy, not simply as a writer and man of culture, but as a human being. "What a thing it would be to try really to recapture him as he was in life; except of course it couldnt be done. All we can do is take pieces of him and distribute them here and there through our books, and all of them together dont add up to more than a fraction of what he was. How could you ever combine the incidental petulance—mainly a boundless capacity for outrage—with the enormous compassion? (11Dec73)"[7]

In the Percy household Foote was exposed to an intellectual climate unusual for any place, much less a small Mississippi town. William Alexander Percy, lawyer, planter, world traveler, had published four collections of poetry, *Sappho in Levkas, and Other Poems* (1915), *In April Once, and Other Poems* (1920), *Enzio's Kingdom, and Other Poems* (1924), and *Selected Poems* (1930). In 1941 he would publish *Lanterns on the Levee,* an autobiography describing in terms echoing Marcus Aurelius his stoical resignation to the disintegration of what he believed to be the best of Western cultural tradition. Something of Percy's dissatisfaction with the modern world surely affected the young Foote, but his influence ran much deeper in at least two ways as Foote often acknowledges. "One was he was one of the greatest teachers I have ever known," Foote recently explained in an interview. "He could read you a poem of Keats that, by the time he finished reading it, made you want to run home and be with Keats by yourself." The second was the "cultured household" Will Percy opened, the household of a "world traveler," which was full of "books and music." To Foote, it was "as if some of that other world had been brought in to this little town." Percy was also "a published writer" and an example: "If he could do it, maybe you could."[8]

The record cabinet in the Percy house had the classics—Brahms, Beethoven, Mozart, and others—even though Mr. Will never learned how to operate his "thousand-dollar Capehart." The library had not only the literary classics—Shakespeare, Dickens, Milton, Tennyson—but also some of the moderns, and sometimes those writers themselves visited— David Cohn, Roark Bradford, Vachel Lindsay, Langston Hughes, Carl

Sandburg, Stephen Vincent Benét, Stark Young, even William Faulkner, whose writing Will Percy did not particularly like.[9]

The Percys were by two generations an older Delta family than the Foote family. They had moved into Washington County before the Civil War and had prospered. The first William Alexander Percy, known as "the Gray Eagle of the Delta," returned after the war to a devastated land and earned a reputation as a lawyer, levee builder, and astute politician in a region that was undergoing rapid economic growth. His son, LeRoy, also active in farming, law, and politics, served two years of the unexpired term of Anselm J. McLaurin in the U.S. Senate. LeRoy's brother, Walker, moved to Birmingham, Alabama; the three boys who moved into William Alexander Percy's household after their father's suicide and a brief residence in Athens, Georgia, were Walker's grandsons.[10] The assumption of noblesse oblige came naturally to Will Percy, and even though his influence on Foote was strong, Foote's mature views differ radically from Percy's. "I differ with Mr. Will in almost every view he has of the planter aristocracy," he explains, "of the rednecks from the hills, and of the position of the blacks—he and I would have fallen out almost certainly if we'd allowed ourselves to overtheorize about society and what's good and what's bad."[11] The Foote family, on the other hand, traced its Mississippi roots to Noxubee County in eastern Mississippi where Shelby's paternal great grandfather owned a farm in the Black Prairie. After the Civil War, Shelby Foote's great grandfather sent his grandfather, Huger Foote, to the Delta to manage three plantations that he had bought there.

A year behind his original class, Foote was finally graduated from the Greenville High School in the spring of 1935, two years behind his friend Walker Percy, who was a year older and in 1935 had completed his sophomore year in Chapel Hill at the University of North Carolina. Foote's choosing to follow his own interests rather than the academic regimen laid down by his teachers and his principal, Mr. Leuckenbach, brought about the year's delay. On several occasions during his high school years, he was expelled from school for pranks and for what Leuckenbach and the staff considered to be insubordination. But Foote had learned to love the English language, and if his reading at times led him away from those "objectives" that the principal and teachers espoused, it amounted to little concern. Walker Percy recalled that "Shelby was always a very precocious reader. A good reader."[12] Foote remembers that as a child he read the usual books, *Tom Swift, Tarzan;* he also remembers being impressed by *David Copperfield* when he was about twelve. "I suddenly got aware that there was a world, if anything, more real than the real world. There was something about that book that made me realize what art is." The experience, however "tremendous" an "impression" it may have made, did not, at the time, cause him to "rush in to read the rest of Dickens nor fan out into reading other things."[13]

That came about four years later. "When I did finally come around to it," he says, "for the next five or six years I read quite literally almost everything I could get my hands on, especially modern things." It was probably Will Percy who told him that "the most important three novels of the twentieth century were Thomas Mann's *Magic Mountain,* Joyce's *Ulysses* and Proust's *Remembrance of Things Past.*" His mother gave him the Proust volumes for his seventeenth birthday,[14] and after that he "paid no attention to school work for the next three years in high school" and failed, he says, "about half" of his classes. "I would not memorize whether sine and cosine were side opposite over side adjacent. . . . Still don't know because I was reading," he says.[15] "That's what, if anything, made me a writer."[16] Leuckenbach might complain, but by the time that Foote was a senior in high school for the second year, he could write with some authority in the *Pica,* the school newspaper, about the work of T. S. Eliot, e. e. cummings, Sandburg, Frost, Robinton, and Edgar Lee Masters.

Will Percy had books that Foote read, as did the public library, not those in the main collection—there were not many in the main collection that interested him—but those in a room upstairs maintained by the ladies of a Tuesday Study Club: "I found I could get in that little room, and I found many books that I had never heard of, that I perhaps wouldn't have been able to get hold of otherwise. I remember one of them was *The Brothers Karamazov.*"[17]

Mr. Leuckenbach disapproved specifically of some of Foote's reading. During his second senior year, he was editor of the *Pica,* working with two teachers, Miss Lillian MacLaughlin and Miss L. E. Hawkins, whom he admired a great deal. The *Pica* had an editorial office where Foote spent most of his time when he could avoid class. When there was no pressing work for the paper, he read books there. Once, in 1934, Mr. Mitchell, the football coach, excused Foote from physical education to work on the paper. Leuckenbach found him reading James Joyce's *Ulysses* in the *Pica* room and berated his pupil for reading a "dirty book" during school time and on school premises. Shelby informed Leuckenbach that, not only was *Ulysses* not a dirty book, it was one of the few books upon which the U.S. Supreme Court had specifically passed judgment. It is possible that Leuckenbach might at times have found his pupil impertinent, if not downright offensive. Foote was apparently not inclined to accept meekly someone else's judgment or to follow without question the dictates of his elders. Leuckenbach perhaps bears some similarity to Professor Rosenback who appears in several of Foote's books: "Professor Frozen Back he was called, for he walked with a stiff Prussian carriage as if he were pacing off the distance between barriers for a duel." Rosenback believed in "memory work. It developed the mind, he said; he frequently referred to the mind in this manner, as if it were a muscle or a savings account or a combination of both."[18]

Foote seemed often to be in trouble with the school authorities. Once, he recalls, Will Percy went to his mother after an expulsion from school and received her permission for Shelby to spend his free week at the Percy house where he could read, listen to the record collection, and escape some of the criticism his uncle cast in Shelby's direction. Percy told Lillian Foote that Shelby was not "a bad fellow"; apparently, though, Mr. Will felt that he could be of some help. Even so, Shelby was accused of a serious misstep—making improper advances to one of the teachers, who a short time after the incident was admitted to an asylum.

Out of school there were pranks and accidents that earned Shelby a reputation. There was a girl, Mary Jane Zeiser, who lived diagonally across the street from Shelby. She had a dog, a wire-haired terrier, one of "those yappy little dogs," but Mary Jane was very proud of her dog Booty. Shelby had inherited a pistol, a 32-caliber Smith and Wesson, from his father, and one day he decided to show the pistol to Mary Jane and her mother and maybe tease them a bit. He was certain that he had inserted the single bullet in the revolver so that the hammer would not strike it. He was wrong. When he aimed the pistol at the dog and pulled the trigger, the pistol fired and the dog fell. Mary Jane's mother screamed, thinking that she and Mary Jane might be his next victims. They put the dog in the car, but there was no point in taking the dead Booty to the veterinarian. Shelby had really not meant to harm the dog or anyone, but he seemed to have one of those self-fulfilling reputations, by design or by accident.

Accidents occurred at the Percy house also, and Foote recalls that Mr. Will's anger could be a "fearsome thing." One day he put some tennis balls in the chandelier, and Phinizy unscrewed the whole thing trying to retrieve them. Shelby and LeRoy trooped down to Percy's law office, where "Mr. Will said 'Goddammit, people who don't know how to take care of good property shouldn't be allowed around it!'—just furious. Roy and I were scared to death of him."[19]

In the fall of 1935, Foote joined Walker and LeRoy Percy in Chapel Hill. Although he had qualified for placement in what the university called the "Flying Squadron," he was not long in determining that he did not want to complete a degree, but there were courses of useful interest for him in history and English. Harry Russell and Dougal McMillen's courses were his favorites in the English listings; P. K. Russell's lectures in medieval European history interested him. There was also the *Carolina Magazine* at Chapel Hill in which he began, soon after his arrival on campus, to publish short stories and reviews. His first short story, a tale about a black Delta farmer titled "The Good Pilgrim: A Fury Calmed," appeared in the *Carolina Magazine* in November 1935. Eight more of his stories appeared there between December 1935 and April 1937. His review of Faulkner's *Absalom, Absalom!* in November 1936 remains one of the finest early surveys of Faulkner's career; he also wrote reviews of *The Big Money* by John Dos Passos, *None Shall Look Back* by Caroline Gordon and Shakespeare's *Sonnets,* edited by Tucker Brooke. One poem by Foote, "Prescription," was published in the March 1937 issue.

During the summer between terms in 1936, Foote worked for the U.S. Gypsum Company in Greenville, "pulling wallboard out of a humidifier and running it through a micrometer" for thirty-two cents an hour. But during summers and other seasons of the year after he left the university, the social life of the Mississippi Delta attracted a good deal of his attention: "I've always been glad that I enjoyed dances and helling around the Delta," Foote told John Jones. "It's where I got much of the material I use now."[20] Because the Mississippi Delta region developed for the most part during the last quarter of the nineteenth century, it had missed much of what the older South had of history and tradition. Delta folk, however, made up for the brevity of tradition with a social life that was intense and industrious. Parties were work as well as fun. Mothers of girls in Foote's generation would drive to country clubs in neighboring towns, even to more distant towns, to join "rocking chair brigades" watching while their daughters danced with boys who had also driven for miles. The music that they danced to was genuine; the blues originated among Delta blacks and then moved down the river to New Orleans and up the river to Memphis, St. Louis, and on to New York.

After he retired from academic life, Foote returned to Greenville where he worked for Hodding Carter II's *Delta Star*, the newspaper that in 1938 Carter combined with the old *Greenville Democrat Times* to form the *Delta Democrat Times*. He worked at times at various other jobs, including a job with the construction crew building the bridge across the Mississippi River at Greenville. He also set about writing *Tournament*, which he sent to W. A. Percy's publisher, Alfred A. Knopf. The editors at Knopf commented favorably on the book, and in rejecting it, they suggested that Foote continue writing, try his hand at a second novel, and send them that one, but the war intervened, postponing his writing for a number of years.

One of his reasons for leaving Chapel Hill had been the inevitability of war. Military tradition is strong in the South, and while he might flout social conventions or the advantages of a university degree, he could not flout military obligation. Even so, the difficulties that he had had with figures of authority such as Mr. Leuckenbach also plagued his career as a soldier. In October 1939 he joined the National Guard and became Private Foote on weekends and at the periodic encampments. The Greenville unit, the 114th Field Artillery Regiment, was called into active service in November 1940. He spent most of 1941 at Camp Blanding; from there he was sent to Officer Candidate School at Fort Sill, Oklahoma, and then to Camp Shelby as a battery commander in the 86th Division. By 1943 Foote, promoted to captain, commanded Battery A of the 50th Field Artillery, 5th Infantry Division, stationed in Ireland fifty-two miles from Belfast.

In Belfast, Foote met and fell in love with Tess Lavery. Visiting her meant that he exceeded the prescribed fifty-mile limit for passes by two miles. Other units in the same military group were two or more miles closer to Belfast, and it was common practice to declare on the official form that one planned to travel forty-eight miles from the base. In spring 1944 a division officer inspecting Foote's battery happened upon a soldier whose equipment appeared tarnished, his leather clean but not shiny. To this officer's inquiry, the soldier replied that he had worked very hard to clean his gear. Foote knew the man had worked, and he was so offended when the officer called the soldier a liar that he told the colonel to apologize to the soldier. The colonel did apologize, but it was probably this incident, coupled with the division's other problems, that led the division officers to watch him more closely. Foote was charged with falsifying an official document, specifically with declaring that he planned to travel forty-eight miles while his intention was to travel fifty-two. Found guilty in the court-martial that followed, he was summarily released from the army. He feels that it was "a real con job!"[21]

In summer 1944 a young man of military age and in obvious good health and not in the service was out of place, a fish out of water, or so Foote felt. Tess Lavery joined him in New York where he was working at the "local desk" for the Associated Press. They were married in "The Little Church Around the Corner" and set up housekeeping in an apartment in Washington Heights. Civilian life was not satisfying to Foote, however, and in January 1945 he joined the Marines. Tess lived with Lillian Foote in Greenville while they entrusted Shelby to the care of one of the most famous of Marine drill sergeants, Lew Diamond. "We hear you were a captain in the Army," they told him at Parris Island, South Carolina. "You might make a pretty good private in the Marines."[22] He did make a pretty good private and was sent from basic training to Combat Intelligence School at Camp Lejeune, North Carolina. The unit to which he was assigned was scheduled for duty in the Pacific Theater, and even though the war had ended before he left North Carolina, they transferred him to Riverside, California. In California he was discharged and sent home to Greenville.

By November 1945 Tess and Shelby Foote had taken up residence in the Allen Court Apartments that would serve him through the rest of his first marriage, all of his second marriage, and through his most active years as a novelist. The return to Greenville did not bring an immediate return to fiction, however; Foote took a job at first writing for radio station WJPR in Greenville. During these years the town offered a great deal for promising writers. There was the memory of William Alexander Percy, and there was Ben Wasson, a writer and literary agent for William Faulkner. Walker Percy was soon to return for a short time and resume the friendship with Foote that the war and Percy's contraction of tuberculosis had interrupted. In 1947 the two traveled together to Santa Fe looking for a better climate for Percy. Later, in New Orleans, Foote was best man at Percy's wedding, and after Percy left Greenville, the two maintained a steady correspondence. Kenneth Haxton, who had followed Foote as editor of the high school newspaper, and Kenneth's wife at that time, Josephine, who writes under the name of Ellen Douglas, also contributed to the cultural richness of the circle of friends. Hodding Carter II, the editor of the *Delta Democrat*

Times, was gaining national attention for the political positions that were soon to earn him censure from the Mississippi legislature. Foote visited often in the Haxton home where they read Shakespeare aloud or listened to music. Haxton, whose family owned a retail business in downtown Greenville, was a composer and music historian; Foote's interest in music can be largely attributed to his influence. Several years later, after Foote moved to Memphis, the two created a game: Foote sent scraps he copied from musical scores (concertos, symphonies) to Haxton who never failed to identify them.

It was after his divorce from Tess in 1946 that Foote took up fiction again. With encouragement from Walker Percy, he retrieved the draft of *Tournament* from the closet: "I . . . looked through it and some of it still looked pretty good to me and some of it looked God-awful;" Foote told Helen White and Redding Sugg, "the Knopf editor had given me good advice."[23] "When I got it out again, I saw that it wouldn't do," he recalls. "It was terrifically influenced by Joyce and Thomas Wolfe and various people."[24] From the draft he first fashioned a short story, "Flood Burial," ironically a tale about a failed Civil War historian, which *The Saturday Evening Post* published on 7 September 1946. With the $750 he received for the story, he left his job at the radio station and set up shop as a writer in a garage at the Allen Court Apartments.

In a 1967 lecture at Memphis State University, Foote regaled his audience with his tale of the subsequent development of his career.

> I didn't want to pull any more out of the book just [then] so I said, "I will write a new story." The one I had sold them was twenty-two pages long. And I said, "The correct way to approach this thing is to write one forty-four pages long and I sent it to *The Saturday Evening Post,* and by return mail I got a letter saying "We do not know whether this is a long short story or a short novelette, and we do not care. Our check for $1500 will come in the next mail." I said, "That's the way it goes." So I said, "I will go on from here. I will write a story sixty-six pages long." This is all the literal truth. So I wrote a story sixty-six pages long and I sent it to *The Saturday Evening Post.* . . . And I didn't hear from them for about a week. And then in the middle of the following week I got my story and a letter back which was a letter that had kind of hurt feelings about it. It said "We do not deal with incest in *The Saturday Evening Post.*"

The "twenty-two page story," entitled "Tell Them Good-by" appeared in *The Saturday Evening Post* for 15 February 1947. It is a story about a jazz cornet player which Foote later revised and retitled "Ride Out." The sixty-six page novelette was called "The Enormous Eye," a version of what later became the novel *Love in a Dry Season*. After the rejection, he told his audience at Memphis State, he "settled down and realized that writing was an important thing and that [he] had better work very hard at it."[25]

The stories published in the *Post* brought Foote to the attention of Jacques Chambrun, a widely respected literary agent whose reader, Desmond Hall, later worked closely with Foote. Hall took the typescript of *Shiloh*, a novel about the Civil War battle on which Foote had been working during 1947, first to Random House and then to the Dial Press. The editors of Dial, Bart Hoffman and George Joel, thought highly of the book but did not think it would sell and asked if he had another novel in progress. Foote told them that he had "in mind" to write a novel named *Tournament*, "a novel about the Mississippi Delta that begins in Recon-struction and comes up to 1914 or so." He reports that the editors at Dial "said they would be delighted to publish it sight unseen—it sounded like a good subject."[26] Dial advanced $1,500 for the project. By 27 September 1948, Foote had completed a second draft of *Tournament*, and almost a year later, on 12 September 1949, the first novel about his mythical, but not-so-mythical, Jordan County and Bristol was published.[27]

Meanwhile, in 1947 Foote had published another extract from *Tournament*, this one a twenty-page booklet, *The Merchant of Bristol*, bearing the imprint of the Levee Press. He had been working from time to time for the *Delta Democrat Times*, writing, among things, book reviews. Bill Yarborough, a typesetter for the *DDT*, agreed to help Foote produce the short booklet. Later Kenneth Haxton, Hodding Carter II, and Ben Wasson decided to form the Levee Press and suggested that Foote and Yarborough use that imprint, which they agreed to do. (The Levee Press eventually published Faulkner, Welty, and a collection of William Alex-ander Percy's poems.)

The last years of the 1940s were good ones for Foote. He had found his craft and believed that he was at the beginning of a promising career as a writer, happy to be sending manuscripts to Chambrun for circulation to publishers and to Walker Percy, living now in Louisiana, for criticism. "My time is coming," he wrote Percy. "No writer ever developed without hard work and disappointment, and I am willing to have my share of both." In the same letter Shelby advised Walker that if he ever expected to become a writer he "had better get to work." Serious writing, Foote declared, requires learning the craft, but the rewards more than repay the effort. "But the most heart-breaking thing about it is: the better you get, the harder youll have to work—because your standards will rise with your ability. I mentioned 'work'—it's the wrong word: because if you're serious, the whole creative process is attended with pleasure in a form which very few people ever know (May Day, 1948)." These years were also good because he was once again happily married. "Give Bunt [Walker Percy's wife] my best wishes, and Peggy's too," he closed his May Day 1948 letter. Peggy was Marguerite Dessommes, the daughter of a Memphis physician, whom Shelby had married in 1948.

Finding his way into print obviously provided Foote an intellectual satisfaction that few other than writers can experience, but it did not always supply him the money he needed. By November 1949 he had completed *Follow Me Down,* a novel based on a sensational murder and trial that had taken place in Greenville nine years earlier. The Dial Press accepted the novel and published it on 23 June 1950, but in November 1949 Foote was waiting, at loose ends, and out of cash. "This is a wretched time for me, between books and waiting to hear from the publishers," he wrote Percy. His "monthly advances" had run out: "I'm hard to live with along through here—poor Peggy." Rereading the paragraph in his letter, he saw that Percy might regard it as "a plea for money." "It's no such thing," he said. "Freedom from money worries will come along with freedom from other things; partial freedom is no good, a negative sort of thing at best." Having no money allowed him "a chance to indulge in just the right amount of fret and self-pity."

That was on 19 November 1949; on the twenty-fourth he received a letter and a check from Percy. "[W]hen I saw it [the check] I intended to send it back," he wrote the next day. "This, however, I was unable to do— too weak, I reckon." On at least one other occasion, December 1950, Percy again came to Foote's financial aid. On 22 December, Shelby was again writing to thank Walker for a check.

Financial worries, however, did not seem to interfere with Foote's writing nor with his confidence and excitement with the writing process. In his 19 November letter to Percy, he had mentioned his interest in writing novels about Civil War battles. "The Vicksburg thing is taking shape," he wrote. "However, I'm going to hold off for a few more years, till I'm good and ready. I know where I'm going, and I know how to get there, too." By March 1950 he had completed a third draft of "Child by Fever," and later in the year he turned to another novel that would be published by Dial on 19 September 1951 as *Love in a Dry Season.*

In the late summer and fall of 1950, working on *Love in a Dry Season,* which he at first called *The Arms You Bear,* he felt extremely confident about his career, of which there were to be three phases. "At the outset," he explained to Percy, "I promised myself three short novels in which to learn how to write; then three long novels, having learned; and finally three novels of undeterminate length, experimental—all this in addition to things of slighter length, most of them tours de force such as *Shiloh* and *Child by Fever.*" The current book ended phase one. "Then Phase Two: which will begin with either the Vicksburg book or a big modern novel—I keep saving that Vicksburg thing: if I dont look out, it will wind up in Phase Three, experimental, and no one will read it: I can see now how it would be—plotless, characterless: really wild, like a shellburst and as unintelligible."[28] The writing of *Love in a Dry Season* went well for Foote. Looking back, in an interview with Evans Harrington over twenty years later, he remembered *Dry Season* as a "great favorite of mine, not *the* favorite all the time, but it is a favorite . . . because of a sort of happy facility I had during the writing of it. . . . And I also thought that it was a funny book, which helped a lot to make me feel pleasure about it."[29] At the time he was writing *Love in a Dry Season,* in December 1950, he explained something of the same thing to Percy, feeling himself to have become a part of an American literary tradition. "Unquestionably this is the best sustained writing Ive ever done," he wrote. "All in all I feel very good about it. I am beginning to feel a part of what comes from being in the American tradition." That did not mean, however, that the reading public would respond: "It's not a book that will sell any more than the others have been," he wrote; "but it will do what I most want it to do—it will add to my stature, my sense of 'sureness' and will add possibly another couple of thousand readers who will remember my name and wait for my next book (22Dec50)."

If fame, or just reputation, were not to be had at home, then perhaps, like Faulkner, he might be appreciated by foreigners. Hamish Hamilton contracted for an English edition of *Follow Me Down* in December 1950 and that gave Foote great hopes. "I may do what other American writers have done—Faulkner for instance—get a reputation abroad before I do at home," he speculated. What he intensely wanted, though, was a French translator; French, after all, is "Proust's language" (22Dec50). *Love in a Dry*

Season was translated by Pierre Singer and published in French in 1953. There were a few other translations during the 1950s, but Foote had to wait almost twenty years for sustained French interest to develop. Then, in the 1970s, Maurice-Edgar Coindreau, Faulkner's translator, along with Mireille Rotfus, Claude Richard, and Hervé Belkiri, translated most of *Jordan County* (Foote's 1954 collection of stories), *Follow Me Down,* and retranslated *Love in a Dry Season.* Foote had complained frequently to Percy that the reviewers had a limited understanding of his work. "If you could read all the reviews [of *Follow Me Down*] you would see why I say a writer can write only for himself," he wrote in August 1950, "hoping that the time will come (after he is dead, alas) when some student will do a critical study that has value." Fortunately, he has not had to wait quite that long. In 1971 the *Mississippi Quarterly* devoted a special issue to Foote, and in 1977 *Delta,* published by Université Paul Valery at Montpellier, devoted almost an entire special issue to *Jordan County.* "You never saw such diagrams, circles, triangles, pyramids, etc.," he wrote Percy. "I found it so fascinating I even studied up on my Chapel Hill French, which covered a period of nearly two months and which I flunked. Now I understand just how I went about putting that book together. I did a much better job than I knew, and any time I have any doubt about my immortality I just go back and limp my way through another of those articles for reassurance (2Dec77)." During the 1970s and 1980s, there was a growing critical interest in Foote's work, including a book in the Twayne Series by Helen White and Redding Sugg, and critical interest in Foote's fiction remains strong in France. In 1950 and 1951, though, Foote was industriously and confidently developing the installments in his three-phase career, each part, like each novel, carefully planned.

Love in a Dry Season, he told Percy, "[W]ill do it: wind up my apprenticeship, forge my middle-period style, set me up to make a dent in American literature (8Feb51)." If this seems ambitious, then it is worth bearing in mind that Foote was a fairly young man, absolutely devoted to his craft, writing in confidence to his best friend, a friend, the letters reveal, whom he was advising to become a writer. Part of Foote's confidence, too, came from the discipline his devotion to his craft demanded of him, and he had learned that, "Writing, when a man is dedicated to it, has such an overpowering pull that the laziest man in the world couldn't keep from doing it." He recommended that Percy get to work. "The only way to learn to write is to write as many hours a day as your hand and brain will let you.

It is an instrument that must be forged in the fire of labor. You discover things one by one, and you only learn by doing (16Feb52)."

With *Love in a Dry Season* finished in late April 1951 and with prospects for the publication of *Shiloh* (it was published on the ninetieth anniversary of the battle, 6 April 1952), Foote was ready to launch into his big book and begin the next phase of his three-part career. "I put the corrected typescript [of *Love in a Dry Season*] into the mail last Tuesday and since then have been working at the plan for a big novel. The story is by no means clear as yet, but I have the subject, the characters, and the form; it will run about the length of my first three books all put together—five parts of 50,000 words each, Parts 1, 3 and 5 being a continuous story, Parts 2 and 4 being separate short novels designed to give the book historical and anthropological depth; . . . All my books are one book anyhow, and this will dramatise the fact. The Delta is the hero and the book will be titled (or subtitled) 'A Landscape With Figures.' You see? (22Apr51)"

"All [his] books are one book," a history of the Delta and Jordan County. He had come to regard himself as "an anthropologist—at least of this little corner of the universe"; and he planned "to get the Delta into [the big novel] as the Delta has never been got before." The new book would have to wait in line for a revision of *Shiloh* to be completed, but by July 1951 Foote was, according to his report to Percy, setting a tentative publication date for fall 1953. "It is my first real book as a writer; the first three (plus "Shiloh") were student works (5July51)." His overall plan for the novel was fairly set by July. It would be five parts and would include "Child by Fever" and other of his earlier work. Actually, as early as November 1949, Foote had envisioned a novel made up of stories that he had written, and ultimately that is what came to be *Jordan County*. In the meanwhile, however, in the second half of 1951, his plan was much more complex, as he explained to Percy:

> I thought, however, that I'd tell you a bit about the book as I see it this early in the game. I think I told you some of it before, but here is what it has come to. Title: unknown. Subtitle: A Landscape with Figures. There are five parts. I, III and V are a continuous story, 90% dialog and without flashbacks except as they occur in conversation. Time: the present. Principal characters: three men and two women, and they are to rush about in a sort of Dostoevskian furor. II and IV are excursions into Bristol's (or Jordan County's) past. II is the story of a Negro, a young man, told from beginning to end, biographical. V is "Child by Fever," which you know. All the Gothic

elements are in these two Parts; the odd-numbered Parts have no such
elements. II is the Twenties; V of course is turn-of-the century. . . . The big
story is all outlined as far as its background is concerned; I have filled fifteen
pages of a ledger with notes on the interrelationships, though so far I have
no idea what the immediate complication is to be. (5July51)

By August he had found his title—"Two Gates to the City." It came
from Book XIX of the *Odyssey*, but meant a good deal more to Foote than
that. "[I]f I were a Catholic this would be a fine Catholic novel," he wrote
Percy in November, "for the immediate situation is a choice on the part of
one of the main characters; which way shall he go? Therefore: TWO
GATES TO THE CITY. All the same, the city's the City of God
(29Nov51)."

His excitement about "Two Gates" had grown as the plan became
elaborate: "Hemingway's right: it isn't good to talk about a book until
youve written it. But I declare I feel awful good about this one (29Nov51)."
"Terrific burst of creativeness!" he reported a week later. "To date, after six
months of futzing round, I have 9/22nds of TWO GATES in first draft,
260-odd pages (6Dec51)."

But then Foote's world began to unravel, and all that he could do would
not seem to make his pattern for life fit. In February 1952 he still spoke
with confidence about his career, but the brightness, the ebullience, in the
tone of what he wrote had diminished. "I have everyday a sense of growing
strength. I have forged this instrument and it's a good one—not so much
for what it is as for my knowledge of what it can be; it is basically the right
one. I know I have what cant be gotten except from within—vitality. Poor
as my first four books may be, they all have that; a lesser writer would have
made five novels out of each of them. . . . Stand by: I'll tell you true—I
am going to be one of the greatest writers who ever lived. Or if I'm not, it
wont be from lack of knowing the requirements and it wont be because I
lied to myself, ever (16Feb52)." If Percy were going to "stand by," he was
to discover that now there was a considerable delay. Shelby's marriage to
Peggy was unraveling; the divorce came on 6 March 1952.

On 5 January, Shelby had confessed to Percy that he felt "like hell." "I'm
confused," he wrote, "and God knows what will come of all this. The only
thing I am sure about is writing," but the writing suffered too. By late
March, he felt that the worst was past. "I am settling down, still with a
mountain of woe upon my head, but I have learned a great deal in this past
month. Dostoevsky was absolutely right about suffering; I always knew

it—but this was the first real suffering of my life. I lost fifteen pounds and came out all gaunt and hollow-eyed, but I would not swap what I got from it for a month of romping in the greenest meadows. I touched absolute bottom; then I came back up. Man, it's dark down there (23Mar52)." He was wrong; what he wrote Percy about "coming out of it" was all about what he would like to feel, not what he actually felt. A little over two weeks later, on April 9 he was writing Percy again. "I am truly in love for the first time in my life and am being kept from the woman I love," he said.

Except for his writing to Percy, there was little writing at all for Foote that spring, but there were moments of relief from the gloom. Dial issued *Shiloh* on the ninetieth anniversary of the battle, and Foote was invited to the battlefield park for a ceremony. On his way there, he stopped by Oxford to pick up William Faulkner who accompanied him for the occasion. Foote's letters often mention writers in whom he had a particular interest. Although he lectured Percy at length about Proust and James and mentioned others occasionally—Tolstoy, Dostoevsky, Joyce, D. H. Lawrence—the most obvious influence on Foote's work is Faulkner. Foote's first encounter with Faulkner's work came in 1932 when he read *Light in August,* "one of the first modern novels." "I suppose," he said, "almost everybody can remember his first modern novel . . . how different it was from what came before it and how it just knocked you off your feet."[30] From Faulkner he learned that "reality within a novel can be realer than reality outside a novel." Faulkner, first showed Foote what Proust called "quality of vision."[31] More specifically Faulkner showed him "a country" that Foote "knew well" but made him realize "how really little [he] knew it compared to [Faulkner]." And finally, there was Faulkner's language. "It was my language—a demotic style of English I was thoroughly familiar with."[32] Of course Foote recognized the dangers of belonging to a "tribe of Will," and the warning he gave students at Memphis State University he has been careful to observe himself. Faulkner's writing, he told them, "will snatch you up and take you with it and you will find yourself writing second- or third-rate Faulkner unless you consciously oppose that influence. . . . What you hope most for is that he will give you what you need of him without taking you over." Then Foote went on to tell the students how Faulkner had once said that Shelby Foote would be his favorite modern writer when he began "writing a little more Shelby Foote and a little less William Faulkner."[33] Foote, naturally, has made a concerted effort to do just that, but at the same time, he finds considerable value in a writer's serving an apprenticeship to another writer whose work he admires. The first novels of "most of the best writers I know of," he told his Memphis State audience, "are written under the obvious influence of some one particular writer." That is a natural process, he believes, and happens in the careers of most writers. "Robert Louis Stevenson gave what I consider a truly excellent piece of advice. He advised people who want to learn how to write to imitate. That is, pick some writer whom you admire . . . and imitate him. . . . Having learned to do that, develop your own style." The great value of that learning process derives from the writer's learning "the form from the inside while you are establishing your own individuality."[34] Foote identified with Henry James in that "the art of the novel and the successful practice of form come from careful observation, experience, and from very hard work." "A man *is* the sum of what he has read and seen; and you would do well not to miss any of the good in the world in the way of writing while you are learning your craft. That's where you learn it, from the writers who came before you."[35]

Faulkner and Foote were never close friends, but the two writers did know each other, and Faulkner read Foote's work. "I was with Faulkner maybe five, six times; spent the night in his house once, took a trip with him up to Shiloh once, had dinner with him and Miss Estelle a couple of times. I liked him very much. He was a friendly, even outgoing man, with certain reticences. His reticences never bothered me; I figured a man with that big genius strapped to his back would be bound to have some pretty hard times."[36] Foote first visited Faulkner in the late 1930s when he and Walker Percy stopped off at Rowan Oak on their way from Greenville to Sewanee. Percy, who had not wanted to stop, remained in the car while Foote made his way through barking dogs to the door that Faulkner answered. Foote asked where he might find a copy of *The Marble Faun,* and Faulkner suggested he write Leland Heyward for a copy. He then told Foote that he had just that morning finished a novel, *If I Forget Thee, Jerusalem* (the title was changed to *The Wild Palms*), about characters from the Delta. Later Foote thought of using the title himself.[37] The trip to Shiloh in April 1952 was apparently an enjoyable occasion for Foote, who arrived at Rowan Oak at about seven o'clock, early for a Sunday morning, knowing that Faulkner would probably have been up for some time. The idea of a trip appealed to Faulkner, but when they reached Corinth, the two realized that they had no whiskey and would probably not be able to find any on a Sunday morning. "We were parked on the square there in

Corinth right opposite the old Corinth hotel and you could see right into the lobby there, and there was a shoeshine stand just inside the door," Foote remembers. Foote was certain that no one at a shoeshine stand on Sunday morning would know where whiskey could be found, but Faulkner disagreed. "It was about 9 o'clock by now, and he said, 'I think anybody getting his shoes shined at 9 o'clock in the morning would know where to get some whiskey.' That didn't ring true to me. I said, 'No, somebody getting his shoes shined is on his way to church.' And he said, 'Well, let's look into it.' So I got out of the car and went over to this fellow . . . and I said, 'Excuse me, a friend of mine and I are looking for some whiskey, and we don't know where a bootlegger is. Can you tell us where one is?' And he said, 'I was just on my way there myself.'"[38]

Although the bootlegger in Corinth and the company of William Faulkner, by then famous as the South's Nobel Laureate, made a bright moment, but Foote still could not write. The gloom of the spring became the settled, not-so-quiet despair of the summer and fall of 1952. Peggy and Margaret, his daughter born in 1949, had moved to Memphis on 6 May, and by July, Shelby had given up hope of remarrying Peggy. In September he wrote to Percy that she was "raising hell—frantic and railing at me"; he could make no progress on "Two Gates" at all. "The new book has already suffered enormous delays, and interruptions . . . I'm sorry I ever conceived it on such a scale and with such complexity." His conclusion was that if he had "stayed drunk these past six months," then "theyd have been more profitable (24Sep52)."

In July money was much on his mind. He considered royalty payments "a hell of a poor index to excellence," but he had at least something of a career to measure during his summer of despair, his "fallow period." The $13,137.42 he had earned in royalties he could consider the mark of a successful beginning.

> Royalty statements for the last six months of 1951 reached me yesterday. They make an interesting subject: the economic outlook for a successful beginner. My first four books have earned $13,137.42 (including the reprint sales), with royalties as follows:

> | | |
> |---|---|
> | TOURNAMENT | $461.21 |
> | FOLLOW ME DOWN | 990.89 |
> | DRY SEASON | 610.32 |
> | SHILOH | 2750.00 —— |

Ive got no kick, except I wish *Dry Season* had done better; what I wanted was a gradual buildup, and except for that, I got it. Ah well—so it goes. (15July52)

The Christmas season that year brought him no relief even though his daughter Margaret had visited during the previous summer. "I'm not doing so good. Still cant write. Maybe I wont care in a couple more months or years—however long. I dont care. One thing nice about it is, if I'm not a writer I'm not anything; so if I ever really decide I'm done with it I can really let go. I'm done with it for now, all right. 1952 was pure nightmare, and here comes 1953. Peace be with us (26Dec52)." When he moved to Memphis in 1953 to settle into a house on the bluff overlooking the Mississippi, he may have been drawn there to be near the four-year-old Margaret. Whatever the reasons for his leaving Greenville, his life thereafter was to be different. His plan, the three parts of a pattern, had fallen apart.

Out of the wreckage came *Jordan County*. Parts of it would have been included in "Two Gates" as Foote had conceived the "big book" in 1951, but now he fell back on the plan he had mentioned to Percy in November 1949. He was planning a trip to New York and would take both *Shiloh* and his plans for the collection along. He commented that the collection would be "a sort of history of Jordan County in reverse."

1950	1. Modern story (short)	20pp.
1939	2. Ride Out (pre-Second World War)	60
1922	3. The 20s (short)	20
1910	4. Child by Fever (Turn of the Century)	200
1872	5. Reconstruction (short)	20
1864	6. Pillar of Fire (Civil War)	60
1822	7. Indians (prehistoric, short)	20
	Total:	400pp. (25Nov49)

Looking back in 1954, Foote could count five published books, four of them set in his Jordan County and the fifth, *Shiloh*, having as one of its major narrators a Confederate rifleman, Luther Dade, who had lived most of his life at Solitaire, a plantation south of Bristol on Lake Jordan. These fallow years were deepened by suffering, and the suffering, he told himself, would make the work that was to come much richer. His commitment to art was undiminished, if anything even deeper. The letter he wrote to

Percy in 1954 is instructive in this regard. One, he felt, had to believe in words, but an artist, any serious artist, should never use them to preach—except, maybe, in letters to friends who were becoming artists.

> We could all be great writers, perhaps, except that we know the cost; and few are willing to pay it. No wonder. For the cost is nothing less than laying down our lives: "Except a grain of wheat fall to the ground. . . . If it die not . . . " (I do not mention the risk of the soul, for I believe in fact that this is the one way of saving it.) Many of us are willing to go half way, some few even three quarters of the way; but there are few who go all the way—Shakespeare, Mozart, and maybe Proust, who (all three) put all that they were into their work; anything else was for extra. They were great men, and must have been charming; but the charm did not really matter and they knew it; basically they gave up love, friendship, even God, because they knew these things were less than art. (To my mind, Faulkner's best claim to belonging in their company is the fact that he hardly exists outside his work—though the worst of him is frivolous, even careless; also I doubt the extent of his suffering, or anyhow his willingness to suffer (witness the Hollywood trips, which he turned to during his dry periods instead of staying home and sweating blood, though he must have known exactly how much suffering had to teach him, provided he would undergo the pain).) It's a rather embarrassing thing to speak of, but I know it well at last. I have never learned the slightest truth from happiness. As for the above, I know it so well that I know I am approaching that renunciation—the crisis you say Kierkegaard speaks of. In the past month I have drawn much closer to it; I may be on the brink, though I wont know until I'm actually over the lip. During this time I have been outlining a tortuous novel, absolutely black and savage, with all the horrors of a nightmare; I intend to work my way through it to greatness. (19Feb54)

Over the next three decades, Foote's stories were reprinted occasionally, and in 1964 Dial issued a collection of three novels bound together—*Follow Me Down, Jordan County,* and *Love in a Dry Season.*[39]

Right as he may have been about art, he was wrong about working his "way through" a "tortuous novel" "to greatness." Instead of fiction, Foote was about to turn to the Civil War, not the novels about Vicksburg and Brice's Crossroads, but a three-volume history of 1,500,000 words. Bennett Cerf of Random House asked Foote to write a brief history of the Civil War for publication during the centennial celebration. The project, as Cerf described it, seemed easy, so Foote agreed: "I figured that I could write about twice as much history per year as I did fiction per year—fiction is hard work; history I figured, well, there's not much to that."[40] He was wrong, as he very quickly discovered. "But I hadn't any more than started before I saw I wasn't the one to write any short history of the Civil War; just a short summary of what happened really didn't interest me. But I was enormously interested in the whole thing."[41] The form of the larger project developed: "[I]t began to open out for me and I was able to outline all three volumes,"[42] and Foote wrote to Robert Linscott, his editor at Random House, sending him the outline. "It must have been a terrible shock to him," Foote says, because Random House had planned that Foote's volume would be the first in a series about important events in the nation's history. Ten days later, Foote received a reply. "Go ahead."[43]

He had found at last an outlet for his Civil War interests that he had been developing from the beginning of his writing career. "Flood Burial," his first *Saturday Evening Post* story, had been about Major Dubose, a Civil War historian, who was buried with his hundreds of pages of flood-damaged manuscript. What is perhaps more important, though, in Foote's comments is that the history "opened out" for him. He had found a form, a shape, for his book, and for Foote that always was a fundamental step in beginning to write. He had found a major publisher; he had at least some assurance that his fate would not be that of Major Dubose, buried in a flood, laid in the chest containing his ruined manuscript. His barren stretch had ended, but he apparently had no idea that his history would take him twenty years to finish and be longer by a third, as he pointed out to Percy in July 1974, than Gibbons's *Decline and Fall*. By April 1955 he could write to Percy that he was busy and, at last, writing productively and learning many things.

> Hope youre fine. I am; have been working hard and steady—about 80,000 words into the thing, approximately one-fifth, and going strong. I think maybe I'm writing a great book; but thats nothing: I always think so. Yesterday I fought (and won) the Battle of Belmont, winding up military operations for '61. When I polish off the Trent Affair I'll be set for A S Johnston and '62, leading up to Shiloh, which I can write in my sleep. . . . I would enjoy talking the war with you, though it could be you wouldnt enjoy listening. Dont underrate it as a thing that can claim a man's whole waking mind for years on end. For one thing, it's teaching me to love my country—especially the South, but all the rest as well. I'm learning so many things: geography, for instance. I never saw this country before now—the rivers and mountains, the watersheds and valleys. (13Apr55)

If he was learning to love the South, then he was also content with Memphis and his house on Arkansas Street on the bluff. Its "three rooms in line like boxcars" were "perfect for work." "I like Memphis and look back on Gville with something kin to horror, though I know I'll feel the tug again (13Apr55)" he wrote.

In 1955 he won a Guggenheim Fellowship, which he needed, as he said, to "visit battlefields . . . as well as eat and pay alimony and rent." The first and shortest volume of his trilogy, *Fort Sumter to Perryville* appeared in November 1958 and "was a History Book Club selection for February 1959."[44] Other things were happening as well while he was writing and visiting battlefields. On 5 September 1956 he married Gwyn Rainer. "[I]t's wonderful when two people find each other, hook atoms, balance frets, whatever," he had written Percy back in 1952, but even then he had gone on to say, "It's not for me but I like to see it when it happens." It was for him, however, and has been up to the present. Huger Lee Foote II was born in 1961.

In addition to writing history, Foote was also writing for Hollywood in the mid-1950s. When Stanley Kubrick asked Foote to work on a film script, Shelby asked Faulkner for advice, and Faulkner said, in effect, that he should take the money and avoid the people. In 1967 Foote told an audience at Memphis State what Faulkner had said. "I thought I'd get out there where all that money is and women and go stark mad, and never be seen again. And so I asked Faulkner if he thought it was a good idea. And he said: 'Well, yeah. Go take their money, but you have to be careful out there,' he said. 'It's the only place on earth where you can get stabbed in the back while you're climbing a ladder.' That was good advice that he gave me, and he said something else: 'And I'm serious,' he said. 'If you go out there, never take the people seriously, because, as I have said, they can hurt you.'" The finished manuscript was never produced: "Gregory Peck decided not to do it, and James Mason decided not to do it, and it was never done. It's sitting on a shelf somewhere. But I got paid for it," he reports.[45]

Gwyn and Shelby Foote left Arkansas Street in 1958 and moved into a house on Yates Road where he finished the second volume of *The Civil War, Fredericksburg to Meridian*, in 1963. Then he took a recess from the history to spend several months as a Ford Foundation Fellow at the Arena Stage in Washington. "I enjoyed it," he remembers. "We got a townhouse in Georgetown with a swimming pool and all that. We spent Mr. Ford's money right and left."[46] Nevertheless, Foote took his work at the Arena "very seriously because," as he says, "I wanted to. And I was there all the time. I went in the morning, or . . . what they called morning which was about eleven o'clock. . . . I stayed right on through or went home to dinner and came back and saw the performance that night." One of his own dramatizations was produced which, according to Foote, proved to him how ill-suited he was for writing drama. "The play was rather successful, but my reaction was miserable," he told a drama class at Memphis State. "These people were out there saying these things some of which were fairly funny. And the audience would laugh. . . . That was all right, but they would keep on laughing and not hear the next funny line. And I did not like that at all."[47]

Not ready to return to Memphis after Washington, Shelby and Gwyn spent almost a year at Gulf Shores, Alabama. In the turmoil over civil rights, Memphis had lost its appeal; in fact, the whole South had lost its appeal. Shelby thought he would find an escape for the evil and ugliness of politicians at Gulf Shores.

> I want to reach out for more of life—not people, really (to hell with people I still say), but the beach and the Gulf and maybe fishing; the sea's edge appeals to me as a notion, the glassy expanse opening out and the salt wind coming off it in the winter. I feel death all in the air in Memphis, and I'm beginning to hate the one thing I really ever loved—the South. No, thats wrong: not hate—despise. Mostly I despise the leaders, the pussy-faced politicians, soft-talking instruments of real evil; killers of the dream, that woman called them, and she's right. Good Lord, when I think what we could have been, the heritage we perverted!—the misspent courage, the hardcore independence, the way a rich man always had to call a poor man Mister, the niggers who stood up for a century under what would have crumpled the rest of us in a month, the women who never lost the knowledge that their job was to be women. All that; and now we trust it to the keeping of Ross Barnett! . . . I want to go live by the Gulf. (13Aug63)

Gulf Shores, the red-neck Riviera, was not as bad as Memphis; it was worse. The house he had had an architect design for them did not work either. "There were two things wrong with that: one, I got crossways with the Ku Klux Klan down there during the George Wallace days, and the other was we had an architect . . . named Adalotte design a house for us. It was [to be] a three-story house with a nine-foot gallery all the way around the two top stories. It was a beautiful house; but we found that in a

sixty-mile-an-hour wind it would fly." Foote's trouble with the Klan came
from his criticism of their use of the Confederate flag. "I told them they
were a disgrace to the flag, that everything they stood for was almost
exactly the opposite the Confederacy had stood for, that the Confederacy
believed the law and order above all things. . . . I created a good deal of
resentment against myself down there until they decided I was crazy and
then they were more sympathetic."[48] By spring 1965 he had moved back
to Memphis, living first for about a year in a suburb, Raleigh, Tennessee,
before moving into the house where he now lives on East Parkway. It was
on East Parkway that he finished the third volume of *The Civil War, Red
River to Appomattox* (1974), and a sixth novel, *September September* (1978).

Writing the three-volume history meant hard work and a great deal of
concentration. It meant reading large quantities of material and traveling
to battlefields—twenty years of careful attention. When the third volume
was finished, he wrote Percy that he felt "extraordinarily good" about the
history, and he wanted people, reading it, to "learn to love their country."

> It's hard to explain how extraordinarily good I feel about my book; little
> things in it, I mean, that others will scarcely notice or just rush by in the
> reading—like the expression on Jeb Stuart's face when they jogged him off
> in an ambulance with a bullet through his liver; or Lee with dysentery,
> tossed about on his cot and crying out of Grant, "If I could just get one
> more pull at him!" Or Forrest at Brice's Crossroads. "Hit 'em on the ee-
> end," he told a brigade commander. Or Mary Lincoln at L's bedside, saying:
> "Send for Tad. He will speak to Tad, he loves him so." . . . So many things,
> and all of them seem to me so extraordinarily *good*. It's quite different from
> any reaction I ever had to a novel, I guess because I didnt make it up. I want
> everybody everywhere to read it so they can learn to love their country.
> (2Aug74)

That pleasure, however, was balanced by the disappointment he felt in
not winning a Pulitzer; nevertheless, the pleasure continued and by December had not abated in the least. "No one knows as well as I how
marvelous the work is," he wrote then, "no one sees as well as I do all its
hidden beauties, no one knows as well as I do how beautifully it's structured, the secret ties with the Iliad, the marvels hidden within iotas in
every page (30Dec74)."

That was in 1974. The completed history was a source of great satisfaction, but the political and economic history of the country was another
matter. Almost exactly four years earlier, he had complained to Percy that

there was seemingly very little about the country to love, and in writing *September September* after he finished *The Civil War,* he gives vent to some of his disgust. Looking back on the 1960s in August 1970, he was angry at the "freaked-out young" and the "stultified old," who, like the nation, "live by (or claim to live by) a batch of myths that never were true to start with." At the same time, as a historian and a novelist, he saw the events of the 1960s in terms of the nation's history, particularly in terms of the Civil War history that he was writing.

> The Civil War is a bloody mess from start to finish, unredeemable even by Lee or Lincoln, and all the "glory" aura isnt worth the death of a single soldier. The cause was bad on both sides, and the worst cause won. We freed the Negro into indignity and serfdom, and turned promptly to every golden calf on the horizon. Jim Fisk won the peace, along with Harriman and Carnegie, while kidnappers were trying to steal Lincoln's body from his tomb in Springfield and Belknap (Grant's Secretary of War) was selling PX franchises for $50 each, cash on the line. This is not a nation, it's a grabbag, an arena where you pay for any trace of decency with your life or by going bankrupt. . . . Our God isnt Christ, it's that iron Vulcan over in Birmingham. (5Aug70)

We have always been, he said, "A nation of halfmad teenagers," a view that he expressed pointedly in *September September.*

The historical accuracy of the setting for his fiction has been important to Foote from the beginning of his career. In a talk to the Southern Historical Association, "The Novelist's View of History,"[49] Foote argues that the "honest" novelist and the historian "are seeking the same thing: the truth—not a different truth: the same truth—only they reach it, or try to reach it, by different routes." *September September,* like all of Foote's fiction, has its clearly established historical milieu. *Tournament* is based on the life of Foote's grandfather and, like "Child by Fever," develops around events that led up to and included 1910, "a sort of watershed year." "In any case," he explained to Evans Harrington, "I see it as a time when all the old America was still there and all the new America was coming on fast—men started flying in airplanes, women started smoking cigarettes . . . a Negro won the championship of the world—many things. I see it as a time when men stood and looked in both directions. . . . Small town America in 1910 is still my notion of the happiest time on earth. And yet I have those people troubled at night in their sleep by the future that's moving against them so fast."[50] *Follow Me Down* is based on the sensational murder committed by Floyd Myers in Greenville in 1940 and the trial that followed in 1941. The depression years provide a backdrop for the events in *Love in a Dry Season*. Concerning *September September,* Foote told John Jones: "The whole book takes place in the month of September in 1957, and I went down and read the *Commercial Appeal* and the *Press-Scimitar* for the month of September 1957 as a way of starting. I took notes on what the temperatures were and how much rain fell on the various days. . . . So I wanted to be accurate, but I always wanted that, even in my earlier books too."[51] September 1957 was another of those "watershed" years; it began with Eisenhower's sending troops to Little Rock and ended (on 4 October, actually) with the Russians launching Sputnik. He took occasion in a talk to the Southern Historical Association in 1964 to answer charges that Kenneth P. Williams had made against novelists in *Lincoln Finds a General.* Williams had asserted that Lew Wallace's description of events was not trustworthy because Wallace was "a writer of fiction." "Whether the events took place in a world gone to dust, preserved by documents to be evaluated by scholarship," Foote argues, "or in the imagination, preserved by memory to be distilled by the creative process, they both want to tell us *how it was:* to recreate it by their separate methods, and make it live again in the world around them."[52]

Foote continued on this occasion to explain that the basic difference between the novelist and the historian is that the latter attempts to recreate the past "by communicating facts" while the former, as Proust had said, attempts to "communicate sensation." The novelist, however, has much to contribute to the historian, and Foote calls that "technique," listing "style" and "plot" as its components. These ideas, and the terms he used to define them, were by no means new to Foote in 1964. They were, in fact, the substance of much that he had written in his letters from the beginning of his correspondence with Walker Percy. They were the formulations of about two decades (probably even more) of thinking about his craft and constitute all that he has published about his theory of art.

As early as 1950, Foote had written to Percy that he thought he knew his purpose as a novelist, a purpose strongly colored by his understanding of Proust. "Some want to teach (or preach): some want to communicate sensation," he wrote. "I suppose I want to share in both of those. Yet I think I know at last what I really want. I want to teach people how to *see.* I want to impart to them a 'quality of vision' (Proust's definition of style)." One does not develop "quality of vision" without considerable work and concentration. "In 34 years I have trained myself through writing to look at the world a certain way, and I think that as a result I see a great deal more . . . than a person who does not concern himself with such (31Dec50)." Eleven months after he mailed these words to his friend in Louisiana, Foote was again explaining to him that "the novelist's principal task is the communication of sensation. If he does this, and does it right, he has rescued something from time and chaos (8Nov51)."

By "teaching" Foote certainly did not mean that the novelist should lecture, and had the text of his 1950 letter recurred to him as he was writing his lecture in 1964, he would probably have regretted the implications of the word. "I learned very soon after first sitting down to write," he told the historians in his 1964 audience, "that no one can really teach—or even tell—anyone anything; not really. . . . [W]ith luck and talent . . . a man can *show* another man something; that is, he can make him see and hear and maybe even feel and smell it."[53] Showing, done with style, and incorporating Proust's "quality of vision," can accomplish much, more than any form of communication that falls short of art. In November 1949 Foote had brought a particular sentence of Proust's to Percy's attention: "As for style, I have tried to reject everything dictated by pure intelligence, to express my deep and authentic impressions and to respect the natural movement of my thought." Abstract philosophy might be "dictated by pure intelligence," but for Foote philosophy had to be such an integral part of the novelist's way of seeing, so clearly a part of his being, that it disappears behind the sensation to which it may be giving direction. Philosophy "must be so much a part of the man that he uses it only as an expression of his being." The result is that a book like *Madam Bovary* "may be the kind of book that teaches us most" because the philosophical basis is integral to the meaning, but at the same time is "submerged (19Feb54)." To Foote, Keats's "Ode to Autumn," like *Bovary*, represented the "best in art." "It makes no slightest attempt, except overtly, to tell anyone anything; it only demonstrates a way of looking at the world ("style"); it is indeed pure art, has no theory to advance (except of course Keats's central theme that truth is beauty and beauty truth), and by never trying to preach does in fact do the most effective preaching of all—the kind done by music and great painting: Beethoven and Vermeer, for example (19Feb54)."

In art one is far more likely to find answers that run deeper and truer than answers found through philosophy or religion, or for that matter

history, if the artist respects the "natural movement" of his thoughts. This
was Foote's argument to Percy, whose conversion to Catholicism brought
with it, apparently, a conviction that religion provided a more reliable way
to truth than the novel, a view with which Foote could not agree. The
artist goes farther, Foote argued, than the man whose "quality of vision" is
shaped by a commitment to the formulations of Catholicism. In a 1951
letter, Foote explained at some length his difference with Percy; his metaphor of the writer's hand seems particularly suitable for his purposes. Percy
apparently had argued that the novel should deliver a philosophical message, but Foote thought otherwise.

> Our difference of opinion over the purpose of the novel is one of degree; for
> while I certainly agree with you that "words exist to communicate mean-
> ings," we dont at all agree as to the nature of meaning. You seem to think
> the novelist is some exalted kind of pamphleteer, and whats more you seem
> to think that his "meaning" is preferably derived from some standard body
> of thought his mind has discovered and accepted as a duty to pass on to
> others—seeking converts to his discovery. As a matter of fact, as I have said
> before, the best novelists have all been doubters; their only firm conviction,
> the only one that is never shaken, is that absolute devotion and belief in the
> sanctity of art which results in further seeking, not a sense of having
> found. . . . Dont tell me you have swallowed that hokum about the writer
> being a Wise Man. As a matter of fact he is stupid to an amazing degree
> about the things that people value; he has a bloc that stops him short of
> acceptance, that makes him examine what others accept; he can be fasci-
> nated by the shape of his own hand, watching it by lamplight holding the
> pen; for him "understanding" is merely description—that is enough. Your
> wise-man says "There is my hand; all right; lets get on to important things.
> How about the relation of God to man?" But the artist, I believe, concentrat-
> ing on the hand itself, without even a thought of God, comes closer to
> finding the meaning simply by observing how the hand, held between his
> eye and the lamp, becomes semi-transparent, showing the skeleton hand
> beneath. (8Nov51)

Percy may find happiness in religion, but in the world of art, Foote feels
confidence. "[Y]ou are in my world now," he wrote Percy, "the world of
art—we've left Jesus and the saints." Then he quotes D. H. Lawrence to
his Catholic friend: "Being a novelist, I consider myself superior to the
saint, the scientist, the philosopher and the poet. The novel is the one
bright book of life." Blasphemy, Foote says, has nothing at all to do with

art: "[W]e've come into another world, and blasphemy exists back in the world we came out of . . . (Foote's ellipsis) (16Feb52)." The bone gives shape to the flesh, and the artist, by describing the hand, reveals the bone within; his is a deeper dimension than that with which religion or philosophy can deal in their abstractions. To the problems of Percy's life, and there were many—the suicide of his father, the death of his mother, his tuberculosis—Foote acknowledges that the "church, doubtless can give . . . highly satisfactory answers . . . as far as they go." "But," says Foote, "the real answers, the answers that will bring you not peace but understanding, can only be found in art (20Jul52)."

The stuff of art, Foote says in this same letter, echoing Henry James whom Foote declares to be his "favorite American writer," is experience, but experience is only a beginning. The artist "comprehends" experience "with his soul" and "trusts" his "intuition, using his style to transform experience into laws." "Intuition," in this sense, one may assume, is the "natural movement" of which Proust spoke. One might also assume that, were Foote somewhat less sensitive to Percy's conversion, he would grant religion, maybe even Catholicism, the same value he grants philosophy in that it can be so absorbed into one's being that it colors the "quality of vision." Neither religion nor philosophy, however, can become the "quality of vision," for the writing thus produced would be less than art, and neither can belong to that high order. The work of art is no less than "the concrete equivalent of a reality belonging to another order (29Oct55)." Art is surely not to be judged on narrow moral ground. "As for pornography I probably dont despise it any more than I do bad writing of any kind," he explained (20Jul52).

The "inner reality," the "something rescued from time and chaos," or the bones of the hand revealed in the light from the artist's lamp, has form, shape. It is a shape that for the novelist may be reflected by plot, the novelist's particular name for form. In his 1964 lecture, Foote agreed with Aristotle that "the management of *plot* [is] the most important element in dramatic composition." A little later he explained, "[p]lotting includes a great deal more than the mere arrangement of events in dramatic sequence. It includes, as well, the amount of space and stress each of the events is to be accorded—and because of this, by the combination of them all, it gives a book its larger rhythms and provides it with narrative drive, the force that makes it move under its own power."[54] He uses the example of Vermeer as a painter who chose his elements well and arranged them dramatically. The sonata form, too, in its classic three parts, is to some of Mozart's music as plot is to the novel.

On several occasions Foote described to Percy the shapes of his plots. "Blocking out" a novel came first. He was particularly upset that Percy did not understand the form—three parts, each divided into three parts—of *Follow Me Down.* But form is common to all the arts. "All art is an organization of experience," he wrote while he was revising *Tournament,* "whatever the form, and in that all the arts are kin: what form an artist chooses to demonstrate his soul, to parade his intelligence, is accidental, even unimportant. 'Child by Fever,' for instance, might have been a string quartet—and a damn bad one too (30Jul48)." Perhaps in this instance Foote does not mean "form" as simply plot, but rather a particular art— music, painting, novel. The form of the novel, the shape of the plot, as well as the style, the "quality of vision," was of enormous importance to Shelby Foote.

It is perhaps only a natural consequence of his convictions about the importance of form in art and the need for a philosophy to be "submerged" beneath the "quality of vision" that caused him, at one point, to anticipate his career as developing in three parts. It is also possible to interpret his self-discipline in light of his convictions, for form determines the very process of writing, the day-to-day working life of the writer. Well into the writing of *Love in a Dry Season,* Foote mailed Percy copies of a "plot diagram" for the book and a "writing-schedule." In the margin of the "plot-diagram," he recorded the estimated page length for particular sections and then the actual length.

The "writing-schedule" began as "a column of page numbers." As the writing proceeded, he entered "notes for incidents" as he came to those pages. Finally, he explained to Percy, "To the left I keep track of how much I get done each day (24Mar51)."

William Faulkner and Marcel Proust have exerted the strongest influence on Foote's work. He once told Faulkner that he had "every right to expect to be a far better writer" than Faulkner because Faulkner's "models were Conrad and Sherwood Anderson" while his models were "Marcel Proust and William Faulkner." Faulkner, Foote recalls, "laughed at that and was kind enough not to say anything about its also depending on who was doing the writing." Proust's influence was large and general, and Foote rates him as "one of the half dozen greatest writers of all time. . . . His idea of the way to tell a story makes me say yes, that's the way to tell a estimate / actual

9·B
PLOT DIAGRAM

estimate	actual	
3½	4	① Amanda in the public eye again— brief but weird; recovering.
3	4	② Briarthrer sold to the Wister boys; Def-Army in Baltimore—the death there.
2	2	③ Duff Conway tried & executed; Nat'l Guard mobilizes without Drew
2	3	④ Expanding horizons: the library, Jeni Hustez, other reading.
2	1½	⑤ The marriage photo in the Sunday section — Charley Drew on Leash.
12½	14½	

story, or delineate a character, or plot a novel, or demonstrate a thesis; anything you want to name, it seems to me that Proust does it better than almost anybody else, certainly anybody else in our time."[55]

From Faulkner, Foote developed ideas about theme, setting, and history; from Proust he derived his deep concern for art. Foote recognizes that his "debt to Faulkner is huge,"[56] and American critics have most often compared him to Faulkner. Helen White, like many readers, has observed, "Mr. Foote is indeed the legitimate heir of William Faulkner," but she,

9-B: WRITING SCHEDULE
(week of 19-24 March)

(PAGE)

MON. { 364 / 365 — Amanda in the public eye again: brief but lurid. Emerging from her shell a 〈—〉 bit, she attends Astor Gala; some public comment on this.

TUE. { 366 / 367

(5) { 368

〈—〉 { 369

WED. { 370 / 371 — Jeff & Amy to Baltimore for plastic surgery; sale of Briartree; the DEATH-THEME.

THU (10) { 372 / 373 — Dan Conway tried & executed; Natl Guard mobilizes w/o Drew

FRI { 374 / 375 / 376 — Expanding horizon — the library: Jane Austen & other reading: Balzac, James, & Faulkner.

SAT (15) { 377 / 378 — The marriage ent: Charley Drew on leash along with George Garrett and others, believes that to read Foote's work through a preconceived notion that he has simply moved Yoknapatawpha about a hundred miles southwest and renamed it Jordan County is to miss a great deal of the unique pleasure of Foote's style and vision. The influence of Faulkner on Foote's fiction is obvious, and no one understands that better than Foote himself. Try as he might, particularly in the early stories, Foote could not escape the influence of Faulkner. Jordan County, after all, opened for development about ten years later than Yoknapatawpha, and because the two writers cultivate some of the same terrain, both the land and the characters have unavoidable similarities. Faulkner used his own family in his early Yoknapatawpha novels, and Foote used his grandfather as a model in *Tournament*. Echoes of Faulkner abound in incident, description, and narrative method, but the influences on Foote's Jordan County are far more complex. As he says, Proust had a great deal to do with his "quality of vision," his basic conception of the function and value of art. If the narrator of "Child by Fever" reminds one at first of the narrator of "A Rose for Emily," one need only examine Robert Penn Warren's "Circus in the Attic" to discover that the powers of influence are various and that Foote has taken in a wide range of modern writing. The monologues of *Follow Me Down, Shiloh,* and some of the tales in *Jordan County* seem to reflect *The Sound and the Fury* on first glance, but on a second look, one is likely to find more of Browning's *The Ring and the Book* than Faulkner. Henry James's *Washington Square* provided character and situation for *Love in a Dry Season*. Foote's understanding of the development of Shakespeare's language and his thorough knowledge of the Old Testament have influenced his diction much more than his mentor from the Mississippi hills has influenced it. Foote worked hard to develop his own narrative voice, and in the process, he subsumed a great deal of modern prose.

The shaping forces in Foote's literary career are typically the forces that have shaped the careers of many modern writers, particularly modern southern writers. First there was the broad intellectual and literary world that began to open itself to Foote during the middle years of the 1930s, and then there was the experience of his family's moving to a new land. Both grandfathers, Morris Rosenstock and Huger Lee Foote, figure in his fiction. Jordan County and Bristol are similar to Washington County and Greenville, and many of the figures who developed the town and county also appear in one way or another in the novels. Historical references in Foote's fiction are usually accurate. Then, of course, there is the wider flow

of history, the region, the nation, and the world. Major Barcroft keeps up
with the early battles of World War II; he has maps and uses pins to mark
the movements of troops. Who the president of the United States was
when the events of the novels take place is generally a matter of some
importance to Foote's narrators. Bristol is no isolated community; important events sweep through the eddies to catch on its sand bars and grow in
the life of the community. And, most of all, there was the Civil War, which
left behind in its flotsam a bevy of majors and colonels, an immense event
that gave the place a new meaning for all time.

Chapter II

Tournament and Shiloh

With reviewers and readers in the United States, *Shiloh* has been Foote's most successful novel. It was the first novel he completed upon his return to Greenville after the war, but the editors at Dial Press did not think it would sell. On 2 June 1951, he completed a third draft, and Dial issued it on 7 April 1952, after *Tournament, Follow Me Down,* and *Love in a Dry Season* had appeared. Nevertheless, in design and conception, *Shiloh* fits with *Tournament* and some of the earlier stories that Foote published while he was a student at Chapel Hill. He had finished the first draft of *Tournament* on 11 March 1940, and in the spring and summer of 1947, worked on *Shiloh,* producing a typescript dated "4 July 1947." A second typescript of *Tournament* is dated 1948. By the time *Tournament* was published in 1949, *Shiloh* had achieved the basic design that it would have in final form. Both books, however, reflect Foote's earlier writing and reading, including the poems that appeared in the Greenville High School student newspaper, the *Pica.*

The *Pica* and *The Carolina Magazine*

By 1933 Foote had begun reading seriously, and at school his interests were almost exclusively literary. The *Pica,* the school newspaper that he edited in 1934–35, won high praise as one of the outstanding student newspapers in the nation. It was there, in 1932, that he began to publish poems. Walker Percy recalls that he was writing a poem the day he met Shelby: "I was writing a poem the first time I saw Shelby," Percy told John Jones. "It was in the study hall . . . he was sitting next to me and said, 'What are you doing?' I said, 'I'm writing a poem,' and he looked at it and read it. It wasn't a very good poem. It had never crossed his mind to write anything either. So shortly after that he began to write some poetry which was actually . . . better than mine, which is to say they were terrible."[1] Foote, too, is rather reticent about his early poetry. "[Y]ou can go back in the files of the *Pica* and read some of it I'm afraid," he told Jones.[2] Foote's poems are imitative of the authors he was reading; the images came more often from books than from his own experience, and the emotions often seem artificial; but this is where most writers begin, and, if anything, Foote's efforts reveal a serious interest in making the language work for his purposes, testing various themes and ideas he would explore more fully later.

Foote's earliest efforts are conventional and imitative as "Embers," published in November 1932, makes apparent.

> Glowing embers, burning low,
> Lend the room a ruddy glow,
> Red and warm 'neath ashes cold,
> Bleeding heart of lover bold.[3]

The association of fire with passion Foote probably found in his reading of Renaissance poets, but his models were soon to be more modern. In January 1934 he published a review of an anthology of American poetry in which he speaks with more than passing acquaintance of the poetry of T. S. Eliot, e. e. cummings, Sandburg, Frost, Robinson, and Edgar Lee Masters. The influence of these poets is present in the poems written at about the same time as the review. The first of "Five Images" reveals his careful reading of the moderns and his attention to their methods.

> I
> The night
> Slips down
> And cool
> Sidewalks
> Slide into the night

Hart Crane's poetry may have suggested the treatment of this image; Robinson is probably the source for the second of Foote's images:

Dawn cracked loudly over the rolling fields
And the sun, like a bloody fist,
Shot from behind the last hill.

"Contract," published in September 1933, treats a theme—the power of women over men—that is central to the fiction he was writing fifteen years later. In the first of these short lyrics, "a country housewife/ Buys halibut from/ A greasy Fish-monger" for a price considerably below what the man wanted. In another "An immense dowager/ Buys orchids from/ An effeminate man," and she also arranges the price to suit herself.

Imitations of Browning's dramatic monologues also begin to appear, first in a short poem, November 1933, in which Mary speaks in rhymed quatrains about Judas's betrayal of Jesus. "Her Knight Comes Riding," published in January 1934, is a more ambitious effort; an unnamed speaker describes the return of Franco Marti, a broken old man, to his village and to the woman, Margot, who years ago would have been his bride, but who has now borne the three daughters of an "old Earl." By 1933 Foote had begun to read Faulkner and would have been familiar with Faulkner's monologues; however, his primary model in these early poems, as it would sometimes be in his later fiction, was Browning.

A Petrarchan sonnet, "Prescription," which appeared in *The Carolina Magazine*[4] for March 1937, shows considerable development in Foote's talent as a poet. The central image is a snake; Foote develops it as a metaphor for mankind, which will "find its peace/ In the eternal hissing of old rain." However, "Prescription" was the last poem he published, for he had found poetry to be too confining.

Foote decided early in his career at Chapel Hill that he would not complete a degree, but rather take those courses that suited his interests. Aided by the library resources at Chapel Hill, he continued his reading and began in his writing to experiment with narrative devices in prose fiction and to develop a number of the themes that would later appear in his major fiction. The writer of prose fiction, he soon came to believe, as he told Evans Harrington, "is superior to the poet and to anybody else."[5] Experimenting with form and technique contributed to the development of his characteristic prose rhythms. "Always, always," he said, "the writer has to have his rhythms." To him "prose rhythms are . . . infinitely more interesting than poetical rhythms;" "the poet," he believes, does not need "as much skill as the prose writer."[6]

Between November 1935 and April 1937, Foote contributed nine stories and four book reviews to the student magazine at the University of North Carolina, *The Carolina Magazine*. One of his reviews, "The Literature of Fury" (November 1936), which he describes as "a placing of William Faulkner's new novel *Absalom, Absalom!* with a relation to his other works," though brief, bears distinction as an early and perceptive critical survey of Faulkner's career and also reveals the depth of Faulkner's impression on Foote. He remarks that the "medicine" of nine of Faulkner's novels is "alike," in that "the final impression is the same: there are the same emasculated lusts and spent desires when the tales have spun their lengths, and the reader is left with the feeling that someone—sometime during the last few pages—has stolen his insides and left him suspirant on the beach of tragedy, with the tale of fury done and the fine proud tall figures gone to dust." Faulkner's "selfspun mesh of rushing language," Foote explains, reveals "how an economy of words—chosen for sound . . . —can create a mood and frighten (or perhaps excite) the reader into understanding the full import of an action or frame of mind." Faulkner's purpose, Foote concludes, mixing his metaphor a bit, is to "look deep into the bowels of the human brain and come up with horrors past some folks bearing." The quality of reality that Faulkner finds places him among the truly great, and the metaphor that Foote finds to describe Faulkner's method reveals a gifted critical mind.

> His presentation of reality is entirely different from any other in all writing; for he does not so much show us stark reality as scare us with the prospect of it. He reaches into the sack and feels about with his hand, all the time describing what he feels and perhaps even suggesting what it might look like—and constantly threatening to bring it out into broad open daylight, while we sit there scared stiff because we know he is capable of doing it. But he does not; even when he tells of the sound a butcher-knife makes on neckbones he does not let us see it. For he knows well that the most tragic figures man has imagined are not Tantalus and Sysephus who were tormented with reality, but Orestes and Hamlet who were tormented with the suggestion of what reality might be. (30)[7]

His other three are brief reviews of Dos Passos's *The Big Money,* Caroline Gordon's *None Shall Look Back,* and Tucker Brooke's edition of *Shakespeare's Sonnets.*

The short fiction that Foote published in *The Carolina Magazine* naturally reflects his reading, but it also reflects his search for subject, setting, theme, and an authentic narrative voice. Sex, race, the conditions of love, and the loss of tradition in the modern wasteland are his themes here. From the beginning, though, Foote saw his short fiction in a larger context. The short story as a separate entity is "a form that is unsatisfactory," he believes, "unless it is tied in with other things." He says that all of the short stories he has ever written are "tied in."[8] Certainly there are some very obvious connections between his early Chapel Hill stories and his later work, for he was already developing Jordan County.

The failure of love in the modern world, particularly in the world of southern whites, becomes the most absorbing theme in Foote's later fiction; however, in his first published story, "The Good Pilgrim: A Fury Is Calmed," the black murderer from the Mississippi Delta finds peace in commitment to his woman. In ideas and images, which echo the wastelands of Eliot and Faulkner, Foote explores the primitive foundations of love and religious experience. Ray, Foote's hero, after almost ten years spent in prison for the murder of the man he had found in bed with the woman Ray had planned to marry, returns to farm the Delta with his friend Charky. In prison Ray had shaped Charky in an image to suit himself. As Ray put it, he had "made" Charky. "Making," he found, "was harder than killing"; to do it "you molded his opinion till it fit yours; then you had a man such as you yourself would like to be—a man with all your best ideas, put forth in your best manner; and yet with something cleaner about him which had first attracted you to him, and which you wished you had for your own but could never have" (5).[9] Charky's life parallels Ray's, but perhaps because Ray had "made" him, Charky's fulfillment comes, apparently, without his suffering eruptions from the mysterious, mythical recesses of his inner self which Ray experiences. Even so, there is no "stony rubbish" here, for Ray and Charky are part of the cycle of nature. "Charky and he had both won their way through that hard first year wrestling with that good ground and almost burrowing down into it to push up the tender young stalks" (6).

Ray swore that after prison he would *"never see another woman but with the eyes of a mule"* (5); but his resolve weakens under the battering of a "pent-up fury" that comes to him first when he is hunting on Christmas morning. Irresistible and ancient, his fury comes "whirring down the icy tundras and sweltering jungles of times past, the silent screams of his race before it was subjugated to cotton and mules and saxophones and dice." On this Christmas Day, Ray calms his fury by shooting a dog and tasting its blood, but the fury comes again and Ray calms it with "a rooster and a pig and another dog" (32).

Charky has married Cora, a "foolishly religious" woman who "prayed for stretches of three or four hours" (7), and in spite of his earlier belief, Ray, too, decides he needs a woman. He takes Sarah home from the barrelhouse to live with him, but is afraid that his fury will seize him and he will kill Sarah "instead of some baser animal" (32). Then one night his fury does come. He reaches for Sarah, and when she does not awaken immediately, he grabs her roughly. Listlessly she falls "over against him," and Ray takes her "as she showed." After that "his troubles [are] all over" (32). Thus, in an agrarian identification with the soil, a quartet of Delta blacks in Foote's earliest story find what is unavailable to the failed white characters in *The Sound and the Fury* and *The Waste Land*. Ray's pilgrimage is not to some ancient holy site; rather, it is a metaphysical journey into the primitive origins of love. It is a pilgrimage that makes the life of the modern spirit worthy and full.

"A Tale Untitled"[10] presents another exploration of the wasteland from which characters again emerge successfully. This time a Bible salesman named Ladyson, who is traveling through the Mississippi Delta, has a vision of the Lady, a vision that harks back to the traditions of the courtly romance. It is at least possible, the young Foote seems to say, that the security and wholeness of being, represented to Eliot by the Round Table and the Chapel Perilous, might also be found in enchanted cabins somewhere north of Greenville. If Jerusalem, Athens, Alexandria, Vienna, and London are all "unreal," as Eliot declared them to be, then maybe the moderns need only to look in the cotton fields of the Mississippi Delta to find what is missing. Late in the afternoon, Ladyson stops at a cabin where he finds Lonzo and a woman whose husband is away from home. They do not buy his Bible, in fact, they do not seem to know that it is a book they might want to buy. As night comes on and it begins to rain, the woman offers the salesman a pallet in the kitchen for the night. Foote's description of the woman's looking down at the man, whose "pale esthetic face" (27) suggests to the narrator the paintings of medieval monks, prepares the reader for the lady's vision of the word "love" which she imagines to be flashing on the wall as though projected by a magic lantern. The salesman does not sleep and finds himself in a room filled with "liquid golden light" (28). In this golden air, "some blind intuition out of some older resource utilized by forebears before barred windows and locked doors, let alone pistols" causes the man to turn his head, and he sees the woman standing in the shadows beyond the door frame. "Clad only in a long white night-gown which fell from her straight shoulder without a fold or wrinkle except for the slight lift of her breasts," she reminds him of "a figure on a church window." His apparition disappears into the golden gloom, but seeing her has made him want "to cry like when he was a little boy, without knowing why" (28). Ladyson's vision of the lady of the manor, or the cabin as it were, is, of course, what would restore health, unity of thought and feeling, wholeness to modern man's fragmented psyche.

City folk are not as lucky as the rural folk in Foote's early stories. "This Primrose Hill,"[11] set in the Delta town that Foote would later call Bristol, has as its main character a young socialite, the latest branch of "a family of statesmen and generals and at least one governor" (9). Nevertheless, the men in the barbershop talk about her and with good reason. One man suggests that perhaps "one o them governors' wives got mixed up with a flag-salesman or something" (10). At any rate, Lurlyne finally grows tired of her promiscuity and sets the date for her marriage to Will Lowery, also of a good family, who has been waiting patiently and enduring for years her refusal even to kiss him good night.

The juxtaposition of failed modernity against the unrecognized and therefore inexcessible richness of tradition provided Foote with a major motif for his early fiction, and because of the abundance and thoroughness of his reading, characters like Lurlyne and Ladyson became more alle-gorical than real. This is true also of Francis in "The Village Killers,"[12] a young man who apparently knows nothing about the saint whose name he bears. Francis hires out to Pozzy as a truck driver and whiskey runner, but he bets the money that Pozzy gives him to pay for the whiskey on the races and loses. Pozzy's henchman leaves him barely conscious in a ditch where all the while he had thought Pozzy was such a nice man. It is the old values that are lost in this story. "Francis's father ran a blacksmith shop" (6) and did not like his son's driving the new-fangled truck; Francis is betrayed by his naive trust in his fellow man and his failure to recognize the deadliness of the sin of greed.

Writing about people in Mississippi, particularly in the Delta, Foote could not easily avoid race. Ray and Charky in "The Good Pilgrim" are black, and Ray's heritage from a primitive past, from those "sweltering jungles," is the cause of his fury, though blacks in Foote's stories are by no means the only ones who possess a primitive past. "All Right About

That"[13] is one of the few stories from Foote's early work in which the relationship between races is a central issue. In this story a little white girl and her black companion, Manny, the daughter of the little girl's mother's cook, are sitting beside a pond when three white boys come to go swimming. Two of the boys are reluctant to strip off their clothes with the girls there, but the third argues that it is not their fault if the girls see them naked. Besides, he says, "We can't help it if she stays," meaning the white girl; "And the other one's just a nigger," he adds. Manny replies, "That's all right about that" (25), reflecting the view that Foote, himself, seems to have reached; race is an unfortunate and accidental difference between human beings, a view that, when expressed almost thirty years later in South Alabama, caused considerable disturbance among the local Klans.

Although racial difference does not seem to make much difference to the young Foote, the differences between the sexes does. Foote's last and most ambitious story in *The Carolina Magazine,* "and the Gay and the Blue,"[14] features a gifted and promising young man, Eben Jaynes, who, having sold his freedom and his soul to an enchantress, is hanged for her murder. Eben's grandfather, Jupe, the narrator of the tale, explains how he knows the details of his grandson's life: "He got along better with me than he ever done with any other man." Eben's mother, Flaunts, sends him off to grammar school, but instead Eben goes down town to shine shoes. Flaunts whips him, but it does no good because Eben is "shining the shoes of whitefolks on the street; just making dime after dime off his smartness and aptness; seven years old, mind you, and dime after dime" (11). Soon Eben is dressed in "yellow shoes and a Stetson . . . just kinging it on the avenue." At twelve, "the hottest thing in Mississippi," Eben deflowers the preacher's youngest daughter. "The women just went hog-wild, and he sho done some sporting," Jupe says. "They called him Pigmeat, he was so mitey small" (11). Eben's first serious trouble comes when the new man who has come to help run the papermill finds Eben with his wife, but it is Kate Mae Tanner who brings Eben's ruin. According to Jupe, Kate Mae "put the grisgris on him proper." "Lord, what a stingaree that woman must have had," he says, "make a preacher forsake the Book, gnash his tooths, forget the Glory, and take up prancing." Kate Mae keeps Eben in her bed and stands at her cabin door smoking and "waiting for his bility, so she could take a little more soul outin him" (13). Day and night, as Eben in his jail cell explains to Jupe, the ritual repeats itself.

I was laying on the bed, like usual, feeling my ribs all empty and her standing there watching the daylight in the street and I says, 'I can again,' and she says,

'Can you?' and

'Yair,' I says. And that the way it went: daytime nightime, bility unbility. You comprehend? [14]

The nights could be worse than the days, though, Eben explains, "with no daylight outside the door, and her sitting there smoking them thousand cigarettes till all my eyes reckoned was a thousand little firedots in the dark separating the minutes, and the long cool dark not firedotted making the sleep, feeling my soul coming back." Then day would come and Eben would feel his "soul leaving" "like it was a leak in between my ribs where it would scape, like a punctured tire does" (14). When Eben can stand it no longer, he breaks her neck: "It made a pop like quick kindling, and then a lot of quick jumping kicking racket, and then it was still-quiet; just me and the darkness flowing over my face and my ribs making a creaking while I breathed my soul back in" (14).

The events surrounding Flaunt's and Jupe's trip to the jail to retrieve Eben's body are described in a way that reminds one of Faulkner's description of Lucas and Molly Beauchamp in Go Down Moses. Flaunt and Jupe have a palpable stoical pride that a white world cannot touch or diminish. Eben's weakness, Jupe realizes, came not from his fear of a dominant white world but, instead, from within his own world. It was his own failure to assert his manhood and independence. Rather than some white man, Kate Mae's calling him "boy" had emasculated Eben by preying on the weakness of his masculinity.

Among Foote's early experiments in fiction are a ghost story, "Sad Hiatus," and a curiously sentimental tale, "The Old Man That Sold Peanuts in New Orleans." The narrator of "Sad Hiatus"[15] watches Willy fall from the docks into the Gulf, but Willy's body is never recovered and only "one garbled shoe" is found. Then Willy appears in North Dakota, and a train apparently runs over him. Again the narrator finds a shoe after both halves of what was taken to be Willy's remains have been buried. Finally Willy appears at Minsky's in New York, and the narrator is not even mildly surprised when Willy disappears with the blond with whom he is supposed to have a date.

"The Old Man That Sold Peanuts in New Orleans"[16] adds a curious and ironic twist to the sentimentality of the O'Henry formula. The Old Man, a shabby peanut vendor, cannot afford to buy a Christmas present, a pair of slippers, for the prostitute who has occasionally offered him a warm place to rest. On the day after Christmas, he has almost enough money to buy the slippers, which are now on sale for half price, so he begs on the street in hopes of raising an additional dime. A little boy, obviously trained in the bourgeois spirit of Christmas generosity, gives him a nickel, but laughs when the Old Man asks for a dime. Frantic lest the shoes be sold, he places his money, still a nickel short, on the counter and grabs the slippers. As the police drag the Old Man out of the store, they pass the little boy who is now not laughing. This time it is the Old Man who cannot control his own laughter. "I was laughing like a fool," the Old Man reports, "and I must have scared the little boy, because he started crying and he hid his face in the skirt of his mother's grey fur coat" (9). It seems that the reader is urged to feel sympathy for the poor, cold, shabby Old Man, but the Old Man seems to laugh at the reader because sympathy, the conventional response, is inadequate and artificial.

Just as Foote experimented with themes and ideas that he found in the writers he had read, so he experimented with narrative techniques. Three of these stories employ rather conventional limited omniscience; the other six are first-person monologues told in the style of William Faulkner. Jupe in "and the Gay and the Blue" is, of course, reminiscent of Molly Beauchamp. The first-person narrator of "This Primrose Hill" has apparently traveled through Jefferson, Mississippi, and talked with Hawkshaw and others in the barbershop there, for he seems to have profited by the conversation in "Hair" and "Dry September." He is even more closely related to the tale teller in "A Rose for Emily." Like Faulkner's narrator, Foote's man speaks for his community. He reports what the town knows and says about Lurlyne and Will Lowery just as Faulkner's narrator reports what Jefferson thought of Miss Emily.

Foote's imitation of Faulkner's technique in "Bristol's Gargoyle"[17] is even more complex. Here he uses the methods of *Absalom, Absalom!* to report events similar to those in "A Rose for Emily." Foote's narrator is a boy who lived with his parents across the street from Miss Esther Weathers, who, when her father died, "nailed herself in . . . [her] house with his body for a solid week" (5). He knows that the town regarded her as aristocracy—blue blood—and on the occasion of her death, the boy and his father speculate on the origin of the bullet in the Bible on the coffee table in Miss Esther's parlor. The father thinks that Miss Esther herself had fired the bullet at her father in anger over Colonel Weathers's having run her boyfriend, Porter Merritt of Virginia, away.

In these nine early experimental stories, it was probably as a result of reading Faulkner that he discovered the importance of place and setting although he also gives credit to other writers. "Place is enormously important in giving validity to writing," he told a creative writing class at Memphis State University[18] thirty years later, and place for Foote was Jordan County, Mississippi. "I was quite consciously trying to cover this county—a county I had more or less discovered for myself by basing it on my home county, Washington County, in Mississippi. It has an industrial north, an agrarian south, and a capital on a river," he explained to Helen White and Redding Sugg. "In each of the novels I tried to reach into some segment of that county with the intention of writing, over the years, a whole series of novels more or less in the manner of Balzac or Zola to show what life there was like over the span of the two hundred or so years that it was sitting there."[19]

Although Foote credits Balzac and Zola for at least some influence on the creation of Jordan County, it was while he was writing under the spell of Faulkner that he first began using the names Jordan County and Bristol. His first short story, "The Good Pilgrim," takes place near Cleveland, which is in the Delta to the north of Greenville. "A Tale Untitled" and "and the Gay and the Blue" have references that seem to place these stories in the Delta, but the first direct reference to a town that continued to appear as a part of the geography of Jordan County occurs in "The Village Killers." Bannard is the town in which Francis buys liquor for Pozzy. This is a town to the east of Bristol and parallel to Leland, Mississippi, just as Bristol resembles Greenville in many ways. The small town, though not named Bristol in "This Primrose Hill," obviously became Bristol when Foote added the text of "The Primrose Hill" almost verbatim to "Child by Fever," a story he revised several times and finally published in 1954 as part of *Jordan County*. Bristol, of course, became Bristol with the publication in February 1937 of "Bristol's Gargoyle."

In addition to "This Primrose Hill," bits and pieces of these early stories crop up fairly often in Foote's later fiction. He had, it seems, almost from the beginning, as he said, conceived of them as a part of something larger. Jordan County and Bristol became the setting for *Tournament* and three later novels. "A Tale Untitled" supplied imagery and theme for *Follow Me*

Down, in which love erupts in a shower of gold. The events of "and the Gay and the Blue" were transformed to become "Tell Them Good-by," published first in *The Saturday Evening Post* in 1947 and later as "Ride Out" in *Jordan County.* The good luck and endurance of the black farmers in "The Good Pilgrim" became the means of Hugh Bart's success in *Tournament,* the novel that Foote began just after he left the University of North Carolina in 1937.

Tournament

In revising *Tournament* in the late 1940s, Foote did not alter significantly the original design; rather, he changed sentences and phrases that he regarded as imitative of Wolfe, Joyce, and Faulkner, and he altered the names of some of the characters, the most significant being the change of the central figure's name from Royal to Hugh Bart. Based on the history of the Mississippi Delta and on his own family's part in that history (in which, of course, Foote was following the example of Faulkner in *Flags in the Dust*), *Tournament* is thoroughly modern in its despair of man's "failure of nerve" and thoroughly southern in its examination of the harmony that southern theorists, of whom Allen Tate is a typical example, believed to be available to "traditional man" in the South.

Because accuracy of historical detail was obviously important to Foote from the beginning of his writing career, the characters in Foote's fiction are frequently based on actual people, as is Hugh Bart and, to a certain extent, Hugh's son and grandson. These characters are set against a historical background that is as accurate as the demands of fiction permit. Foote has described *Tournament* as "a young man's attempt to deal with what he imagined might have been his grandfather's life."[20] The life of Huger Lee Foote, Shelby's grandfather, seemed to him to be typical of the Delta: "I don't personally know anybody who was around that part of the county, when I was born that hadn't had a grandfather or great-grandfather who amounted to something considerable." "[T]hose down had been up, those up had been down," and Foote's grandfathers, both Hugh Foote and Morris Rosenstock, fit the form: "Both of my grandfathers were worth close to a million dollars in the course of their lives; they barely had the money to dig the holes to put them in when they died."[21]

Foote's great-grandfather, Hezekiah William Foote, sent his son Huger Lee to the Delta in the 1870s to manage four plantations—Egremont,

Mounds, Hard Scable, and Mount Holly. Hezekiah Foote, a Confederate veteran who had had his horse short from under him at Shiloh, had become a substantial land owner in Noxubee County in the Black Prairie region of eastern Mississippi. To prepare Huger to manage the Delta plantations in which he was investing, Hezekiah first sent him to Chillicothe Business College in Ohio, then to Texas to learn the cotton trade. Mount Holly became Huger's favorite of the four plantations, and he arranged to buy it from his father, only to find later that Hezekiah had willed it to him. The large plantation house at Mount Holly, which became the Solitaire of *Tournament,* had been built by John Irwin, who resembles Isaac Jameson in *Tournament.* Foote says that his father was raised at Mount Holly as a "sort of rich man's son that never thought he would do anything in this world." However, at about the time that his father married, his grandfather sold Mount Holly, moved to Greenville, and lost his money at the poker table in the Elks Club.[22] These are the general outlines of Foote's grandfather's life and the general outlines of the events in *Tournament.* However, *Tournament* is fiction and not biography, as Foote has carefully explained. "My first novel *Tournament* is written out of sort of a conception of him, but it is only a conception. It's not even founded much on fact. I'd never seen him, I'd never talked about him a great deal with his widow or my mother, except for small things."[23]

If *Tournament* was "a young man's attempt to deal with what he imagined might have been his grandfather's life," then it also needs to be pointed out that this young man had read the most important of the modern writers and had taken them so to heart that he was inclined to interpret his grandfather's life in terms that these writers had employed. *Tournament,* Foote says, "was an attempt to understand the homeland I came out of. I knew then, way back in the dark ages of the '30s, there was something dreadfully wrong with that land that needed looking into—though I knew of many things that were good about it and could be enjoyed. So I tried to examine it."[24] It is usually not accurate to label a fictional character as the author's mouthpiece, and certainly Parker Nowell (a lawyer possibly based on Faulkner's Gavin Stevens), who appeared in *Follow Me Down,* "Rain Down Home," and the drama based on the short story, is not Foote's mouthpiece, but Nowell does identify what was "dreadfully wrong with that land," even though his emphasis is far more negative than his creator's might be. "Love has failed us," Nowell said. "We are essentially, irrevocably alone. Anything that seems to combat that loneliness is a trap—Love is a trap: Love has failed us in this century. We left our better destiny in '65, defeated though we fought with a fury that seems to indicate foreknowledge of what would follow."[25] Nowell's words resemble those that Hugh Bart uttered on his deathbed; both men faced a meaningless loneliness.

Foote set this history of family and region in a two-dimensional understanding of time; there are the actual events in which family and neighbors are caught up, even the weather that Foote seems to represent accurately, and there is the ancient, almost timeless, history of man's experience that has found its way into myth and religion. Allen Tate identifies these two as the dimensions of "historical imagination" and "religious imagination" in an essay, "What is a Traditional Society?" The "religious imagination," says Tate, "can mythologize indiscriminately history, legend, trees, the sea, animals, all being humanly dramatized, somehow converted to the nature of man." The "historical imagination . . . is the religious imagination *manqué*—an exercise of the myth-making propensity of man within the restricted realm of historical event." According to Tate, the "higher myth of religion" and the "lower myth of historical dramatization" are necessary for both happiness and action, but he finds that happiness and action are not possible in the modern world because of the disparity between the way of life and the earning of a living. "The middle-class capitalist does not believe in the dignity of the material basis of his life; his human nature demands a homogeneous pattern of behavior that his economic life will not give him. He doubtless sees in the remains of the Old South a symbol of the homogeneous life. But the ante-bellum man saw no difference between the Georgian house and the economic basis that supported it. It was all of one piece." Life in the antebellum South offered a unity of being that is, in Tate's view, increasingly unavailable to modern man. "Antebellum man," Tate concludes, "insofar as he achieved a unity between his moral nature and his livelihood, was a traditional man."[26] Hugh Bart began his career as a traditional man, though he was unaware of it, but the forces of his world gradually destroyed him.

The comments of Hugh Bart's grandson, Asa, open and close *Tournament*. Asa comments on his own interest in Bart's life and what he, Asa, has learned or, perhaps more significantly, has not learned from it. Asa explains that, from various sources, he has drawn three conclusions about Bart and, to some extent, about all human experience. First, he has learned the facts of Bart's rise from obscurity to prominence and then to self-destruction; second, he has learned how the stages of Bart's life were "punctuated by experience which made him what he was and were explained by his trying to be what he was never meant to be"; and, finally, Asa concludes that, after all of his efforts to find out about his grandfather, he knows no more than he had known before he began. Bart, Asa finds, was a figure "cast in the heroic mold, whom facts shook and conditions altered, and the thought, the conviction which rose out of the roiling cauldron, that each man, even when pressed closest by other men in their scramble for the things they offer one another with so little grace, is profoundly alone" (xiv).[27]

Being "cast in the heroic mold" means personal, social, and financial success for Bart, as long as he maintains an instinctive harmony within himself and with the world around him—as long as he obeys his inner "spark." His rise to the top of Delta life comes naturally, almost inevitably, to him. Soon after his arrival in the Delta, he becomes sheriff of Issawamba County, voted in "because of some inner hang for making the small farmers and tradesmen admire the way he sat a horse and picked a crop" (xiv). Bart's principal opponent in the election, Judge Wiltner, soon becomes one of his most ardent admirers, so when the Union Prudential Insurance Company writes asking his advice about Solitaire, a large bankrupt plantation on the banks of Lake Jordan in Jordan County and just to the north of Issawamba County, Wiltner recommends that the holders of the defaulted mortgage contact Bart. In 1887, nine years after arriving in the Delta, Bart has charge of one of the largest plantations and ten years and six months after that he has cleared his title to Solitaire—five square miles of some of the richest farm land in America on which a forty-room mansion sat. Big men and little men, bankers, sheriffs, and sharecroppers alike admire him. Almost as soon as he begins farming "other planters and cotton men" begin coming "from nearby counties to see the Solitaire crop" (15). Billy Boy, Bart's long-time companion and servant, imagines him to be "immense and knightly and Biblical in the rich, unreal glare of hero-worship" (xiii), and Bart provides an image that men of lesser fortune believe they themselves would fit had Mistress Fortune dealt them a better hand.

It is more than luck that brings Bart success and makes these men admire him. Bart has a "spark," an "inner quality, a combination of simplicity and insight" that enables him to recognize and instinctively do the right thing. It "made his advances possible and was the mainspring of his reaction when choice was necessary, which enabled him to reach out in the dark and touch Right when other men, lacking the spark, would not have been able to distinguish it from Wrong in broad open daylight" (67–68).

Judge Wiltner, one of the first to recognize Bart's "spark," is one of the first to remark Bart's decline. Three weeks before his death, the judge calls Bart to his bedside and explains, though Bart does not understand, the conditions under which Bart will fall. Wiltner tells Bart that, because of the sources from which he sprang, he needs to "keep growing." His success at Solitaire was to have been "a step along the way," as were his wife and children, but now Wiltner sees that these were not "steps," but that they were developing into the whole "edifice." Instead of advancing through and beyond the pattern of life in the Delta to some larger goal, Wiltner fears that Bart considers the style to be goal enough. It is possible, Wiltner believes, that Bart, for all his worth, will "snarl up the whole business." "Youre made another way, son. If my reasoning is right (and I know men) and if youre half what I took you to be, you cant stop like the rest of them. You cant loaf on a slope, no matter which way youre heading; youve got to keep moving. If you stop youll fret; youll lash out for action. And you wont pick an action that will carry you toward the things your life points to; youll just grab the first action that comes to hand. And if it isnt the kind that will carry you along the way you were born to travel, youll snarl up the whole business. Youll undo in a hurry all youve done. Youll bungle, son; youll bungle. Youll die with the whole thing gone crash in your lap" (53). Listening to his oracle, Bart feels "like a prize pupil told by his professor that he had done well in an examination, but less well than was expected" (52). Riding home to Solitaire he thinks that Wiltner has given him "a long speech . . . veering from consideration of what the dying man had said, occupying his mind with awe for the number of words rather than their import" (53).

Bart suffers his "failure of nerve" during the early years of the new century, about 1910. In his lecture at Memphis State on the poetry of John Crowe Ransom, Foote defined "failure of nerve," a theme he found important to the understanding of Ransom's work, as "the feeling that in modern times we are not able out of the complexity of our lives to cope with situations as well as our forebears could who were not pulled to pieces by the jangle of modern life." Foote thinks that the failure is by no means unique to modern times but that "if you had any time in the history of the world where people could with the most justice complain about the quick increase in the tempo of living it seems to me to have been around then [1910], not since then."[28]

Failure was not a necessary condition for Bart, however. Continuing success with his land, family, wealth, and the games seemed almost by definition possible, but success depended on recognizing a difference between patterns that are the natural resources for the "religious" and the "historical" imagination and those that are artificial. Intuitively Bart felt the natural, the "essence" of his "spark," and as long as he followed it, he would be right. His life would harmonize those timeless resources of being that give meaning to pattern and style. Unfortunately, Bart mistook the superficial for the permanent, which, Foote suggests, is a recurring problem for modern man, "pulled to pieces by the jangle." Near the end of the novel, Bart engages in conversation with a peddler, an event that treats concisely the terms of Bart's failure. The peddler's name, Arthur Sunday, represents both dimensions of the imagination that Tate identifies—"Sunday" is the religious dimension and "Arthur," the name of the mythical British king, is the historical. By September of 1914, technology and progress have ruined Arthur Sunday. In 1907 he had earned a very comfortable living in Hattiesburg selling "carriages, buggies, anything in the horse-drawn line," but by 1914 the automobile had driven him to peddling soap from door to door. Bart wishes to buy ten bars of Lavender Flowers shaving soap, but even this small wish is denied the defeated Bart. Instead, because Sunday does not have the lavenders that he wanted, Bart ends up with ten bars of Blue Waltz.

Ransom's treatment of the theme of failure of modern man caught Foote's attention; another theme, the irony with which failure accomplishes itself, is obviously another parallel between the two writers. In *The Poetry of John Crowe Ransom,* Miller Williams points out that in Ransom's poetry "a sense of irony is the abiding realization that every human statement contains its own contradiction and that every human act contains the seeds of its own defeat."[29] The growth of the barriers that enclose is one of the central metaphors through which Asa explores Bart's fall; the other metaphor is the tournament, the game. Both metaphors contain the ironic dimension that Foote no doubt observed in Ransom's poetry. The success that provides Bart with material wealth, the fat of the land as well as that of the body, and the games at which he seems to excel provide the means and the conditions of his ultimate defeat. His successes, ironically, are the means by which he fails.

If Bart were to "lash out" against the prospect of his failure, as Wiltner predicted he would, his lashing out would need to penetrate the barriers that thickened around him. Leaving Wiltner, Bart "wore the dignity and detachment which the insecure assume to guard against intimacy and possible insult, and he had begun to put on weight, flesh building a barrier about the robust frame, incasing the still-hot blood." It was then that he "took sanctuary within inaction, his invulnerability left him with a rush like wind; gallantry fell from him like a garment; the open simplicity of his mind went like smoke. It required another ten years for him to realize what had happened, as if grossness of the flesh had insulated his mind's quick, but that was the day it began" (53).

The term *tournament* brings to mind the games of knights in Arthurian romances, games usually played according to rules of long-established custom. Nineteenth-century British and American writers—Tennyson, Walter Scott, and even the black writer Charles Chesnutt in a novel, *The House Behind the Cedars*—found the tournament a useful substitute for war, a crucible from which heroes emerge. Allen Tate's novel, *The Fathers,* features a tournament, and Mark Twain's comment on 'Walter Scott's responsibilities in bringing about the American Civil War is well known. Bart's games are described in terms that are often associated with American and European culture in general, but especially with the South.

Bart's awareness that his life fell into a pattern grew. He accepted the challenge that Solitaire offered him and, at first, he won, making success at Delta farming and its attendant grand style his goal, but "when he first reached" his goal, Foote's narrator says, "he was like a man who, overcome by a desire to leap into a whirlpool, thrashes about inside it, too busy to analyze his present sensations, let alone the nature of the impulse that prompted the leap" (66). Bart found that his life seemed patterned; "as if the whirlpool had ebbed or the thrashing became accustomed, Bart could look about and see his days following a pattern, alike within their separate seasons" (66). At first the pattern was both natural and sufficient for Bart—the farming, hunting, shooting, cards, social life. These games sufficed for his drive and his unselfconscious innate ability, but the flux of events and what they offered proved insufficient as Bart's self-consciousness grew, as he curbed his spontaneity. Facing the twentieth century, Bart needed something that he did not have to preserve his "spark." Perhaps he needed a bigger game, a larger plan, an inquiring mind, a more imaginative intellect, the sensitivity of an artist; these he did not have and so he was lost. He grew content to measure himself by other men's patterns, rather than become the hero of his own dream. As Wiltner said, he "stopped growing."

Bart's games were emblematic of more fundamental challenges and obviously were played according to clearly defined rules. For Bart, the young and successful planter, hunting was a source of recreation and relief from the ritual of his schedule. He loved "the hard recoil of the gun, the acrid smell of powder blown back across his face, the feathery explosion of birds in midair, the sound of brush breaking as the dogs went bounding for the quail" (35). As game in the Delta became less plentiful, hunting gave way to trapshooting. The Ithaca Gun Club was organized and began to hold contests that drew crowds from across the region. "Bart was a favorite with the crowd; it was so exciting to watch him shoot. His style was spectacular and sudden; the act of firing was quick, almost savage in contrast with his manner" (122). Bart soon won the tri-state competition in Memphis "against a field of two hundred marksmen from Tennessee and Arkansas and Mississippi" (125). Finally, in November 1911, he won the national trapshooting championship in Louisville, Kentucky, and that earned him the opportunity to shake hands with President Taft. When the weather was too cold for hunting, the planters played poker in the hunting lodge on Lake Jordan, and Hugh Bart won. The "first night, playing his cards well enough but betting with little ability, he won five hundred dollars" (81). He "took to" poker, not out of some theoretical interest, but out of the same exuberance that made him win at almost any contest he entered. "He played with a sort of ruthless joviality, laughing and raking in pots with both hands and gibing at the losers" (82). At all of these games Bart won, but the winning was not enough. The shooting skills eventuated in his refusal to defend his national championship in trapshooting because he found the championship meant nothing to him, his luck at amateur poker led him to play away the remainder of his meager fortune night after night at the Bristol Elks Club.

For Bart farming Solitaire was a game governed by the rules that money and banks had established; mother nature set the odds. Bart bought Solitaire for $96,000 in 1886; ten years and six months later, he had paid off the mortgage. He worked hard at farming, and success led him deeper into the rituals of planting, selling, and banking. It was only a matter of time before he began to fret at the limitations these rules imposed. When he began at Solitaire, farming had meant "rising before dawn" and "being able to get a maximum of work out of fieldhands," but as he became more successful, farming "meant balancing money against labor and risk; it meant sitting at his desk to make decisions." When his patience would run out with visitors who "discussed the market and uttered sums with reverent voices signifying their worship," and when the walls of his office seemed to close in on him "like the walls of a torture chamber, restlessness and resentment would fill him to the bursting point, and he would rise, shouting for Billy Boy to saddle the stallion" (34–35). After he had paid the mortgage and had established himself in his role as a planter, when he, in short, had, it appeared, won his game, he was as unsatisfied as before. Bart developed only "a vague, uneasy feeling of having accomplished what he had set out to do," now that the hard work and risks were "all behind him." "Excepting the growth of the bank account, a year's work brought him exactly where he had been the year before. . . . The striving was not new and strange; it brought no fatigue to the mind, displaced no fretfulness, calmed no discontent" (75). Nature, the seasons, provided, too, a ritual for the planter. Each spring there was planting, chopping in summer, ginning in the fall. The excessive spring rains that ruined neighboring farmer Patterson's crops or the flood that killed Major Dubose, the historian, did not destroy Bart. His "spark" tamed and harmonized the natural world.

The banker's world was not natural, however, and soon Bart was dissatisfied with the bankers' rules that set the terms of his success. After Bart had sold Solitaire, moved to Bristol, and was living on the proceeds from the sale of the plantation, the Memphis bank that held the proceeds failed. Bart thought he should have forseen this disaster, but his disgust was not limited to the bank failure; it extended to the system of banking as well. "I should have known a man cant live on printed paper that he never even sees except the little he draws at a time to keep the creases out of his wallet and a bulge on his hip" (197). Earlier, when Solitaire was still increasing his fortune, Bart had had an experience that proved to him the worthlessness of banking. "It was the beginning of the antagonism he was to feel for all who made their livelihoods by the manipulation of nothing but money." Lawrence Tilden, who ran a bank in Ithaca, convinced Bart to lend money through the bank to Abraham Wisten, "an Austrian Jew," who was opening a dry goods store in Bristol. Tilden seemed to know that Wisten would fail and simply waited for the event, showing crass indifference to the man but strict concern for the rules of banking. In fact, Tilden had arranged to sell Wisten's interest at a considerable profit for Bart and himself months before formal foreclosure and before Wisten shot himself. Bart realized for the first time "how the desire for money . . . could make men go any lengths, face any indignity. . . . His reaction resembled a desire to secede from the human race" (63). Bart demanded that his money be returned without interest or profit.

His "spark," when he followed it, gave him the earmarks of Tate's traditional man, but instead of becoming deeper in Bart's sense of being, the harmonies of nature and tradition deserted him. Solitaire became the means of Bart's defeat because he did not make it into his own place. Of course, he owned the land and its forty-room mansion, but he never saw these as part of a vision that was uniquely his own, or as a means toward the ends of accomplishment and fulfilling himself. Rather, Solitaire remained integral to a pattern already established, so what Bart bought were the remains of another man's failed dreams. "Cast in the heroic mold" as he was, Bart's dreams should have been his own. Loneliness, Solitaire, was Bart's final despair.

Solitaire had been Isaac Jameson's place. He had cleared the land, and his son, Clive, had built the house there in 1855–56. Isaac Jameson had come to Lake Jordan in 1818, and even though Isaac "had named his plantation Solitaire to express his bachelor intentions" (34), he married the daughter of an inn keeper in Ithaca. Clive, born in 1833, became a general and a hero of the Confederacy; he married the daughter of a Bristol lawyer and they had three sons and a daughter. The sons were born before the war, but the daughter, Florence, was born in 1871 when the general was already in his decline. When the general died in 1882, "ex-planter, ex-Beau Sabreur, ex-everything," the Memphis bank foreclosed. Mrs. Jameson moved to Bristol with Florence and two of her sons to live with her "firstborn, who had left the lake in something kin to disgrace . . . to manage a sawmill" (25). In May 1890 Hugh Bart married Florence and took his bride back to the house her father had built.

Bart's experience repeated that of Clive Jameson. Like Jameson, Bart grew fat in his declining years (25, 52). Both men's lives were strongly affected by the failures of their eldest sons, both of whom worked at menial jobs for a lumber yard in Bristol. Both Jameson's and Bart's failures ended in the hands of bankers. When they left Solitaire, both men moved their families into "rented property," as Mrs. Jameson called it. Both responded in similar ways to their wives' announcements of their final pregnancies. In 1871 when Mrs. Jameson made her announcement, Clive, the general, was already consumed by his imminent ruin. For Clive there was no joy, no excitement, no interest, only indifference. "'So?' He was looking down at the tablecloth" (24–25). Florence's announcement to Bart, "We are going to have our fourth child, Mr. Bart" (91), met with a similar response.

Even though Bart did not arrive in Jordan County with preconceptions about the grand style, as Thomas Sutpen had arrived in Faulkner's Yoknapatawpha County, he was not long in finding abstract patterns into which he thought he should fit, patterns and rules already established there. The baronial plantation style of the South probably had always been a product of the imagination rather than reality; even so, whatever usefulness it had in the older, tidewater, traditional regions—as Tate and the Agrarians argue, an eighteenth-century tradition—was lost in the Mississippi Delta because of the newness of the land. The region was sparsely settled before the Civil War and developed as a cotton empire during the last half of the nineteenth century. Therefore, the roots of an antebellum southern ideal, a plantation tradition, were historically shallow in the Delta. It was an ideal imported into the Delta from older regions of the South to lend order, elegance, and the trappings of a tradition that the region lacked but loved to imitate. The ideal was the belief of a culture that was not ultimately interested in whether its tradition had any basis in nature and history, in myth and romance. The tradition provided entertainment and a sense of noblesse for those who were able to afford it.

Bart accepted the pattern as he found it in the world around him, and that pattern, of course, proved too constricted for the man he should have been. He did not recognize that men admired him because he was Hugh Bart, that they saw beneath his superficial styles a more substantial being. Wife, children, manners, and style were as important to him in the accomplishment of his plan as were his other possessions.

As soon as he moved to Solitaire, he began to pattern himself on what he found around him. The "grand life," as Bart conceived it, was "composed not so much of large actions and possessions but rather of small, undiscussed and apparently birth-acquired habits and gestures" (18). Bart watched those around him and began to imitate them to the point of "stodginess"; he was saved only by those innate qualities he could not control. "He watched, and as he watched he began to acquire; from this man he took one thing, from that another. The result was a stodginess an aloof mien which began to resemble misanthropy, except that he was saved by one of the strongest tendencies in his make-up, albeit this was one he battled hardest against, believing it to be part of a grosser heritage—sheer camaraderie" (18).

Bart tried carefully to preserve his "air of gentility," and he thought that men admired him for it. Like his new fifty-dollar jacket, his manner was a garment. "He thought [men] liked him because of the garment, while actually it was because of the glimpses of what the garment was meant to cover" (19). Thus, manner became for Bart an enclosure, a garment, a shell. "The minute he found himself thus, coat spread open, belly shoved forward, he would know that he had dropped what he believed was his air of gentility, and he would snap shut like a turtle jerking back into its carapace. Later he learned to slide back into the other at such times like a good dancer recovering from a misstep" (19). Alien as banking was to what Bart felt himself to be, his appearance nevertheless resembled that of a banker (75).

In Bart's conception, wife and family were next in importance to the plan. He observed carefully the surrounding life so that, after his experiences on Christmas Day in 1888, he "knew perfectly what it was he wanted to duplicate" (22). Bart had spent the day with various families on the lake and he liked very much what he found there. Imitating their way of life would, first of all, mean finding a wife, so in May 1890 he married Florence Jameson, who was not to be his companion in romance, but the keeper of Solitaire and the mother of his heirs. After the wedding ceremony, Bart "thought: Bride, I have a bride; but the word meant nothing, brought no image until he changed it and thought: Wife, I have a wife; and the image rose perfect, actual—of a woman like those others he had seen in homes on the lake, each with a ring of keys at her belt and efficiency at hand like a mule skinner's whip. But when he said bride and even wife, he was translating: what he meant was chatelaine" (23). Florence became Mrs. Bart, chatelaine of Solitaire, the keeper of the keys like other Delta women of the style who "called their husbands Mister all their lives" (35). For Bart "the marriage license . . . was the seal set on his invasion of the planter kingdom" (36).

After "wife" the plan called for children, who would be raised according to "the strict formula whereby life was simple because conflicting thought did not cloud it and no battle raged between conception and execution" (36). It was the failure of his children, and Bart's willingness to measure that failure by the Delta plan, more than anything else that brought him to ruin. "Bart had four children to build his hopes on, three sons and a daughter: Hugh and Clive and Clive and Florence," Asa, his grandson, tells us. "The first son," as Asa puts it, "turned out dreamy and ineffectual; the second son was dead before he was one day old; the third son broke his body and filled his soul with hate; the daughter turned out perverted" (xvi).

At first, though, Bart expected that his children would follow the usual pattern, the purpose of which, says Asa, "was the repetition of a cycle," and "the maintenance of a static life-way" (92). The boys, after a time in the one-room school in Ithaca, were sent away to "military preparatory schools, then either to Ole Miss or Sewanee." After that, if "they had chosen a profession . . . they went to an Eastern university, Harvard preferred, or Virginia" (92). Away at school these boys would tell grand tales about life in the Delta, but when they returned for Christmas there were disappointments. "There would be the Negroes and the lake and the house and the Christmas fireworks, all more or less as they had described them: but the overtones of romance, the colors with which their imaginations had tinted it, were gone. With the frustrate yearning of boys wanting to be men and men wanting to be boys again, all during their school days they talked about home and all during their holidays they talked about school" (94). They learned to farm cotton at home, and they learned the "avocational" life of the Delta there too—hunting, cards.

The girls of the Delta were raised to follow the roles of their mothers. "They followed their female share of the pattern, exciting at first only contempt" from the boys just after the latter had made their first hunting trip, "then indifference, then mystery, then love, and then respect" (95). They became the chatelaines, "sharp-tongued and predacious" (95), and they were, in truth, the backbone of the Delta life. In a civilization where the men were given to farming, hunting, poker, and drinking, and were inclined more than the women to imagine and interpret their existence in terms of romance, it was the "character of the women" that "made the planter society hold together as long as it did" (95).

By the terms of the established patterns, Bart's children failed. Hugh at fourteen, "a pale reproduction of his father, blond, with more delicate features and a shyer manner," was "easily the best wing shot among the boys on the lake" (123), but looks and a love of shooting and hunting were about the only traits Hugh shared with his father. The commandant of the military academy in Tennessee where Hugh was enrolled regularly, "complained of Hugh's failure to apply himself; his indolence, the commandant said, was a sort of tactical inertia by which he avoided exertion in all its forms" (133). When Hugh "finished at the academy," he had no idea what he wanted to do next. "Bart, who had worked so hard all his life, always with his goal set plain before him . . . could not conceive of a dormitory filled with boys who were not spending all their time planning their future" (142–43). Two eastern universities refused Hugh because of his poor marks at the academy, but he finally entered the University of Mississippi, where, after one year, he was still a freshman. During the Christmas vacation of what should have been his sophomore year, Hugh married a Bristol girl, Kate Bateman, who was generally regarded as a "would be." Kate had descended from one of the original settlers of Bristol, but her father, "whose wife notoriously domineered him, was scraping the bottom of the fortune" (159). Marriage ended Hugh's career at the university and made a farmer of him, temporarily, at least, but in a year he had failed at that too. Hugh could explain easily why he did not want to farm. "It's not so much wanting to as it is I cant. I cant. Ive been here more than a year now, farming, and I know I cant—unless you say I have to" (178). "If you dont want Solitaire, I reckon Solitaire dont want you," Bart told Hugh. A week later Bart had arranged to sell the farm for the quarter of a million dollars that he later lost in the failure of the Memphis bank. After the family moved to Bristol, Hugh had no better luck with the job that his father's friend, Ireland, had arranged for him at the lumberyard. Hugh "just lost interest, stopped caring" (185).

Florence and Clive were no more successful than Hugh. At twelve Florence had become "calculatingly disobedient and would go into tantrums if she was denied her way in the smallest matter" (123). At fourteen she was a confirmed tomboy, not like the other girls on the lake; "there was nothing willowy in her nature. . . . She had no use for boys, however, and was more at ease fighting them behind the barn than she was receiving them as callers in the parlor" (132). Bart was afraid of her; he "knew in his heart that he was afraid of her—actually afraid" (144). At seventeen, Florence "had bloomed without softening." She attended dances, but unlike other girls, she "saved no dance cards, made no scrap book, kept no romantic diary" (158). When the letter arrived explaining that Florence had been expelled from a Virginia boarding school for lesbianism, Bart was about to go to Kentucky to defend his trapshooting title, but he gave it up, forfeited.

He was defeated at farming by his older son's failure; at shooting, by his daughter's expulsion from school; and his financial failure was coincidental with Clive's maiming. Clive had been Bart's favorite, but he was spoiled and very unpopular with the other children who attended school at Ithaca. "He preferred the admiration of grown-ups; they were the ones who ran the world, who handed out favors and laid down restrictions; they were the ones to cultivate" (133). Even though Clive was only a boy, Bart knew when he sold Solitaire that Clive "was not worth the powder it would take to blow him up" (177). A month before he was fourteen, Clive fell from the high roof of the rented house in Bristol. Although the fall did not kill him, it doomed him to a wheelchair for the rest of his life. In his delirium Clive pictured Bart as chasing him: "I fell off the roof and he laughed. He pushed me" (196). It was on that same day that the Commercial Bank of Memphis failed, leaving Bart with only the eight thousand dollars he had deposited in Bristol.

Bart's fondness for the grand Delta style precluded his dealing with his wife and children with any warmth and abiding affection; the camraderie that made him a favorite among men, because it was only camraderie, was insufficient to fill the deeper human need we sometimes call love. At first he thought he wanted "*romance*" with Florence, but the narrator makes clear that "he was fooling himself about the desire he felt" (29). Their courtship was brief: "He saw her twice before he spoke of marriage." The wedding was in May, just when Solitaire needed him the most. He had planned a week-long honeymoon in New Orleans, but it lasted only two days.

Sex with Florence became no more than a hollow ritual, a shabby affair without feeling, "careful and controlled" because the expression of real passion might have been distasteful. "He would cross to the bed and blow out the candle. . . . And sometimes, if she was awake, he would put one hand in a groping motion, fumbling like a man in a strange dark room, and lay it flat against her far thigh. That was the signal. Then he would hitch up both their garments, avoiding any show of haste or urgency, and mount. It would be careful and controlled, Bart holding his weight on knees and elbows and maintaining an even breath because any display would be distasteful, until the end was accomplished and he could turn his back and sleep" (84).

After the death of the first Clive, the pattern changed for a brief time, and it was Florence who effected the change. "Now it was she who made the overture. Spurning their old signal, she would roll against him. . . .

She made little throaty sounds of passion, she writhed. Bart was aghast and did not understand" (91). The change was temporary, though; it lasted only until she conceived again and had some promise of a replacement for the boy who had died.

Even this formal and passionless pattern disappeared after the plantation was sold and the family moved to Bristol. After his "poker-and-whiskey" evenings, Bart would climb into bed and sometimes remember the old ways, being aware of Mrs. Bart beside him, awake. "Feeling the awareness, the revulsion, the tenseness communicated by the sheets and mattress and bedsprings—a taut, almost imperceptible trembling: *Dont touch me! Dont touch me!*—he would wait for sleep to come down like a cloud, and would wake in brilliant sunlight, alone on the wide bed" (222).

The family, too, became family in name only. He had enjoyed spending time with his children when they were young, but as they grew older, relationships became more distant, and near the end there was only "estranged regard" for them. As his interests began to draw Bart away from Solitaire, the camraderie that served him so well in his relationships with men drew him away from his family and became, ironically, the source of his isolation from them. There were social events in Bristol beside which "the Lake Jordan life paled" (125). There were the trapshoots that took place in Memphis, Louisville, and all over the South, the hunting trip to Canada, the reception at the White House where he shook hands with President Taft. By Christmas of 1907, Bart had filled Solitaire with trophies, but the cost of his being so often away was that "he hardly knew any of his children" (132). After the sale and the move to Bristol, family life continued its decline. "Bart was away from home even more than he had been during the last months at Solitaire. Poker was everything now" (189). The family was hardly a family, a family in external appearances only. "He moved cautiously, like a hostage among enemies, into and out of Mrs. Bart's stolid contemplation, Clive's accusing stare, Florence's disinterest or sometimes glaring hate" (213).

In a conversation with his grandson, Asa, Bart seemed, near the end of his life, to reflect briefly on what had gone wrong. Asa's mother, Kate, the outsider who had provided what semblance of cohesion the family had, indicated that Asa had meant little to Bart except occasionally to remind him of an old trapshooting pal, Asa Gold, for whom he named his grandson. To Asa, Bart was that "vengeful god who lived in an upstairs room and caused the rest of the household to move on tiptoe and speak in whispers while he slept" (224). But one morning Bart found Asa on the top step of the front porch, and the two struck up a conversation for the first time. "I didnt even know he could talk," Asa later told Kate, who had come upon "Bart sitting on the top step with Asa in his lap, laughing, nodding his head rapidly, and speaking with that mock-serious verbose cajolery grown-ups adopt when trying to talk with children" (225). At Christmas Bart had purchased the Santa outfit and decorated a tree as a surprise for his grandson, but his fatal stroke occurred as he tried to place the star atop the tree.

In his "Foreword" to the Summa Publications' reprinting of *Tournament,* Louis D. Rubin, Jr., points out Foote's debt to Proust in his depiction of Bart. "It is only through art—time regained—that the relationships between our otherwise perishable moments of existence in time can be recognized and joined together into a reality that may endure free of chronology,"[30] Rubin writes, summarizing Proust's comments in the final volume of *Remembrance of Things Past.* Proust's words indeed diagnose succinctly Bart's cultural illness. To find the answer to his problems Bart needed what he did not have; he needed an artist's sensitivity. As he talked to Arthur Sunday near the end of the novel, he seemed to glimpse briefly, but without much understanding, what his problem may be, as Rubin points out. The "facts" of one's life, Bart seemed to recognize, stand apart, joined only in the succession of events in time. These "facts," Bart concluded, "were only individual beads; the hidden string was what made them into a neckless" (222–23). It would take the power of the artistic imagination, however, to find the string, to see in the disparate events the "essence" that makes life whole and makes it more, in the end, than one man's life, makes it a part of the experience of mankind. That artistic sensibility Bart had never developed: "The abstract was a trap: his brain was not meant for such work" (223). "How could documentary realism have any value at all, since it is underneath little details such as it notes down that reality is hidden?" Proust's Marcel asks. The everyday impressions "have no meaning if one does not extract it from them," and he questions where the writer who deals only with "a repetition of what our eyes see and our intelligence notes . . . finds the joyous, energizing spark that can stimulate him to activity and enable him to go forward with his task."[31] Bart once had the artistic possibility that Proust identifies, the "joyous, energizing spark," but he did not become the artist because he did not develop imaginative insight in either the religious or historical dimension that, tied to the agrarian metaphors of the land, planting and reaping, would have sustained him and enabled him to flourish as Tate's "traditional man."

Perhaps if Bart had been a closer observer, he would have known of the superficiality of his tournament, of any tournament not continually nourished by the imagination. Bart had Clive Jamesona and Abe Wisten, whose example he disregarded, and he also disregarded the examples of Major Dubose and Cassendale Tarfeller, the "last male of a line that included some of the original settlers of the Lake Jordan country" (39). Tarfeller inherited a plantation and the wealth that accompanied it, but he took little interest in farming; "neither the concentration nor the labor required by farming was possible for a person of his temperament" (39). But Tarfeller dressed for his role of the Delta planter, and he possessed the requisite gentility. "Poor, he might have lapsed into the role of village ne'er-do-well, but rich as he was—his clothes neat and carefully fitted as only the New Orleans tailors knew how to make them, his manners perfect because they achieved at the outset the ultimate aim of good behavior by never making him obtrusive—he was part of the society formed by the lake planters" (39).

Tarfeller's younger daughter, Bertha, "a romantic, violent girl" who, observing how her mother dominated her father, grew up telling herself that he was "not a man." Seeking refuge from his effeminancy, she offered herself to Downs Macready, an itinerate gambler. Tarfeller's wife decided that Tarfeller had to challenge the man who had "defiled" her daughter. In Tarfeller's imagination the duel was to be conducted in a manner described by "the elder Dumas or Walter Scott; Tarfeller was given to such imaginings, such dreams of things as they never were" (44). Since he was ill-prepared for the role that his wife and his code had forced on him, he was easy prey for the gambler, and Bart himself was wounded coming to Tarfeller's defense. Bart killed the gambler, but not before the man had shot Tarfeller. The demands of the tournament had forced Tarfeller to do what he never should have attempted, and, except for his wife's insistence that he follow the romantic conventions, he never would have pursued such a course.

The example of Major Dubose was another ready source of insight that passed Bart by without recognition. In the spring of 1903, the levee broke and the lower Delta was flooded. During the previous winter, a landing that the planters had built on the Mississippi had been destroyed by high water, but against the advice of Dubose and a few others, the planters had hired an engineer from Memphis to design and build another landing. The engineer bragged that his landing would be the last one that the lake planters would ever build: "[I]t'll take a damn sight more than water to wash this one away." Dubose knew better; the river "is a damn sight more than water," he told the engineer. When the flood came in May, the landing was swept away, but so was Major Dubose and his lengthy history. Bart gave Dubose a temporary burial in the chest with the water-logged, ruined manuscript, and the wet paper held the corpse until the water receded and a more decent burial was possible. What men can build (and even what they write about their deeds) can never be as permanent as the river and the land. Bart's game, its design, and its rules in the face of time were as impermanent as the landing and the major's history. Mistaking the surface, the style, for the deeper substance of the religious and historical imagination, Bart fell easy prey to the "failure of nerve." Those things which, in light of the active imagination, might have provided him a fair field for glory had instead become the means by which, finally, he was enclosed, solitary, within himself. Even in the end, when he had lost everything and even the enclosure of the flesh was of no use, he could only despair: "The four walls are gone from around me, the roof from over my head, I'm in the dark, alone" (xviii).

Shiloh

William Faulkner admired *Shiloh*. Malcolm Franklin, Faulkner's step-son, remembers that Faulkner once asked if he had read *Shiloh*. "It's the damnedest book I have ever read and one of the best," Faulkner told Franklin and added later that *Shiloh* is "twice the book that *The Red Badge of Courage* is."[32]

Foote says that he conceived of *Shiloh* first "as a short story about a young Confederate soldier who went into battle for the first time and in the course of that battle gave his first rebel yell." The story quickly grew into something more. The yell does ring out but, as Foote puts it, "he gave his first rebel yell and I had left it behind me before I knew I had written it." He described *Shiloh* to Helen White and Redding Sugg as "an attempt to examine a battle through a series of monologues by people engaged in the southern side and on the northern side." The battle, he said, "is one of the most confusing battles the world has ever experienced; I was trying to penetrate that confusion and at the same time communicate it."[33] Foote employs seventeen narrators in all to "penetrate" the "confusion" of Shiloh. Sergeant Polly, Private Dade, and Lieutenant Palmer Metcalf speak for the southern experience; Metcalf opens and closes the book, providing a framework as Asa did for *Tournament*. Captain Fountain, Private Flickner, and twelve members of a squad from the 23d Indiana Regiment represent the Union side. The northerners' monologues alternate with those of the southerners. In all there are seven sections.

Foote assigns Lieutenant Metcalf the duty of providing the reader with background information about the Confederate army at Shiloh. The nineteen-year-old Metcalf was in a position to know a great deal: his father was a close friend of General Albert Sidney Johnston, commander of the Confederate Army of Mississippi; Metcalf had been a student at the Louisiana State Military Academy, where William Tecumseh Sherman was superintendent when the war began, and at Shiloh, Metcalf served as a junior officer on General Johnston's staff, where he helped write the battle orders. His opening narrative takes place Saturday and Sunday morning, 5 and 6 April 1862, and supplies significant details of the war leading up to Shiloh. It pleased Metcalf, just as it seemed to him to please Johnston as they watched the army file past, that finally the Confederates were assuming the offensive. "And now, standing beside the road and watching his troops start out on their march against the army that had pushed him back three hundred miles while the clamor of the South rang in his ears, accusing him of incompetence and even treason, there was satisfaction for himself and justification in the eyes of the people" (19).[34] Because Metcalf's father had been so closely associated with Johnston—fighting with him in Texas and Mexico, serving as a second in Johnston's duel with Felix Huston, who had taken offense at Johnston's being promoted ahead of him in Texas—Metcalf's pride was a clanish, familial pride. He imagined capturing Sherman and making Sherman admit to poor judgment. His eagerness to watch the army execute the battle plan he had helped "write" (by supplying punctuation) emerges in his report of Johnston's overruling the more cautious Beauregard. "I'd fight them if they were a million," Metcalf heard Johnston remark.

Captain Walter Fountain, adjutant of the 53d Ohio, was not as enthusiastic about his Union leaders—Colonel Appler, his regimental commander; General Sherman, his division commander; and Ulysses Grant, commander of the Army of the Tennessee. Fountain's views, though, may have had some relation to Appler's having assigned him duty for the night of 5–6 April; Fountain did not believe that an adjutant should serve as officer-of-the-day. The narrative duty that Foote assigns Fountain parallels Metcalf's—to provide background information leading up to the battle. Fountain grew up in Georgetown, Grant's home town, where he had watched Grant drill the militia. He knew something about Grant's failures at farming, at soldiering in California, and at selling leather for his brothers in Galena, Illinois. Now, he had also followed Grant's career as a Civil War general, and, to some extent, he had followed Sherman's career. Fountain had confidence in his generals; "Fighting for Grant meant winning victories." Colonel Appler, though, was a different matter: "All day Saturday Colonel Appler was on tenderhooks. We felt really ashamed for him" (55). Nobody believed, as Appler did, that an entire Confederate army was about to throw its might against Sherman's front, and it was Fountain, more than anyone else, who should have been attentive to potential danger. On Saturday night he had responsibility for guard, but he spent the night between his rounds, which he performed perfunctorily, writing to his wife while the regimental mascot, a dog named Bango, slept at his feet. The Confederate skirmishers with "their wide-brimmed hats" and "butternut trousers" interrupted Fountain's mediations just after dawn, Sunday 6 April, and that is the last we hear from him.

Private Luther Dade, rifleman, 6th Mississippi, tells the third part of the story. Dade (Foote's middle name) grew up in Ithaca at the southern end of Jordan County and was the genesis of *Shiloh*, the young Confederate giving his first rebel yell. His observations are those of a private who knew little of the grand strategy. The reader meets him as Dade is waking up on Sunday morning, the first day of the battle, and he tells us his experiences—charging into battle (successful at first, eating the Yankees' breakfast), being wounded in his arm, and wandering behind the lines looking for the medics who would amputate the arm. But there is also humor as Dade watches General Cleburne ride his spirited horse into a bog that the foot soldiers had avoided, making a gap in their line. Cleburne waved his sword and yelled at his troops to no avail until the horse tired of him too and threw him into the mud. "We could hear his cussing across two hundred yards of bog" (73), Luther says. There is no humor in his watching General Johnston bleed to death. Even more poignant, though, are Luther Dade's impressions of his experience of battle, one of the most destructive battles in history to that time. Luther, basically an innocent and peaceful fellow, must work himself quickly into an irrational engine of death. High purpose and fine, abstract, high-sounding words dissolve into the concrete reality of killing: "[T]hey may warn you there's going to be bleeding in battle but you dont believe it till you see the blood" (81), and at first there is enough of a scared little boy in Luther for him to be horrified at what he saw.

"There was a great crash and clatter of firing, and over all this I could hear them all around me, screaming and yelping like a foxhunt except there was something crazy mixed up in it too, like horses trapped in a burning barn. I thought theyd all gone crazy—they looked it, for a fact. Their faces were split wide open with screaming, mouths twisted every which way, and this wild lunatic yelping coming out. It wasnt like they were yelling with their mouths: it was more like the yelling was something pent up inside them and they were opening their mouths to let it out. That was the first time I really knew how scared I was" (75). He stopped to consider: "Luther, you got no business mixed up in all this ruckus," but then a big man ran into him and knocked him forward. "He looked at me sort of desperate, like I was a post or something that got in the way, and went by, yelling" (75). Reflection detained Luther only a minute, for he quickly became a part of the 6th Mississippi that was hurling itself to destruction. "We were running and yelling, charging across the flat ground where white canvas tents stretched out in an even row. The racket was louder now, and then I knew why. It was because I was yelling too, crazy and blood-curdled as the rest of them" (77).

Private Otto Flickner, a cannoneer with the 1st Minnesota battery, tells the fourth part of the story. Flickner's unit began the day facing the Corinth road, and it displaced twice to the rear before taking up a position with Prentiss's division at Sunken Road. There, for four hours, Flickner was a part of the bloodiest fighting of that first day, and he may well have heard Luther Dade's rebel yell. The Confederates, he says, "took killing better than any natural men would ever do, and they had a way of yelling that didnt sound even partly human, high and quavery, away up in their throats, without any brain behind it" (110–11). When orders came for the 1st Minnesota to displace a fourth time, Flickner became "demoralized." He walked away from his gun and joined the ten thousand others who were likewise "demoralized" and had deserted their units, fleeing to the river where a high bluff protected them from the fighting. There Flickner encountered Bango, the dog, covered with Captain Fountain's blood.

Courage in the face of danger remains an admirable human quality; the northern cannoneer like the Confederate private confronts his fear. "You think strange things when something has happened to you that you know is going to change your life," Flickner tells us. His sergeant, Sergeant Buterbaugh, had said that the men walking away from battle "werent necessarily cowards; they were just demoralized from losing their confidence" (103), but Flickner knew better. He had watched others finding shelter from the battle: "I got the notion they were not only trying to get away from the fighting, they were trying to walk right out of the human race" (114). Under the bluff Flickner came to terms with his fear: "I wasnt demoralized back there at the sunken road: I hadnt even lost confidence. I was just plain scared" (120). Fear, though, is internal and that "meant I would have to do something about it, or live with it the balance of my life" (121), so Flickner set out in search of his battery and finally found what was left of it.

Sergeant Jefferson Polly, the third southern narrator, a seasoned scout with Forrest's cavalry, climbed an Indian mound overlooking the Tennessee at sundown on Sunday, and from there he saw Buell's troops unloading from boats and marching up the bluff. Polly knew he was seeing the reinforcements that would turn the battle for the Union on Monday morning, and he set out to find Forrest. The two had no success in finding a general who would order the night attack that both Polly and Forrest knew to be the only chance for the Confederate army. Polly had fought with Forrest from the beginning of the war, and the Colonel had become his hero: "I followed him and watched him grow to be what he had become by the time of Shiloh: the first cavalryman of his time, one of the great ones of *all* time, though no one realized it that soon except men who had fought under him" (150). To Polly, Forrest had something of Hugh Bart's "spark."

The combined voices of several members of a squad in the 23d Indiana Infantry Regiment and Palmer Metcalf's second monologue cover the events of Monday, 7 April. The Confederates, having driven Grant almost into the Tennessee River but unable to prevent Buell from reinforcing Grant, were driven back on the second day of Shiloh just as Polly knew they would be. By mid-afternoon there was no option for Beauregard and Bragg, who had succeeded Johnston, but to break contact and withdraw to Corinth, retreating along the roads by which they had advanced.

The 23d Indiana belonged to Lew Wallace's division; the squad was a part of Company G. Although it was under Grant's command, Wallace's division did not participate in the first day of battle because it was at Stony Lonesome, five miles north of Pittsburg Landing. About mid-day on Sunday, according to Corporal Blake's account, Wallace was ordered to the battlefield but took the wrong road and had to countermarch. On Monday, however, Wallace took up his position on the right flank of Grant's army, next to Sherman's division. A hard day's fighting took Wallace's division to the positions that Sherman's division had occupied on Saturday night before the battle. Company G of the 23d Indiana lost two of its members and two were wounded.

The twelve members of the squad have monologues of varying lengths. The longest belongs to Corporal Blake, who tells us what Wallace did on Sunday. Blake, "in charge of the baggage detail" that took the extra equipment to Crump's Landing early Sunday morning, saw Grant come by aboard the *Tigress* on his way to Pittsburg Landing from his headquarters at Savannah. He saw Grant lean over the railing of the boat and order Wallace to have his men "under arms" and "ready to move at a moment's notice" (177). The shortest monologue, "Tell my wife—" (186) belongs to Pettigrew who was shot in the throat.

The individual speakers are not always clearly identified, but occasionally it is possible to discover their names in the monologues of other squad members. Winter, the first speaker and the first man to be killed, is the only member of the squad to say anything about his childhood. Klein is the squad's jokester; several speakers believe that Sergeant Bonner, squad leader, is ambitious for promotion and exposes the squad to danger unnecessarily. The voice of the squad, though, is a corporate voice. They have been together for some time and have shared most of the first year of war together. In fact, the final narrator for the squad, probably the one named Pope, has some difficulty justifying their being at Shiloh at all. The war is "much easier for the Confederates" for they believed they were fighting for independence and their land was being invaded. Pope also thinks that "it must be lots easier to fight *for* something" than it is "to fight *against* something" (192). The matter of right and wrong, of historical inevitability or free will, Pope recognizes finally, lies beyond him, even though, as Corporal Blake once argued, the Confederate soldiers might stop fighting when they learn "theyd been misled by bad men." "Winter and Pettigrew were lying dead out there in the woods and I was not," Pope tells us. "What right did I have thinking it was up to me to say why?" (192).

Tuesday afternoon found Palmer Metcalf, now unattached since Johnston's staff had disbanded following his death, walking on blistered feet
toward Corinth. For help he held on to the rear of a wagon carrying the
wounded, including a delirious Luther Dade whose left arm had been
amputated. The stump of Dade's arm "extended about four inches below
his armpit" and hung in a rag, "a little bloody sack of bloody meat" (196–
97). In his delirium Luther repeated periodically what he had told his
company commander just after the charge: "It dont hurt much, Captain. I
just cant lift it no higher than this" (85). Metcalf had chosen not to
accompany Johnston's body to New Orleans where it would be buried.
There was still a battle to be fought, but having no general to serve, all that
Metcalf could do on Monday was watch Beauregard until the battle ended
about four o'clock. Then, on Tuesday, he watched Forrest cover the Confederate withdrawal before he joined it himself. In characteristic fashion,
Forrest looked for ground that would be favorable for an attack on whatever Federal forces might be following, and at the Fallen Timbers, he
found the right place, "a mean-looking stretch of ground nearly a mile
across, with jagged stumps and felled trees crisscrossed and interlaced with
vines and knee-high weeds" (208). Almost as soon as this ground was
found, Sergeant Polly reported to Forrest that, indeed, a force of Federal
troops was approaching, and Forrest formed his cavalry for battle. At first
Metcalf did not belief that Forrest would attempt to hold his ground
against a superior Federal force, and he was incredulous when he heard
Forrest order a charge, but Forrest knew what he was doing, although he
was seriously wounded when he charged quite alone into the main body of
the Union brigade. Forrest's prisoners explained that the Union general
that Metcalf had seen, whose forces were then retreating under Forrest's
attack back toward the Tennessee River, was Sherman. At Fallen Timbers,
Metcalf lost his horse and had to walk back to Corinth in boots that were
not made for walking, but now he, like Polly, had a hero—Forrest.

There has been some critical objection to Foote's handling of technique
and point of view in *Shiloh*. Allen Shepherd's critique, "Technique and
Theme in Shelby Foote's *Shiloh*"[35] is the most thorough consideration of
the problem. Shepherd acknowledges the many comparisons that have
been made between *Shiloh* and Stephen Crane's *Red Badge of Courage,* but
he is careful to point out that Foote's use of multiple narrators is somewhat
more "modern" than the narrative Crane had employed and that Foote's
scope, his treatment of the history of the Civil War, is much broader. The

seven segments of narrative span a little more than two days, and yet the narrators provide a general history of the conflict from its beginnings in the West until April 1862. "Such an overview," Shepherd points out, "is exactly what Stephen Crane did not, and did not wish to provide."

The breadth of interest, however, raises questions about what, within reason, the narrators could know about the details of the battle and the lives of the generals. "One danger to which Foote is not immune," Shepherd observes, "is that of bringing together, in somewhat unlikely fashion, among tens of thousands of participants, his few selected soldiers." The example that Shepherd selects to demonstrate violation of point of view is Flickner's knowledge of Grant's activities on the battlefield. Foote's source is Grant's own account, and it seems somewhat strange that Flickner would stumble on a sleeping Grant on Sunday night and that he would know that "earlier he'd tried to get some sleep in the log house." "Point of view," Shepherd points out, "whose integrity is the making or unmaking of the novel, is violated here and in a number of other places." In the interest of Foote's art, in extenuation at any rate, it is worth pointing out that the time of narration is not uniformly established. Three of the Union narrators die in the battle, Fountain, Winter, and Pettigrew; they obviously could not tell their stories from some time distant, looking back on events from days, months, or years hence. It is obvious, though, that other narrators are telling their tales from a later perspective. Flickner clearly is not telling his tale on the sixth or seventh of April 1862; when he found the remnants of his battery among a group of huge siege guns, he tells the reader that he "later . . . heard that a colonel by the name of Webster . . . had placed them there" (121), but it is not altogether clear just how much later. The shifting time of narration makes some confusion, but Foote has at least attempted to deal with the complexities of his narrative method.

Shepherd has also found the imbalance in the novel between the southern and northern narratives to be an "artistic deficiency." "Some of the narratives, however, are considerably more effective than others, and this unevenness deserves examination. Southern characters are more successful, and more attractive than Northern. I have in mind no literary code of equal justice and interest, but lopsideness is an artistic deficiency" (4–5).

Southern narrators and southern interests do dominate *Shiloh*. One of the northern narrators even sympathizes with the southern cause, and because Palmer Metcalf narrates both the opening and closing sections of the book, the southern narrators employ many more pages in which to explain their presence. Thus, *Shiloh* is a southern book. The northern narrators provide a counterpoint, representing, perhaps, General Sherman's vision of the North as an industrial and mechanical force, against which the efforts and the beliefs of the southerners stand in a tragic relief. *Shiloh* takes its stand in the interest of the southern cause and southern history. Seen from this perspective the artistry of the book is perhaps less defective than it is when we demand of it, as Shepherd does, objectivity and balance. The technique of point-counterpoint may, in fact, have been suggested to Foote by the alternating narratives in Faulkner's *The Wild Palms;* and the narratives of the squad members suggest that, when Foote came to write *Shiloh,* he had not forgotten *As I Lay Dying,* or, perhaps, a reading of William March's *Company K.*

When Flickner left his battery on Sunday afternoon to hide under the bluff with the thousands of other "demoralized" Union soldiers, he encountered a survivor of Fountain's guard and the dog, Bango, covered with Fountain's blood. Such coincidences, however, occur much more frequently between the southern narrators and give their part of the tale greater internal coherence. The southern army seems to be more of an organic whole, and Luther Dade from Jordan County plays a crucial role. First, Dade saw Metcalf when Johnston and his staff rode by the 6th Mississippi on Sunday morning. "There was a little blond-headed lieutenant bringing up the rear, the one who would go all red in the face when the men guyed him back on the march" (69–70). Metcalf, in his first paragraph as narrator, complains about this teasing; soldiers cheered Johnston, he says, but "they jeered at me especially, since I was the youngest and brought up the rear" (3–4). Polly encountered Dade at Beauregard's headquarters and Shiloh Meeting House. Dade had been wounded and was looking for a doctor; Polly was there helping Lieutenant Strange locate Beauregard. "While I was standing there," Polly reports, "a tow-headed boy wearing a homespun shirt under his jacket came up to me. He was about seventeen, just beginning to raise some fuzz on his cheeks" (141). Polly told Dade that he might find doctors nearer to the fighting, and a dazed Luther Dade wandered away. Finally Metcalf, on his way back to Corinth, held on to the rear of the wagon in which Dade, his arm now amputated, rode. "The only face I was really conscious of was the face of a boy in the rear of the wagon; he looked out over the tailgate, our heads on a line and less than a yard apart. He wore a checkered homespun shirt

which was half gone because of the way the surgeons had slit it when they
took off his left arm" (196). Both Polly and Metcalf noted Luther's sudden
maturing; "he had a dazed look around his eyes, as if he'd seen things no
boy ought to see" (141), Polly comments. To Metcalf, Luther looked "at
once young and old, like the boy in the tale who aged suddenly because of
some unspeakable overnight experience in a haunted house" (196). Both
Polly and Metcalf reflect what Dade himself knew: battle "was like being
born again, coming into a new world" (75). Luther Dade's experience at
Shiloh stood, in its way, as representative for all southerners. He had given
almost the full measure of his devotion to the southern cause and had been
forced to come to terms with his own human limitations and those of his
fellows. If Dade had ever suffered from a romantic idealism, he was
quickly cured of it. There was no victory to provide escape or consolation.
At the end of the book, Dade's mind clears, and Metcalf reports:

> Facing me over the tailgate he suddenly seemed to realize where he was,
> that the column was heading for Corinth. . . . For the first time, except for
> the raving, he spoke. "Lieutenant . . . " His voice was weak; he tried again.
> "Lieutenant . . . "
>   "Yes?"
>   "Lieutenant—did we get whupped?"
>   I said I supposed they would call it that. [222]

Defeated in battle, Luther Dade must return to Jordan County to live
out his life without an arm. Defeat, after all, means change. It is not
coincidental, of course, that Metcalf's father also had an empty sleeve, his
arm lost fighting under Johnston in Texas.

The southern narrators are more reflective than their northern counter-
parts; they have, for the purposes of the action of the novel, a more
significant past on which to reflect, and as Metcalf's father asserted, they
were in love with the past. Their prose is more lyrical and flowing. Just as
there are closer ties between the southern narrators themselves, there are
also closer ties between the narrators and the officers under whom they
serve. Fountain knew something about Grant because they both came
from the same section of Ohio, but his knowledge came only from hearing
people talk and seeing Grant once as he drilled a militia unit. Flickner had
also heard talk about the generals and later he may have even read something about Grant's leadership at Shiloh. The southerners, on the other
hand, were much closer to their leaders. Metcalf's father had known

Johnston intimately enough to serve as a second for Johnston in a duel in
Texas. Sergeant Polly had made something of a study of Forrest, but, then,
the relationship between a colonel and his scout is by its very nature close,
and Polly was under Forrest's direct command. The close ties of the
southerners are counterpointed against the more distant relationships of
the Federals, and the comparison suggests that the South is a more uniform and coherently ordered civilization, that the conditions of its existence and its purpose are more clearly defined.

One reason that these ties stand out more clearly is that the past has
deeper meaning for the southerners. Their past is more closely connected
to who and what they are. We know that Union officer Fountain was
married to a lady named Martha and that Martha came to Paducah with
him, but that is about all we know of his past. Two members of the squad
are from the same area, but that information is really incidental. Among
the Federals, only Flickner comments on the past and that is to deny as
much of it as he can. His father told tales of his grandfather's having
fought against Napoleon, but to Flickner tales of the past seemed out of
place, irrelevant. "This is a new country," he told his father. "We dont
need those stories from the old one" (112). Even though Flickner wore the
watch his father had given him, the same one his grandfather had worn
when he fought Napoleon, on a string around his neck, time did not seem
to matter to him.

There was no break, however, between Metcalf and his father; both
were soldiers and both in their own ways were "incurable romantics."
Metcalf had been a student at the Louisiana Military Academy where
Sherman was superintendent in the days before the war. Because he had a
case of measles, Metcalf could not go home for the Christmas holidays in
1860, but as soon as he was well enough, Sherman moved the lonely
Palmer into his own quarters. There, on Christmas Eve, Metcalf overheard
Sherman's reaction to the news that South Carolina has seceded. The
South is bound to fail, he heard Sherman say: "You are rushing into war
with one of the most powerful, ingeniously mechanical and determined
people on earth." The agricultural South, Sherman knew, did not have the
means to defeat the North. "You are bound to fail. Only in your spirit and
determination are you prepared for war. In all else you are totally unprepared, with a bad cause to start with." Dipping even further into his
past, as Metcalf drifted off to sleep on Saturday night before the battle,
images of his mother, whom he knew only from a painting hanging in the

house in New Orleans, floated into his fading consciousness. "I thought of my father, who had been a soldier himself and lost an arm in Texas fighting under the same man I would fight under tomorrow, and of my mother who died when I was born and whom I knew only as a Sully portrait over the mantel in my father's study and some trunks of clothes stored in the attic of the house in New Orleans. It seemed strange. It seemed strange that they had met and loved and gone through all that joy and pain, living and dying so that I could lie by a Tennessee campfire under a spangled reach of April sky, thinking of them and the life that had produced me" (26).

Johnston's death gave Metcalf pause; he reflected on the South's temperament and cause. Others had told him how Johnston, just before he was hit by a stray shot in the leg, had ordered his surgeon, Dr. Yandell, to look after the wounds of a group of captured northerners. Johnston's concern for the wounded Federals reminded Metcalf of his father's prediction of southern failure. "I remembered what my father had said about the South bearing within itself the seeds of defeat, the Confederacy being conceived already moribund. We were sick from an old malady, he said: incurable romanticism and misplaced chivalry, too much Walter Scott and Dumas read too seriously. We were in love with the past, he said; in love with death" (200).

Polly, too, had a past that was important to him. He had joined Forrest's cavalry in Memphis during the summer of 1861, had fought in Kentucky and Tennessee with Forrest, and had followed him out of Fort Donelson. Polly's father, a Baptist minister in Houston, Texas, had planned for his son to follow him into the ministry, but when Polly and his roommate in the Baltimore Seminary were caught with a woman and whisky, Jefferson's career as a divine was brought to an abrupt conclusion, much to the young man's relief. During the six years following his disgrace, Polly jumped from one job to another—sailor, card dealer, cowboy, field hand. June 1861 found him in Galveston, where he intended to go to Houston and admit to his father that he had "done as poor a job at making a bad man" as he "had of making a good one" (149), but the war had come and he decided instead to join the Confederate navy. In Memphis, on his way east by train, he read Forrest's advertisement for volunteers in the *Appeal* and decided he had come far enough.

The southern narrators feel not simply the presence of their own personal and regional past but also, beneath that, the bedrock of a European past that prompted their being at Shiloh. This appears most clearly in Metcalf's narratives; he worked on a battle order patterned after Napoleon's Waterloo order, he thought of himself as a sort of "latter-day Shakespeare," and he consciously quoted Keats—a tall order for a nineteen-year-old. Metcalf helped Colonel Jordan of Beauregard's staff prepare the battle order; that is, he supplied "the commas and semicolons which made it clearer." When the plan was finished, Metcalf thought of it as high art: "I began to understand how Shakespeare must have felt when he finished *Macbeth*" (13). Even while he was writing the order, he recognized that battle orders "would all result in victory if they were followed," but this plan seemed to Metcalf to be "so beautifully simple" and "somehow so *right*." "Colonel Jordan was proud of it to," he said. "I believe he really thought it was better than the one by Napoleon he used as a model, though of course he didnt say so" (13–14). Later, after the plan failed, Metcalf recognized some of its shortcomings. "Lying under that big, tattered sky and looking back over the last two days of battle, I saw that it had gone wrong for the very reason I had thought it most apt to go right. The main fault lay in the battle order I had helped to prepare, calling myself a latter-day Shakespeare because I had supplied the commas and semicolons. . . . Attacking the way it directed . . . divisions and regiments and even companies had become so intermingled that commanding officers lost touch with their men" (205).

Then some lines from *Macbeth* welled up in Metcalf's consciousness.

> we but teach
> Bloody instructions, which being taught, return
> To plague the inventor.

Even the common soldiers in the Confederate army compare Shiloh to Napolean's battles. Dade hears his fellow soldiers speaking of Shiloh as "the sun of oyster-itch" (Austerlitz), a comparison Dade obviously did not understand.

Lines from Keats and Shakespeare give a poetical and lyrical quality to Metcalf's prose, but even without these quotations, his own language has a lyrical quality. He lay down under "that big, tattered sky" (205); rain fell in "slanted, steely pencilings" (195); when the sun broke out there was a "sudden burst of gold and silver weather" (3). His images of Sherman sleeping in his tent on Saturday night are typical of many passages in his prose. "Now somewhere beyond that rim of firelight, sleeping in his headquarters tent on the wooded plateau between those two creeks, he probably had long since forgotten me and all the other cadets. Certainly he never imagined some of them were sleeping in the woods within a mile of him, ready to break upon his camp before sunup" (27).

Dade's prose, too, has a poetical quality, some of which is concerned with his realization that war is a horrible, grotesque affair. The dead and dying litter the field "like bundles of dirty clothes" (86); Dade yelled as "crazy and blood-curdled as the rest of them" (77). The fever that developed from Dade's wound affected the later portions of his narrative, and toward the end, he felt as though he were "somewhere outside" himself. In his wanderings in search of a doctor, his observations took on a hallucinatory quality. At one point he had a vision of God's disposing of the defective men He had created. "God was making men and every now and then He would do a bad job on one, and He would look at it and say, 'This one wont do,' and He would toss it in a tub He kept there, maybe not even finished with it. And finally, 6 April 1862, the tub got full and God emptied it right out of heaven and they landed here, along this road, tumbled down in all positions, some without arms and legs, some with their heads and bodies split open where they hit the ground so hard" (89–90).

Even Sergeant Polly, the most practical of the southerners, demonstrated something of this lyrical quality. As he stood on the Indian mound in the blowing rain and watched Buell's troops coming across the river, the trees seemed to him "like keening women;" they were "trembling along their boughs." For Polly the rebel yell was "like fox hunters coursing," but the sound that the Federal soldiers made as they charged was "like surf on a stormy night" (157).

The Yankees do not quote Keats or Shakespeare, and Flickner would like to forget about Napoleon, but he has no way of knowing that he too, in a way, is fighting Napoleon or the memory of Napoleon. The northerners are more prosaic and matter-of-fact. Although Fountain describes the rebel yell as sounding "like screaming women" and the advancing Confederates looking "like quail hunters" (60), his images lack the color of Polly's "keening women" and "fox hunters coursing."

These images also lack the depth. The interests that the southerners have in their past, together with Metcalf's awareness that the Shiloh experience must be dealt with within the dimensions of his European heritage, suggest that they are aware of the working of the "historical imagination."

Their observations, captured in Foote's lyrical prose, also suggest the larger dimension of Tate's "religious imagination." These characters oper- ate within a web of nature and history as complex as that of Hugh Bart in *Tournament*.

The battle order was to have established a pattern, a plan by which the southerners could carry out their mission and annihilate Grant's army, but that pattern failed from the weight of its own artificiality. There are other patterns, systems of order, at work, however, which are now working inexorably, patterns that the characters, most especially the southerners, glimpse only partially if at all. Although they may feel the force of these deeper, more primitive, and illusive forces, they fail to understand them. Tragedy, history, and nature are only approximate terms that name those patterns, and against such mysterious power, language fails.

Metcalf's quotation from *Macbeth* and his comparing himself to Shake- speare suggest that recognition of the formal pattern of tragedy might lend some understanding to the southern condition at Shiloh. Metcalf, of course, did not see those patterns and could not interpret his role in the larger design; he was satisfied with Napoleon. His response to Sherman's prediction, however, establishes an essentially tragic framework for the action of the novel when that action is seen, as it should be, from a southern perspective. Metcalf might have fared much better had he put his faith in Shakespeare rather than in Napoleon.

Proust is also instructive here. Marcel, Proust's hero, speaks of patterns, distinguishing the patterns that immediate experience give us, which are superficial, from the deeper rhythms that give these patterns their shape and meaning. "No matter what idea life may have implanted within us, its material representation, the outline of the impression it has made upon us, is always the guarantee of its indispensable truth," Marcel says. Patterns that are simply the products of individual minds "have only a logical truth, a potential truth," but the "book written in symbolic characters not traced by us is our only book."[36] Metcalf, like Bart, is not sufficient as an artist. He places too much confidence in the "material representation" of pattern and cannot, or does not, see the "essence" that gives the representation its form. Metcalf's superficiality is Proustian.

A consciousness of the fatality of the southern cause failed to daunt the bold nineteen-year-old warrior. Metcalf had heard Sherman's prediction of southern failure: "If your people will but stop and think, they must see that in the end youll surely fail." For Sherman the South's rushing into war constituted "a crime against civilization" (216). Metcalf's father had no more hope for the South than Sherman had; there was a sense of awareness in his saying that the South was rushing to oppose the inevitable forces of time and history. The South, Metcalf's father believed, had within it "the seeds of defeat"; the Confederacy had been born dead.

A sense of fatalism pervades Polly's narrative. He had been the first to see Buell's army, and he knew that the battle on Monday would not go in the favor of the southern army. His commander, Forrest, knew this too: "We'll be whipped like hell," Forrest told Chalmers, knowing that his prediction was accurate. There is an even deeper strand of fatalism and the inevitability of the flow of history in Polly's narrative. In *Tournament*, Asa explained that Hugh Bart was trying to be something he "was not meant to be," and almost identical words appear in Polly's narrative. When he was caught with a prostitute at the seminary and expelled, he felt a sense of relief. His expulsion "meant an end to trying to be something I was never meant to be" (147–48).

If Shakespeare's words fail to provide a means of insight for noble Metcalf, so also does the rather obvious metaphor of the loss of arms. His father had lost an arm in Texas, Luther Dade loses his arm at Shiloh, and so it will be that the South will lose in armed conflict because, quite literally, it loses its arms. Palmer Metcalf will not give up his cause, however, not in 1862. The reason is Nathan Bedford Forrest.

It is, of course, tragically ironic that Metcalf, in his dedication to the romantic warrior, Forrest, repeated his father's somewhat cynical and contradictory romanticism. Metcalf realized that, although his father "enjoyed posing as a realist and straight thinker," he was nevertheless "a highly romantic figure of a man" who "talked that way because of some urge for self-destruction, some compulsion to hate what he had become: an old man with a tragic life, who sent his son off to a war he was too maimed to take part in himself." Metcalf says that his father's action was motivated by a "regret of a particular regional form" (200). Whatever knowledge or insight these words might have had for Metcalf is lost, for he plans to join Forrest's cavalry after Shiloh and possibly repeat his father's experience. No matter what "reality" each confronts, the lure of romance—dashing, swashbuckling courage—overwhelms both father and son.

Luther Dade also encountered a situation that reveals to the reader, if not to Dade himself, the same truth that Metcalf's father observed. Just before the charge in which Dade was wounded, the Federals repulsed the

6th Mississippi. The retreating rebels found cover under a ridge and halted to reform their ranks. Dade saw one of the running men shot, killed, but continuing to run. "I saw one man come over, running sort of straddle-legged, and just as he cleared the rim I saw the front of his coat jump where the shots came through. He was running down the slope, stone dead already, the way a deer will do when it's shot after picking up speed. This man kept going for nearly fifty yards downhill before his legs stopped pumping and he crashed into the ground on his stomach. I could see his face as he ran, and there was no doubt about it, no doubt at all; he was dead and I could see it in his face" (79–80). The dead man's running "scared" Dade "worse than anything up to then"; it was "somehow so un-religious for a dead man to have to keep on fighting—or running, anyhow" (80). The dead man resembled in a way the southern cause that Metcalf's father had described, moribund before it had a chance at life.

The foolishness of these young men's challenging the larger historical forces out of ignorance or lack of vision lends a heightened tragic quality to their actions. These inexorable forces in history, however, give way to even more natural sources of existence against which these men act out their futile courage. The historical imagination gives way to the more elemental and timeless religious imagination and its origins in the natural world. Shiloh, conveniently for these purposes, was fought in early April, that "cruelist month / breeding lilacs out of the dead land." Foote's "lilacs" are the pink blossoms of peach trees and the early redbud blooms. The rebirth of spring has been ritualized in religious belief over many generations of life on earth, so it seems appropriate that Dade, even in the horrors of April 1862, would describe his growing awareness in terms of rebirth, even if that rebirth meant the terrible awareness of death: "It was like being born again, coming into a new world," he says. It is equally appropriate that the battle, which began in the warmth of early spring, should end, for Metcalf and the southerners, with the sudden, unexpected return of cold and winter.

Metcalf's first words describe the southern army's marching toward battle in spring warmth—green grass, golden sun, and April heat.

"The sky had cleared, the clouds raveled to tatters, and at four oclock the sun broke through, silver on the bright green of grass and leaves and golden on the puddles in the road; all down the column men quickened the step, smiling in the sudden burst of gold and silver weather" (3). For Metcalf, on 5 April, the earth seemed to burst with new life.

"This was mainly a brown country, cluttered with dead leaves from the year before, but the oaks had tasseled and the redbud limbs were like flames in the wind. Fruit trees in cabin yards, peach and pear and occasional quince, were sheathed with bloom, white and pink, twinkling against broken fields and random cuts of new grass washed clean by the rain" (4).

Three days later both weather and fortunes had changed for Metcalf. He marched back to Corinth in a rain that turned to sleet. "As twilight drew in, the wind veered until it came directly out of the north, whistling along the boughs of roadside trees. Thunder rumbled and the rain was like icy spray driven in scuds along the ground. It grew dark suddenly, not with the darkness of night but with the gathering of clouds, a weird, eerie refulgence. Thunder pealed and long zigzags of lightening forked down, bright yellow against the sky. The air had a smell of electricity; when I breathed it came against my tongue with a taste like brass" (220–21).

The southern narrators' response to nature and the poetic quality of their observations imply that, although they do not fully understand their inarticulate awareness of the differences between the natural order and the directions in which their own jarring purposes lead, they, nevertheless, recognize, by indirection, hints of their condition in various images. To Sergeant Polly, that second day at Shiloh meant "that blasted field where the dead lay thick as leaves at harvest time" (158). His describing the sound of northern troops as "surf on a stormy night" suggests that, behind the appearance of men on a battlefield, there are larger, more elemental forces. Metcalf, in his images of spring and ice, seems almost at times to know what he does not want to know.

Against these larger forces, Napoleon's battle order is a tawdry thing indeed. It is an attempt to find in history, in time past, a plan by which the contemporary can be arranged, but following Napoleon is no better than following Scott or Dumas or any other artificial pattern that men can attempt to impose on nature and time. In Foote's vision of things, men cannot manufacture history in this manner, or if they attempt it, history becomes the record of their failure. The northerner Flickner sees this rather clearly: "It seemed so wrong," Flickner says of his father's tales of the old country, "so out of place, hearing about Napoleon, when I could see right through the living-room window the big rolling Minnesota prairie with the tall wheat shimmering in the sunlight" (112). Even though Flickner wore his grandfather's watch on a string around his neck, he knew that the hands of the watch could not be returned to 1815.

Fleeting time and nature mock Metcalf and his fellow Confederates. On Saturday, on their way to battle, an entire Tennessee regiment cannot hit a deer. Nature is illusive and not to be contained in any plan that men draw up. "West of Mickey's, within two miles of the Federal outposts, I watched an entire regiment bang away at a little five-point buck that ran the length of the column down a field adjoining the road. They were Tennessee troops who prided themselves on their markmanship, but so far as I could tell, not a ball came within ten feet of that buck; he went into the woods at the far end of the field, flaunting his white scut" (24).

As Metcalf on Tuesday night walked toward Corinth, a brown thrasher on a fence beside the road made him uneasily self-conscious. "On a rail fence beside the road a brown thrasher sat watching the column go past, and for some reason he singled me out, the steady yellow bead of his eye following me, the long bill turning slowly in profile until I came abreast: whereupon he sprang away from the rail with a single quick motion, his wings and narrow tail the color of dusty cinnamon, and was gone" (221).

While the modern southerner may find in the remains of the old South, or rather in his image of it, strands of a cultural lineage with ancient European origins, the events of regional history force him to recognize the superficiality of the causes that led to a destructive Civil War and an impoverished twentieth century. This knowledge forces the modern southerner to a recognition of the deeper, more universal resources of cultural heritage, and the tragic edge of this awareness gives him a richness and depth of being that he otherwise would not have.

Chapter III

A Jordan County Trilogy

I n February 1951 Foote was confident that he had learned his craft and that, with the publication of *Love in a Dry Season*, his apprenticeship had come to an end. "This one will do it," he wrote, "wind up my apprenticeship, forge my middle-period style, set me up to make a dent in American literature (8Feb51)." The apprenticeship Foote delineated in winter of 1951 included the three published novels—*Tournament, Follow Me Down*, and *Love in a Dry Season*—that were set in Jordan County. He did not anticipate that several months later Dial would schedule *Shiloh* for publication; that, much to his delight, served as lagniappe to the apprenticeship. *Shiloh* had been completed in its basic form on 4 July 1947. When Dial accepted *Tournament*, on the basis of reading the typescript of *Shiloh*, Foote turned to revising that book and completed his revisions on 27 September 1948. He had to wait fifteen days short of a full year for *Tournament* to appear as a book; 12 September 1949 was the official publication date. Meanwhile he had begun work the preceding February on his second Jordan County novel, *Follow Me Down*; it was completed in manuscript in July 1949 and published by Dial on 23 June 1950. *Love in a Dry Season*, which Foote says he began in the afternoon of a day in mid-July 1949 after finishing *Follow Me Down* in the morning, appeared from Dial on 19 September 1951. Foote had been at work intermittently on a novella, "Child by Fever," and a series of stories, some of them developed from portions of *Tournament* and published in the *Saturday Evening Post*.

Follow Me Down appeared to a mixed, but generally favorable, reception. Foote could not understand why the *New Yorker* called the novel "amoral," nor could he understand the reviewers' response to *Love in a Dry Season.* "I am puzzled," he wrote Percy in November. "No reviewer has pointed out that the book is (what I think it clearly is) 'the best-constructed American novel since Gatsby.' Thats what I'm waiting to hear them say. Looks like I'll have a long wait." The writing of "Two Gates to the City" filled the fall of 1951, and Foote's enthusiasm, confidence, and sense of purpose are reflected in almost all of his many letters to Percy. At Thanksgiving he had some advice for his friend: "If you ever take a notion to do a four-generation book, prepare yourself for some long hard hours of drawing outlines, boning up on history, and working out genealogies . . . none of it comes easy (24Nov51)."

Still he was in love with his hard work. Love, though, as Foote's lawyer in *Follow Me Down* pointed out, has failed in the twentieth century, and so it was in a sense with Foote himself. By the winter of 1952, his writing had come to a halt and his enthusiasm was completely gone.

Out of the wreckage of what he had believed to be the beginning of his major phase, Foote salvaged a collection of stories, *Jordan County: A Landscape in Narrative,* published by Dial in 1954. For *Jordan County,* Foote fell back on a plan that he had first described to Percy in a letter dated "25Nov49." Some of the stories, including "Child by Fever" and "Ride Out," clearly had been intended for "Two Gates to the City." What he had wanted to be the first novel of his maturity had become, at least in part, but salvage from his apprenticeship. Ten years after *Jordan County,* the Dial Press issued the three major Jordan County novels in one volume, *Three Novels by Shelby Foote,* published on 19 October 1964.

Follow Me Down

Follow Me Down[1] concerns an unfulfilled self that wanders aimlessly in a world of jumbled and contradictory values, a self in need of wholeness; it is about one character who finds "what she was meant to be" but looses her life in finding it. Luther Dade Eustis (Foote again uses his middle name) suffers the loneliness and separation that result from his failure to find harmony with an elemental force and flow of history; to live a life that is tempered by those traditions whose foundations lie in the timeless shaping power of myth. Beulah Ross finds an inner harmony, but Eustis drowns

her. The novel, evidence of Foote's hard work and improving crafts-
manship, is related nevertheless in theme and technique to *Tournament*
and *Shiloh;* here too is the interest in actual events of southern and Mississippi history, the contrasting narrative voices, and, in a modified form, a
framing device for the action of the novel.

The source for the plot for *Follow Me Down* is the trial in 1941 of Floyd
Myers for the murder of Imogene Smothers. The murder had stirred the
curiosity, not to mention the imagination, of Greenville; it was "big news."
Although he moves the time to 1949, Foote follows rather closely a
number of the details as the *Delta Democrat Times*[2] reported them, beginning with the headline from the issue for Friday, 21 June 1940—"Gar-
roted Body Found in Lake."

Myers, a fifty-year-old chimney painter from Jasper, Alabama had come
to Greenville with his girl friend, eighteen-year-old Imogene Smothers.
Tiring of Smothers and perhaps pained by conscience, he told her that he
planned to return to his wife and family in Jasper, and she, like Beulah in
Foote's novel, swore that she would follow him there. While the couple
was swimming in Lake Ferguson, on 17 June 1940, near Greenville, Myers
strangled Smothers with a willow branch; he then "wrapped her body in
wire, fastened it to a big rock and tossed it into Lake Ferguson." Myers, "a
member of the Holiness Church and a frequent reader of the Bible," had
grown tired, he said, of "the way we had been living." "The body," the
newspaper reported, "was found floating on the lake north of Greenville
by Mrs. John Dillon, wife of a fisherman, as she paddled a rowboat laden
with groceries on the afternoon of June 20." Myers and Smothers had
boarded with the Dillons, identifying themselves as Sue and James
Holcombe. Mrs. Dillon identified the corpse by the "double small toe on
her left foot." The sheriff of Washington County traced Smothers and
Myers through a laundry mark in a dress "Sue" had given away, and on 23
June, Sheriff Crouch arrested Myers near Jasper.

Myers came to trial, finally, after two postponements, in July 1941. The
Delta Democrat Times took note, almost with pride, that the case had
"attracted nationwide attention. Three articles have been written in detective story magazines about the case and the investigation." Carl A. Elliott
from Jasper and Ben Wilkes from Greenville defended Myers. The testimony of "Dr. E. G. Meriwether, psychiatrist of the Mississippi State
Hospital at Whitfield," was crucial in Myers's plea of insanity. "When the
defense attorney, Ben Wilkes, painted a word picture of Myers as a re-

ligious fanatic with several cases of insanity in his family and queer actions, Dr. Meriwether said, 'Assuming all these things, he is crazy,'" the paper reported. On Saturday, 25 July, the jury deliberated for two hours before giving Myers a life sentence. During the same term of court, Myers's cellmate, J. A. Yount, was given a death sentence for slaying F. C. Pope, chief of police in Hollandale, Mississippi.

Foote, who attended the trial,[3] used a number of the details of the Myers case—some names, newspaper headlines, and quotations from the trial. Yount becomes Lundy in *Follow Me Down;* the double toes become a gold anklet with a heart-shaped charm. The delay in trial is omitted— Luther Dade Eustis kills his "Sue" in June and is tried in September 1949. Myers and Eustis are religious fundamentalists, and Wilkes's defense is very close to Parker Nowell's defense of Eustis. The plot of *Follow Me Down* is very similar to the actual events, as Foote explained to Percy:

> [A] tenant farmer from down on the Lake takes a girl to an island, lives alone with her in a deserted shack, abandoning his wife and three daughters. The only other people on the island are a fisherwoman and her deaf-and-dumb son. In the course of time (about two weeks) remorse sets in; he tells the girl he has to go back to his wife. She says no, and whats more if he goes she will follow him and tell his wife where he has been. So he drowns her in the lake and returns to his wife.
>
> Three days later the fisherwoman finds the body: it came up with the concrete slabs he had wired to its neck: but she doesnt recognize her until the coroner takes a tiny anklet off its leg. They still dont know who the man was or where he had gone (he had given a false name). But Dummy, the fisherwoman's son, saw his name and address in the Bible the man brought with him; Dummy informs the sheriff, because he had fallen in love with the dead girl. The sheriff goes down to the lake and arrests him, brings him back to Bristol and locks him up.
>
> He is tried in the September term; his lawyer proves insanity, and he gets life at Parchman. (May Day 1948)

These are the events, but Foote was writing a novel, not journalism. In this novel, as in *Shiloh,* he employs a series of narrators to tell his tale— the circuit clerk, Ben Rand; a reporter, Russell Stevenson; the deaf-and-dumb son of the fisherwoman, James Elmo Pitts, usually called Dummy; Luther Dade Eustis, the murderer; Beulah, the victim; Eustis's wife, Kate; the lawyer, Parker Nowell; and Roscoe Jeffcoat, the turnkey. Ben Rand, Roscoe Jeffcoat, Dummy, Beulah, and Kate each serve as narrator for one

```
1 -- I ----- the bailiff (trial scene).
2}
3}-- II ---- a news reporter (finding of body).
4 -- III --- the dummy (informing of sheriff)
5}
6}-- IV ---- the murderer (how he met & killed her).
7}
8 -- V ----- the murdered (life seen backward).
9}
10}-- VI ---- the murderer's wife (his background).
11}
12 -- VII --- the fisherwoman (life on island).
13}
14}-- VIII -- the lawyer (defense plea; man after crime).
15 -- IX ---- the turnkey (jail scene).
```

section. The reporter and lawyer, Stevenson and Nowell, each tell two, and Eustis narrates six sections. The structure is formal and balanced. "Here is the way I have cast it for my purposes," Foote explained to Percy, "each of the Arabic numerals in a 7000-word Section; each of the Roman numerals is a narrator."

"The story, you see, has facets, like a diamond," he explained in this same letter, "has themes, like a piece of music; gives me room to really show what I can do. . . . The form makes it possible to heighten interest by the use of nine different styles." It is a form, as Foote explained in a letter to James Kibler, derived from Browning's *The Ring and the Book.*

> The notion, as I recall it, was to penetrate to the heart of an event and then emerge, by means of monologs that became increasingly and then decreasingly involved in the story being told. The first and last speakers, for example, are involved as minor officials of the law; they speak in the vernacular. The second and next-to-last, a reporter and a lawyer, are involved by their professions, and both speak in a more or less professional manner. The third and third-from-last are intimates of the principals, and their tone is lyric. So much for Parts One and Three. Part Two supplies the deepest penetration, the victim's monolog flanked by the two monologs of her killer—led up to, then down from; into and out of. The intention, as I said, was to give an impression of penetrating and emerging. Beulah's

seven-page paragraph at the heart of her monolog (a seven-page autobiography, really) supplies the keystone of the arch; the narrative slopes off in
opposite directions from there.[4]

Ben Rand, the circuit clerk, introduces us to the principals and gives the
general outline of the plot leading up to, but omitting, the verdict. From a
mildly cynical, humorous point of view, Ben gives us Bristol's general
views. His narrative opens with a description of the courtroom in the
September heat, and then he summarizes the events that led up to the
sentencing on that Saturday morning. Ben had first heard about the
murder on the Friday just after the body had been found. He and Willy
Roebuck, the deputy sheriff, were in the Greek's cafe for lunch when
Roebuck told him about what had happened. Ben was not in town on
Sunday when Eustis was arrested and brought to jail, but he did read the
reports that Stevenson ran in the *Clarion* on Monday afternoon. Ben
reports that it seemed a guilty verdict was a foregone conclusion. He could
see that the owl-like Eustis—"hornrim glasses, sharp little beak of a nose,
a tuft of hair on each side of his forehead"—had been well coached for the
trial, but, as he puts it, nobody could blame Parker Nowell, Eustis's lawyer,
for his coaching, "considering what hung in the balance was a seat in the
old shocking chair and a trip to the big beyond, where every imp in hell
had polished the tines of his pitchfork shiny bright and old Satan himself
was planning to handle the damper" (4). The middle-aged Eustis, showing
signs of a man who has spent the better part of his life hoeing cotton under
a hot sun, does not look to Ben like a man who could "entice a girl into a
soda shop, much less off on a wild abandoned island to live in a voodoo
shack" (9). Apparently most of Bristol would agree with Ben.

Tolliver, the young and inexperienced district attorney, handled his case
fairly well in Ben's view. When he had finished with Beulah's mother's
testimony, Ben says, "You could almost hear the hum of the electric chair,
see the little blue crackle of fire, the spiral of smoke that corkscrews up
when everything is over" (16). Between Eustis and hell, though, stood
Parker Nowell, and whatever else Ben Rand may think of Nowell, he has
respect for him. Nowell, a young man from a prominent family, had
shown every promise of greatness—successful lawyer, member of the
legislature, even mentioned for the governorship—until his wife deserted
him. Then he retreated or, as Ben says, he went "sour." Coming home to
Bristol after a long binge, he began to take the most hopeless legal cases.

Nowell lived alone in a huge house behind a wall of music: "Youd pass the house at night—the big old house on Lamar Street that his grandfather built, Judge Nowell: the social center of Bristol in its day—and the curtains would be drawn and all youd hear would be highbrow music booming out of a thousand dollar phonograph he ordered from New York City, New York" (12). Nowell won his cases, "getting outlaws in circulation" (13). One outlaw, a gambler, had committed "a cold blooded killing," but Nowell's client pleaded self-defense and won "because the dead man had been cleaning his nails at the time with one of those little knives that you wear on the end of your watch chain." Another outlaw, this time a black man who had run "amuck with a razor at one of these sanctifyings down by the river," received a reduced sentence "because by the time Nowell wound up his closing argument, the jury was blaming the Holy Ghost for getting the nigger wrought up. Manslaughter, they called it, and managed to keep a straight face" (12). But, even though Ben does not believe Nowell can save Eustis from the chair, he can imagine what the jury will face in Nowell's performance.

> Everybody knew what he was doing: it was the talk of Bristol. But it was one thing to condemn him when court had adjourned and you looked back on what he had done, and it was another different thing entirely when you were sitting on the jury with a man's life in your hands and Nowell was walking up and down in front of the rail in that crisp white linen suit, stopping every now and then and leaning forward to speak in a voice that was barely above a whisper, the courtroom so quiet you could hear your neighbor holding his breath and every time Judge Holiman raked one of those matches across the bench it was like the crack of doom, Nowell throwing law at you with one hand and logic with the other, until finally you got to thinking you were all that was left in this big wide ugly world to save a poor victim of malice and circumstance from being lynched by the State of Mississippi. (13)

Roscoe Jeffcoat, the jailor, closes the narrative and, like Ben Rand, represents the community's view, a view somewhat removed from the center of the action but, nevertheless, one that allows for comment on the events and the other characters. Roscoe is not as cynical as Ben and has a great deal of sympathy for Eustis. Perhaps Roscoe's own experience has mellowed him; he is a country boy like Eustis, and his wife, Martha, who covers her goiter with a towel, provides little enough companionship for him. "It takes real trouble, something worse than a goiter anyhow, to make people know how much they mean to each other" (265), he concludes after he has watched Kate and Eustis in a tearful reunion after the verdict.

Russell Stevenson and Parker Nowell occupy the second level of narration. Both are, as Foote explained, more involved and closer to the action, and both have a more complex perspective because of their learning and experience against which they can measure the significance of the events and their own relationship to them. This does not mean, however, that either narrator at this second level is more admirable than Roscoe Jeffcoat or Ben Rand. Stevenson's involvement with the crime began on Friday morning at the *Clarion* when the sheriff called for Lonzo, the community photographer, to come to Bachelor Bend to take a photograph of the corpse that Mrs. Pitts had found. Russell went along to get the story and was able to interview Mrs. Pitts who had identified the corpse on the basis of the gold anklet and heart-shaped charm. Confident that the man Mrs. Pitts had identified as "Luke Gowan" had fled and that no information would be available about him before the deadline for Monday's paper, if even then, Stevenson wrote the story for the Friday evening paper and a follow-up for the Sunday paper. He was quite surprised on Sunday to hear talk of the murderer's having been captured, and he telephoned Jeffcoat to learn what had happened.

The impression that Russell Stevenson leaves is that he has no fixed vision of the world in which to order events and assign values. In a person less self-centered than Stevenson, tolerance might be a virtue, but he reflects, without giving the matter much thought, the commercial values that surround him, even though he has the tools to do better. His world is cluttered with references to the past, allusions to important cultural and historic events, but these references fit into no pattern, show no evidence of conviction. Stevenson does not particularly care about Luther Dade Eustis. His profit from the events will go into his billfold or his bank account.

Without a trace of embarrassment, Stevenson tells us at the beginning of his narrative of a trick he has played on Gladys Triplett, the society editor of the *Clarion*. She had corrected "lice" to "lace" in her copy, but Russell had destroyed the corrected proofs so that the bride wore "a collar of white lice." Russell thinks he can collect ten dollars from the *Digest* when Glady's article is quoted in its column "Slips That Pass in the Night." When he sees Beulah's corpse spread out at Bachelor Bend, he wonders how Gladys might describe the scene.

Miss Whatever Blank comma *debutante daughter of Mr and Mrs Nemo Blank of this city* comma *attended a swimming party on Lake Bristol last Saturday evening* Stop. *Miss Blank wore an appropriate ensemble consisting of eight or nine yards of bailing wire and a pair of matching pyramidal concrete blocks pendant one beneath each ear* Stop. Paragraph. *Today Miss Blank received a select gathering at Bachelor Bend and was the cynosure of all eyes* dash *what was left of her after her week end with her kinsmen west of Bristol* comma *the Shrimps and the Gars* and so on for three galleys, down to the 30 she puts at the end to prove she's a newspaperman. (28)

If Nowell has, as Ben Rand says, "gone sour," then so, obviously, has Stevenson. He was grateful to Roebuck for calling the paper, but he sees most of what other people do as self-serving. For example, after he had talked on the telephone to Roscoe Jeffcoat and after Jeffcoat had given him a great deal of information, Stevenson casts what seems to be Jeffcoat's sincere helpfulness in a different light, a light that perhaps reveals more about Stevenson's motivation than about Roscoe. "I'd hate to try to think of something Roscoe wouldn't do for the sake of getting his name in the paper" (44), he tells us. "Human vanity and curiosity," Stevenson reminds himself, "created my job and keep it going" (46). A hard-core realist, Stevenson believes, "No matter how they dress it up with rouge and a sewed-in smile and highflown words, the final scene in any life is always an indignity, a return to matter, slime" (36). Death, he says, "has almost no connection with that bill of goods the preachers and poets and undertakers hand us" (36–37). But "nothing warms the cockles of [his] heart like the chink of cash," Stevenson admits. He looks forward to the ten dollars he thinks the *Digest* will pay and is encouraged in the belief that *True Detective* or some other magazine will pay sixty, "maybe seventy," dollars for the story about Eustis that he has already begun. (Later, we learn, that Russell's fellow worker, Benny Peets, the sports editor, has already sewn up this market.)

The frame of reference that Stevenson has available does not provide him with the depth of vision that it might provide. The text of his narrative is rich in figurative language; Mrs. Pitts's eyes, for example, "were yellow, like a goat's, and hard as agates." Eustis had "the hands of a workman, splayed and callous, with thumbnails thick as little oyster shells" (51). He knows good writing; Eustis's confession, which he read on Monday morning in preparation for his story in the afternoon paper, is the object of envy: "If I could write like that, I told myself, I'd be at the top of the ladder by now. The trouble is, you have to have lived it first. No thanks: it isnt worth it" (47). Events remind him of passages from Shakespeare and Milton; his knowledge is superior to the other narrators in the book, with the exception of Nowell, but unlike Nowell, Stevenson's knowledge does not lead to any depth of insight. Beginning with his Greek-like association of the Friday morning events with Fate, his knowledge is apparent: "I was . . . thinking what a thing Fate is—that will let you get up in the morning believing this is going to be a day like any other . . . and then the phone will ring" (30). Russell knows that the tale of the Bible-reading Eustis, living in a shack built by a Negro voodoo conjurer, has a rich store of "angles": "Black magic: Love—Bible-reading: Pagan rites" (37). He also knows something of the history of Jordan County. Eustis lived at Solitaire Plantation: "Everybody knows Solitaire; it's written up in the books. That was where General Jameson's father, old Isaac, first settled in 1820 before there was any such thing as Jordan County" (42). Then there is the old brick jail, "built in '73," which had, before the concrete was applied to its exterior, "a beauty only Time can bring." Stevenson looks at the present ugly concrete facade and thinks "of the brick building crouched inside, the Old South under the garish facade of the New" (45). Milton's fallen angel comes to mind as he recalls his first visit to Eustis in the jail, but "he resembled nothing less than he resembled an angel, fallen or no, and he'd never known a paradise, much less lost one—unless he was playing Adam to Beulah's Eve on the island opposite Bristol. If so, he certainly jumped the script on the final scene" (52). This framework, against which the reader may judge Eustis, seems lost on Stevenson. The reader can throw Eustis into some sort of historical light, but Stevenson does not seem to care. He is, Parker Nowell observes, "hard-faced already from living off the misdeeds of the people" (220).

Nowell, Eustis's lawyer, whose two sections in part three balance those of the "hard-faced" Stevenson in part one, seems to care intensely, and yet in his way, Nowell, too, has a hard face, and his caring has more to do with his intellectual satisfaction and enjoyment of perversity than with a genuine concern for Bristol. He is a disillusioned, frustrated man, pointedly aware of the modern world's shallowness of spirit, yet he uses his learning and his skill at artifice to frustrate Bristol's needs and expectations. A man less disillusioned, less aware of the modern dilemma, might employ his skills to some high purpose, or, at least, he might join Stevenson's preachers and undertakers to proclaim some high-sounding purpose. Nowell is one of Foote's most complex and highly significant characters.

Names of his fictional characters are for Foote often as important as the names of Henry James's characters. Stevenson, in fact, points out the significance of the name Eustis adopted to conceal his identity while on the island: "Bristol, Jordan County, Mississippi, had had its final look at him, Gowan or Go-on or Gone, whatever his name was" (39). Stevenson was wrong about Eustis, of course, but the name is significant. His name was not Gowan and he was not gone; at least he had not gone far enough. Nowell's name, too, says something about his character—"know well" or "no well." He is one who has said "no" to Bristol rather emphatically, but also because of his knowledge of music and literary art, he "knows" well from what modern malaise Bristol suffers. He has the skills in language and music to recognize and understand but also to use and explain. His knowledge of language and art makes him an artist, or at least an artificer, even though the purposes to which he puts his skills do not necessarily qualify him as a man exercising his talent in a living tradition.

Keats, Browning, Chaucer, Emerson, and most especially Shakespeare, constitute a portion of Nowell's literary background, which, along with his music, provides him with a frame of artistic and historical reference, a kind of reflecting mirror, in which he can see and thus judge the present. When Eustis's wife, Kate, appears in his office in the Mannheim Building (suggesting the Mannheim school of composers, although of all the characters in the book, only Nowell would make such an association), he has expected that she would appear. And as she sat telling him her story he was "reminded of all the others so much like her, who came and sat where she was sitting and slid their misery across the polished walnut of the desk." Her tale reminds him, too, of Troilus and Cressida and of Emerson. "It's true we have an affinity for evil. What she told me had occurred in an atmosphere much like that of *Troilus and Cressida,* in which the faithful are betrayed and the brave are slain. I was reminded of Emerson's 'Our faith comes in moments; our vice is habitual'" (219).

The polished walnut desktop, he thinks, is "our twentieth-century confessional," and later, thinking about his defense of Eustis, the image of reflection recurs. "The air-conditioner purred, breathed moist and cool, and I sat with my arms on the desktop that gleamed dully as if it had been polished by all the tales of wretchedness that had been slid across it, breathing the used breath of the machine" (233). The image of reflection and its association with confession suggest that Nowell's informed consciousness is also a mirror of much wider, deeper dimension.

At the beginning of his narrative, we find Nowell reflecting on the Violin Sonata in C Major, Kochel 296, by Mozart, "the one he wrote for the little Serrarius girl, his landlord's daughter." Nowell knows a great deal about music history and musical form, and this, too, contributes depth to his consciousness. He knows, for example, that Mozart had "hooked" the "main theme of the second movement, andante sostenuto . . . from one of the Bach boys" (217). Foote includes four measures of the theme in the text, and to close and frame Nowell's two sections, Foote prints two measures from the *molto adagio* of the *Heiliger Dankgesang* from Beethoven's Fifteenth String Quartet. Nowell listens primarily to the music of classical composers—Haydn and Mozart—although during the trial he upon one occasion admitted to listening to "Ravel's left-hand concerto."

Nowell's accomplishments might provide him with the means not only of understanding Bristol's narrowness—in his own terms if not those of the author—but of escaping it. Music to him lays bare its soul; his listening is more than simple appreciation. Mozart's Fortieth Symphony for him is "music so limpid, so pure, that after repeated hearings you begin to be frightened by it, not so much hearing the melody, the music itself, as experiencing the impulse that brought it into being" (243). Yet Nowell knows well that Bristol lacks the cultural maturity to understand; it is too dumb and deaf, too inarticulate, too stupid to fear. Rhythm, melody, harmony, form, cannot coalesce with history to humanize and enlighten the rootless, modern world. The result is that music and the arts form a barrier that, as Ben Rand observes, isolates behind a wall of sound. Nowell knows and experiences, apparently, the Proustean "essence," the string that holds the beads, in High Bart's words; but it does not make a better man of him.

Also contributing to Nowell's isolation is his distrust of Bristol's commercial values and its response to technological development. In his office he breathed the "used breath of the machine"—his air conditioner. The main street in Bristol's business district, Marshall Avenue, is, Nowell observes, "a brick- and glass-walled canyon, an oversized trap laid by merchants (and by doctors and lawyers, too) for the Negroes and country oafs blundering in with money clinched in their fists" (218). The owners of those stores are, in all likelihood, optimists of a shallow sort who believe that technological progress will make life better, a view that Nowell abominates. Walking down Marshall Avenue, he glances at the sun and then "automatically" checks his watch: "We've progressed so far in our mechanistic materialism," he thinks, "that now we look at our watches to check on the sun" (220). Shortly thereafter, Nowell, with other "automations," waits at a corner for "the wink of the mechanical eye"—a stoplight (225–26).

In such a world as that which Nowell describes, art is, of course, cheapened—even to some degree in Nowell's own consciousness. As he waits for the light he thinks "of that pathetic little figure from the G minor Quintet, adagio molto non troppo, descendent, giddy, arabesque, forlorn: K. 516" (226). Mozart is Nowell's retreat from the mechanical world. While he is waiting for the stoplight, across the street at the theater a billboard "displayed Rita Hayworth, low-bosomed in a strapless gown, being embraced about the knees by a young man with patent-leather hair who pressed the point of his chin against her stomach and looked up at her through the neat fringe of his eyebrows, at once suppliant and frozen, like the lover on Keats' urn—*Yet do not grieve; She cannot fade*—except that in this case a Moslem prince had got her, whisked her clean away to l'Horizon" (225).

Patterns and forms constantly affect Nowell—stoplights regulating pedestrians and vehicles, parked automobiles "racked fender to fender along the curb, obediently within the yellow stripes," and parking meters selling time—*"Time for sale. Step right up! Buy ten minutes of Time"* (225). But his knowledge of the forms of classical music provides him with the sharpest insight and the basis for his skill in not only understanding but furthering his manipulation of Bristol. As Tolliver was presenting his closing arguments, Nowell was "sketching Mozart themes on a scratchpad" (251), and when his time came for closing arguments—summation—Nowell "gave it to them straight sonata-form: Exposition, Development, Recapitulation" (253). With his watch on the rail of the jury box, he carefully measures the time for each section of what he called the "busy little symphony of Time" (253).

Nowell points out that he was very much aware that he was consciously using his understanding of form to shape his case to its best advantage, stirring the affections of the jury and measuring out their responses. As soon as he knows the facts, he can "shape the case to fit almost any pattern the jury might seem to want." He believes that, regardless of the reality involved, his duty is "to make the jurors think they understood him." He knows at the same time that he must provide the "terms" for that "under-standing"—the context—and is aware that he "had to do it in simple terms, which was only doubtfully possible because the facts were far from simple." If the jury "saw how truly complicated it was, the case was lost." These judgments lead him to the plea of insanity. "So I had decided to do it the easy way. Make them believe he was insane and the scales would fall from their eyes; they would 'understand'; the fear, the hate would be gone, evaporated. 'So that's it,' they would say; 'he's crazy. I knew it all along.' They might even begin to pity and sympathize. Good old Hollywood Christianity: God's gift to the Defense" (237). During the course of the trial, Nowell knew he was providing good theater. Of Kate's testimony, he says; "This was no fable read second-hand out of a newspaper: this was Life. We had them." And when she had finished, he shaped her comments like "something out of the *Ladies Home Whatever*. They ate it up. There wasn't a dry seat in the house, as Ive heard theater people say" (245).

Just as Nowell senses that beneath the form of Mozart's Fortieth Sym-phony there is the terrifying impulse that brought it into being, so he senses that beneath these affairs in Bristol runs a primitive level on which one might find the legend of the scapegoat. It is a sense of time and history in which the almost constant repetition of the forms of human action give way to the deeper rhythms of history. The turnkey identifies the theme in the final section: "Maybe we ought to be thankful. Maybe the world is in a balance: so much sin and evil, so much good. Maybe we ought to be thankful to the ones that get in trouble. Maybe they draw the evil like a billy goat in a barnlot draws the fleas. Yet here they were wanting his blood, as if the fleas that were eating him werent enough" (263).

It is a theme, however, of which Nowell is intensely aware. He knows that the people of Bristol want "to see Eustis get the chair" because they are envious. "Eustis had done things they had always wanted to do, beyond the pale, but didnt dare" (229–30). The trial would have been a "show" for Bristol, "at least an epilog, though it's true the audience would be limited and tickets hard to get." What they could not do themselves they wanted to see exorcised in the sacrifice of Eustis. "Everyone has an island," Nowell observes.

Nowell is contemptuous of the "Good old Hollywood Christianity"— the religious convictions of the average Bristolite. The problem of the modern world is, as Nowell observes, "Love has failed us," and goes to some lengths to explain, giving historical dimension to his cynical observations.

> Love has failed us. We are essentially, irrevocably alone. Anything that
> seems to combat that loneliness is a trap—Love is a trap: Love has failed us
> in this century. We left our better destiny in '65, defeated though we fought
> with a fury that seems to indicate foreknowledge of what would follow if we
> lost. Probably it happened even earlier: maybe in Jackson's time. Anyhow—
> whenever—we left the wellsprings, and ever since then we have been
> moving toward this ultimate failure of nerve. Now who has the answer? The
> Russians? The Catholic Church? Or are we building up to Armageddon, the
> day they drop the Bomb? God smiles and waits, like a man crouched over
> an ant-hill with a bottle of insecticide uncorked. [233]

Kate, Eustis's wife, narrates the section that opens part three of the
novel, and Dummy, James Elmo Pitts, closes the first part. The two brief
narratives balance each other in length. These narrators bear similar relationships to Eustis and Beulah and are more intimately involved with them
than are Stevenson and Nowell.

Life on the island, where the people he knew as Luke and Sue Gowan
spent about ten days in June, was for Dummy a rather rigid isolation.
Dummy and his mother had lived alone on the island for several years,
making only brief trips to Bristol. "Sue" was one of the few young women
he had ever had occasion to know very well, but he had an intuitive notion
that "Luke" and "Sue" were not what they represent themselves to be. He
watched what they did in the voodoo man's cabin and, entranced by the
fornication, wanted to do that too. He hoped "Sue" would show him how.
On one visit to the cabin, he found Eustis's Bible, and the names on its
leaves confirmed his suspicions. When he learned from his mother what
had happened to "Sue," he knew what he had to do.

Dummy is both deaf and dumb, and neither his island world nor the
interior of his consciousness have been invaded by a Christian understanding of evil or any other influence that might make him feel guilty for what
he felt about Beulah. He can read and had read at least parts of the Bible,
but the import of the story of the Fall meant little or nothing to him until a
newspaper, thrown overboard from a passing boat, bearing news of
Beulah's murder floated toward him on the water "like a swimming snake."
Until then, Dummy's associations were only with the natural, innocent
world surrounding him on the island, which even Eustis tried to see as

Eden. "No one can know what a word means till he feels it" (61), Dummy explains.

The outside world brought him pain and imposed upon the idyllic quality of his interior world. On his way to find the sheriff in Bristol, he had two dreams. In the first he was visiting Beulah's shack on the island; she told him that she would make love with him and that they must hurry. In the second he dreamed that he was walking under water "on the golden sandy bottom" and that Beulah was floating above him. "A current rocks her gently on her side, hair writhing; one arms snakes out, limber as an eel, the hand performing that beckoning gesture [he] feared so much." But as he approaches "the water is filled with invisible sparks" and he believes she is "guarded by pain." Then awake he realized that the "sparks" were tiny red ants from the rotten stump against which he was leaning. "I had not brought the pain out of my dreams," he realized. "It had seeped into my dream from the conscious world" (71–72).

Kate, Eustis's wife, tells us about Luther's past and as much of the Eustis family history as she knows. Her frame of reference is almost as restricted as Dummy's for she has passed practically all of her life hoeing cotton crops in the southern part of Jordan County and raising children— Rosaleen, Myrtle, and Luty (Luther) Pearl. A brutal, unremitting silence surrounded her; she seldom talked to anyone and few people spoke to her, including Eustis, and their conversation was limited only to the essential.

Eustis, according to Kate, had a "double heritage of lust and murder." His mother, Lucy Dade, daughter of the Luther Dade who had lost his arm at *Shiloh,* gave the appearance of "primness," but "behind the properness . . . there was something bold. It was faint; it barely glimmered through—so faint, whoever saw it thought he was the only one to see it: a promise of something un*holy*" (198). Perhaps Kate saw something of that same power in Eustis, just as his father, Pascal, had seen it in his wife Lucy. But that was long after Pascal had burned his house with his family in it, saving only the grandfather and Eustis, because he, Pascal, knew that Lucy's newborn was not his child.

Rosaleen, Kate and Luther's first child, had some of the Dade heritage, and it was a relief that she had married at sixteen. Myrtle was plain and grew plainer; at twenty she was an old maid. Luty Pearl, born during the 1927 flood, was retarded. Because she embarrassed her family by masturbating, even in church, they had a chastity belt made for her. During the day she wore the belt; at night they tied her hands. Luty Pearl was Luther's

favorite. It was after the family learned that she would never be more than
an infant mentally that Luther began attending church, but it was only
after Brother Jimson came that "the Lord . . . reached him." Until Beulah
came along and Luther began playing a role similar to the one his mother
had played, the family, Kate felt, led the life they "were born to lead"
(211).

The middle section of *Follow Me Down* belongs to Luther Eustis and
Beulah; Eustis narrates six sections that surround a single central section
by Beulah. His tale begins on Easter Sunday at a revival that Brother
Jimson had held at an empty dance pavilion on Lake Jordan. The services
failed to come up to Jimson's expectations because three soldiers and two
women riding noisily by in an automobile disrupted it just as the saved
were beginning to quake with the spirit. Eustis saw Beulah for the first
time in the automobile, and again that same evening when he and Jimson
came upon the five reprobates having a picnic. After that Eustis began to
see Beulah everywhere. Finally, in mid-May on the floor of his cotton
house, believing he was at work for the Lord, he had sex with her for the
first time. He thought of himself as a lamb bent on salvation: "*Teach her
what it means to be a Christian*"; but she smelled a different beast: "You
smell like a billy goat, honey."

In the following weeks, Eustis dedicated his penis to what he felt to be
the Lord's will. In June, Eustis and Beulah decided to run away to the
island in the Mississippi that Eustis remembered from his boyhood visits
there with his grandfather. He had imagined that the island "might have
been the world the way it was before God made creatures to walk it"
(97)—an Eden, "a promised land." He also questioned his motivation—
was he acting out God's will or was he simply fifty-one and afraid of
missing something. "*Youre scared youll wake up dead in the by-and-by to find
there aint any heaven, or hell either, and you wont have a thing to regret, much
less hope for*" (99). The island, however, was no Eden. At first he thought it
had changed, but then he realized it was himself who had grown older,
and, more importantly, Dummy and Mrs. Pitts had claimed the paradise
before him.

Mrs. Pitts's story of her marriage, the birth of Dummy, and of her
husband's desertion of the family when he discovered that his son was deaf
and dumb and his wife now barren made Eustis think of his own situation.
Her story reminded him of Kate and Luty Pearl. Luty Pearl had seemed to
be a burden (he had envisioned himself explaining to St. Peter that he had

spent his life carrying her around), but now he dreamed of her. Beulah increasingly appeared to him to be the temptress.

After he had drowned her in the "covy pool" and disposed of the body, he rowed Mrs. Pitts's boat over to the Mississippi side and slept the rest of the night under the levee. The next morning two black women carrying fishing poles awakened Eustis from his dreams, and a little later he frightened them away so he could eat the three fish they had caught. He spent Wednesday on the levee "like one of those oldtime hermits in the desert, fasting in the wilderness," and Thursday night he made his way to Bristol, which at night took on the appearance of a mechanical underworld. The houses and the people in them seemed to Eustis to be "a series of pictures out of a printing machine." He imagined them to be "lying limp in their beds, bellies up, breathing darkness, like batteries being charged for another tomorrow" (154). To Eustis, Bristol was even more of an urban wasteland than it was for Nowell. "Lampposts came out of the concrete down both curbs, like iron trees," and out of "a music machine . . . with tubes of rainbow-colored water running up and down its front" in the cafe that Eustis entered, a "machine man" sang *"Take me where the concrete grows"* (155).

After a night in a flop house with a gonorrhea victim, Eustis spent the remainder of his money on a set of clean used clothes, a bath and haircut, presents for Kate, Myrtle, and Luty Pearl, and a train ticket home. By Friday afternoon he had joined his family hoeing in the cotton field, but on neither Friday nor Saturday was he able to serve Kate with a proper erection. "I hadnt only lost my purity," he says, "I'd lost my manhood." Sunday afternoon he was arrested. "She [Beulah] came up, blocks and all," he said—he knew.

Beulah's mother had told her that when she met the man she was "born to meet" that she would know it—sense it intuitively. Mrs. Joyner (Joyner by her third husband), by trade a prostitute, had moved about the lower South, but she was, nevertheless, very proud of having sent her daughter to a prestigious school in New Orleans. The summer just before Beulah's fourteenth birthday, Mrs. Joyner arranged for a Mr. Iverson, who had made a fortune on the cotton market and who was entertaining Beulah and her mother at his summer cottage in the Ozarks, to be Beulah's "first." Mrs. Joyner collected four hundred dollars for her daughter's virginity. By the time Beulah had met Luther Eustis, she had become a regular in her mother's trade and had had one abortion. Sex, though, bored her. "And all this time it was like I was searching for something, I didnt know what, and couldnt find it," she says. "All the fun I'd ever got was seeing them get excited, and it seemed to me there ought to be more than that" (135). When she met Eustis, she believed she had found what she wanted. "When the time really came, I knew. I could see it as clear as I saw the star hung in the doorway, pale yellow against the purple sky; I could feel it as plain as I felt the cottonseed under my back, like pebbles on a beach. I been so miserable all my life, I said" (137).

Beulah's narrative occupies the center of the novel and takes place as Eustis is drowning her. Her life flashes before her as she watches the bubbles rise, and she thinks that she will tell Eustis that they are going to have a child when he pulls her up, as she believes he certainly will. At the center of Beulah's narrative is the long seven-page paragraph summary of the important events of her life, culminating with her meeting Eustis on the cottonhouse floor.

Beulah is the truly successful character in the book in that she achieved at least something of the satisfaction, the wholeness of being, that eludes the others. Unlike them, she found the man she was "born to meet," and because of that she achieved, at least momentarily, a harmony with the more elemental forces of history and time that operate in Foote's fictional world. At the very center of the novel is a character who, in finding what she has been searching for, possesses what the other members of the community so sorely need, and yet she is never able to communicate this to the others.

In his "May Day, 48" letter to Percy, Foote commented on the central theme in his novel, which he had first titled "Vortex." "The current novel (Vortex) has taken on implications I never dreamed of when I first conceived the plot—nothing less than the Fall of Man; entails a complete analysis of the sense of guilt in a man's soul, from all angles as well as from inside it." Percy did not like *Follow Me Down*, however, and apparently called it a dirty, sex-ridden book, which continued to trouble Foote. Over two years later, he was still defending his novel and particularly Beulah to Percy.

> The whole purpose of that capstone section (the seven-page one-paragraph autobiography of Beulah) was to show what she emerged from when she found Eustis, her father-lover. To have omitted the excitation, to have ridden herd on it as a moralist, would have been to wreck it and rob it of its point. Surely no one, not even your "sinful" reader, could miss my intention of showing it as grim and sordid, hell in fact, something she was better off

dead than returning to; and in fact she chose death. I claim the disapproval,
the shocked dismay, is implicit in every word. What could underline this
better than the fact, baldly stated by herself, that she never even experienced orgasm until Eustis took her in the cotton-house? As for the hairless
Mr Iverson, she says herself that he was the one "good" person she came in
contact with. It is even true, in a way. Dont you remember how he wanted
to hurt her for the excitation, but actually regretted having to inflict the hurt
itself? Angels dont exist in the flesh; the selfblame of the sadist is the holiest
thing I know. Why should he blame himself? What is it in him that makes
him tremble with selfblame and concern? If youre looking for God in my
books, there is where youll find Him. (20Jul52)

Allen Tate's distinction between the historical imagination and the religious imagination has rather obvious application to *Follow Me Down* as it
did in *Tournament* and *Shiloh*. Although Nowell believes that the ills of the
modern South are traceable to events surrounding the Civil War, he also
recognizes, as the reader must, that Eustis's "insanity" represents the
disease of the entire culture and that the modern artist, the only effective
physician for these ills, must distill the medicine to cure them from a
recognition of human need that is embodied in primitive fertility myth.
Religious ritual and the form of art are at once a metaphor for, and a
celebration of, man's basic sexual nature and his dependence on the flow of
the seasons and their operation on the rich Delta earth. Effective religious
expression recognizes man's dependence on the earth and harmonizes that
dependence with his sexual nature.

The three levels of time with which these characters deal are very much
out of sync, and the text abounds in ironies that grow from the characters'
failures to understand the cacophony they hear. For example, Eustis recalls
a sermon of Brother Jimson's: "There had to be a balance in the world, so
much corruption to so much sanctity, or everything would come undone.
People were little wheels in one big clockwork, so when one wheel turned
in one direction, the one alongside it, meshing, had to turn too, in the
other direction: for if once a wheel turned so much as a tiny fraction of an
inch and the meshing one stood still, the strain would be too much; the
clock would fly apart, explode" (99). The murder Eustis committed obviously was an explosion; the clock for him failed. The first level of time in
Luther's clockworks is his personal past. His memory and the habits of a
lifetime bear upon his actions. For example, a farmer all his life, he
naturally falls to work beside Dummy in Mrs. Pitts's garden. Next, there

is historic time, the dimension that the references to English literature make available and the history of Jordan County. Luther's family, the Dades, have been a part of Jordan County history almost from its beginnings; they have sharecropped part of Solitaire from the Jamesons, Hugh Bart, and other owners for three generations. Bristol tends to mythologize the historic past; Civil War veterans are constantly promoted in rank, and Billy Lillard, who never did more than serve on KP in Tampa during the Spanish American War, has bought a chest-full of medals and calls himself captain. The jail that Stevenson and Nowell describe, its garish modern exterior covering the warmer brick beneath, marks the corruption of historic time.

However important these first two wheels of the clockworks may be, it is the third wheel that causes the most serious malfunction. Time, this third dimension, is related to the "impulse" Nowell feels in Mozart's symphony; it is the need Bristol has for its billy goat. There is a pervading sense among all of the narrators that time is not haphazard but that fate, the stars, God, or some other force gives it design and purpose. Beulah feels she has found the man she was "meant" to find (130, 135); Stevenson believes that "fate" has to do with his being present at Bachlor Bend (30); and Nowell thinks that "providence" may have brought Kate to his office (218). According to Kate, she and Eustis were leading the life they were "born to lead" (211). Beulah observed a star in the doorway of the cottonhouse when she knew she had found her man; the Dummy followed the stars to find his way to Bristol; Brother Jimson fought the soldiers under the stars; and stars reflected in Beulah's "covy pool": "We undressed on [the] bank. His face and neck and hands and wrists were dark; the rest was pale in the starlight, paler than ever. It was as if he bleached whiter inside his clothes these past four days. He stood with his back to me and I waded in, then turned and saw him coming toward me, knee-deep, thigh-deep, waist-deep in the water. Starlight gleamed on the whiteness; against the dark background of the tress" (144).

Eustis feels forces operating beyond his control, but he cannot see them in any form or order in his description of events. Stevenson's first impression of him is that he is "disconnected." He seems never to doubt that the Bible he always had with him contains truth, but he is never certain what the truth is. In the beginning he is convinced that he is following God's will. "It was God's will I was led to her, for it was God's work I was attending when I saw her that first time at the pavilion" (77). Doubt follows

quickly in Eustis's recollection of Jimson's fight with the soldiers: "A thing
like that begins. Then something grows out of it and you look back.
Chances are, you tell yourself it was all foretold in the seeds of that first
beginning, if you could only have read them. But that was not the way it
was with us. I took no more part in the fight than she did, just as earlier at
the lakeside she had not done the driving nor I the preaching. We were
caught up in events concerning others, like a man out for a holiday swim
that paddles full tilt into a whirlpool, never suspecting it was there" (86–
87). Soon, caught in the vortex, he is ready to believe that he has lost his
faith or that he *never had it* (99).

At the moment of crisis for Eustis, the Bible has nothing to say to him;
he feels that his God, after all the praying and reading, has left things up to
him. "Then Tuesday, late, it reached me plain what God was saying. *I'll
leave it to you, Luther Eustis,* He was saying; *I'll leave it to you.*" If God lets
Eustis follow his own inclinations, then he is inclined to murder.

The excuses with which he provided himself along the way sometimes
countered his doubt. He felt drawn to Beulah because "a godly man feels
drawn to sin every time" (87). About to commit his first act of fornication
with her, he heard God say, "*Teach her what it means to be a Christian*"
(93). In an earlier age he might have been a Red-Cross knight "pricking"
his way across a plain, for the modern Eustis knows that "a man with
sanctity wears armor; he breaths sin like fire. Every time he moves he
clanks, and every breath he draws is a breath of pain" (93).

Eustis's emotional balance finally ran out: "God hadnt been my guide,
hearing my prayers and telling me what to do: the devil had—old Satan.
And now I had to live with that, unable to blame it on God" (193). He
discovered that his island-garden had long since been corrupted and that
the golden age was remote. Peeps, the derelict with VD who had provided
Eustis with a place to sleep in Bristol, commented when he saw the money
in Eustis's cigar box, "Youre heeled, by Christ." Such ironies abound in the
text. Eustis, like Peeps, is a sick man indeed, anything but "healed," and
certainly not "by Christ." It is, in fact, "the Bible that betrayed him" (252),
as Nowell observes.

Like the stars or fate, the cyclic passing of the seasons is one of those
great forces and may be associated with the impulse manifest in Nowell's
"symphony of Time." Nowell takes note of the passing seasons, yet he
seems to find nothing sacramental in them—no god planted in the garden
in springtime to be resurrected, or reborn. Instead, the seasons in the

Mississippi Delta are "repetitious, immemorial, and grim" in Nowell's lyrical cynicism.

> The year moved into August. Whatever breeze stirred, and that was little, was like a breath from an oven, the earth baked powdery, ash-gray between the rows of dusty cotton stalks whose bolls were beginning to split and spill their whiteness. Soon now the pickers would be moving across the fields, enormous insects translated out of a Biblical curse and dragging nine-foot sacks. Saturdays the Bristol streets would be filled with Negro and Mexican shoppers crowded shoulder to shoulder from curb to store-fronts, the length of Marshall Avenue. Then, agriculturally speaking, a lull would follow. The gins would hush their perpetual whine; cold weather would bring hog-killing time with a tang of wood-smoke in the air. Finally the autumn rains would lower a curtain, like the darkness after fireworks Christmas night. It was the age-old cycle of the Delta year, repetitious, immemorial, and grim. [230–31]

Nowell's sterile rituals not withstanding, 1949 was a strange crop year in the Delta. It began with a cold Easter (78), which was followed by late planting (90) and an unusually wet summer (266). Whatever the conditions of the year in *Follow Me Down,* the seasons, nature itself, fail to give time form. Instead, time has become merely a ticking abstraction—something the parking meters in Bristol can sell. If anyone should find sustenance in the vegetation myth that the moderns find so important to religion, then the farmer is most likely, but the seasons pass lightly over the modern land and do not bring, even to the most remote fringes of consciousness, a suggestion of religious or mythical fulfillment. It seems to matter little that the God was planted on Good Friday, germinated, and sprang from the earth on Easter. Even Jimson, the preacher, is only a poisonous weed, and who wants weeds in his garden?

Jimson's religion relies upon emotional extravagance, and just as the religious practice is out of order with respect to nature, so revivalism is out of order with respect to sex. Among the sins that the sacrifice of the goat or the innocent lamb is supposed to address is the guilt caused by sexuality. Man's own reproductive capacities have a relationship in religious myth to the growth of the crops and the passing seasons. Yet sex, in the evangelical exuberance, remains superficial, even vulgar. Eustis observes that Jimson "had a way of standing that showed off the bulge of his crotch," but he also reports that "nobody took it amiss" because "they knew that was part of what he meant when he spoke of the strength of the Lord" (79). Luty Pearl is not allowed to masturbate even in her own bed at home, but the sexually suggestive behavior of the redeemed, when the fit of the Lord is upon them, is approved. At the revival a woman from the southern part of the county had such a fit: "her body began to rise and fall in the middle, her bottom thumping, and every time it hit she would move down the slope six inches or so, like a measuring-worm" (81). The sexual expressions are as abstracted from their foundation as the time that Nowell's parking meter sells, as remote as the jungle is from civilization. One of the songs that the machine is playing in the cafe while Eustis is there has lyrics very much to the purpose; the lyrics are from "Civilization," a song by Bob Hilliard and Carl Sigman which was current in 1949: *"Bingle-Bangle-Bungle / I'm so happy in the jungle . . . Bingo-Bango-Bongo / I dont wonna leave the Congo . . . Civilization."* The primitive, natural jungle is a part of the past that the moderns need, for to forget it is to make civilization an abstraction in which murders such as Eustis has committed are possible. Eustis would love for time, the past, to be of no consequence—"calendars," he says, "wont do for measuring time." His life is in two parts, nine days on one side and all the rest on the other. A calendar will not take that into account. Nevertheless, even though he tries to rid himself of every vestige of his life on the island, his life in the jungle, the sheriff, Roebuck, and the Dummy ride up to his house and he is caught.

Beulah alone among these characters achieved a moment of harmony and a sense of wholeness. She, almost literally, glimpsed the meaning of the star framed in the doorway of the cottonhouse as intuitively she seemed to recognize the impulse that gave form to time, and she felt in that impulse the harmonization of the great natural forces of the earth. Because of her sense of the rightness of her relationship with Eustis, she would not let him go. In a seemingly sterile world, she had conceived. Even more obvious, though, is the praise, the ecstasy, the letting go that came with her orgasm on the cottonhouse floor. "I didn't know whether we went in by the door or the window or down through the roof, it happened so fast," she says. She thought she heard horses nickering but realized that it was Eustis praying. "I had forgotten him; I had my eyes closed, not even remembering where I was. When I opened them I saw him framed against the doorway, on his knees, unhooking a strap from the bib of his overalls. The smell came strong and rancid through the musty smell of cottonseed: Like a billy goat, I told him; I was lying on my back, my knees drawn up. He struck like a stallion lunge; My God; he even neighed and nickered, hands like hoofs. I only realized afterwards he'd been praying all the while: what I had thought was whinnying was praying. I should have known" (129).

But then, Beulah was praying too, and her praying was not blasphemous swearing. It was the deepest praise she could give, and all of time focused on that climactic instant.

> Because something came out of somewhere to reinforce him, whatever makes thunder and lightning, fires and floods; no one man was ever like that in all this world, alone. The whiskey grogginess left me like the flame will leave a candle in the wind. All there was was Now: the swoon and surge and swoon and surge—I swung back from somewhere off in space, again on the floor of the cottonhouse with the seeds like pebbles under my back, and heard my voice calling Jesus, calling His name with a high thin eerie wail. I was cussing, but I wasn't; I could tell by the sound. I was praying. I was praying too.
>
> . . . This was a brand new different world, and nothing in it would ever be the same—all because of a little man in overalls I'd thought to kill fifteen minutes making fun of, lying on my back with both knees drawn up, whiskey-sodden, relaxed, with time enough even to tell him he smelled like a goat: one last half-instant before the thunder clapped, the world hung still, and everything pointed to Now. [129–30]

Beulah, because of her intuitive sense of fulfillment, should be of great value to this civilization, and yet that value, precious as gold, goes largely unrecognized. Eustis often associates Beulah with gold, and yet the notion that she has heightened value is lost. The golden charm, a heart with the word "love" engraved on it, implies another relationship between gold and love, perhaps the golden rule. In any event the word on the charm describes what Nowell believes has failed. Not only the charm but Beulah's physical self is golden—her golden hair, when wet in the "covy pool," fit her "like a helmet," Eustis thought (177).

Except for Beulah's ecstasy with Eustis, sexual relations in modern Jordan County are not a joyous celebration of an intuitive sense of harmony with the "broadcast doings of the day and night." Sex for Eustis is fornication, sin, at best a duty that he, a godly man, is compelled to perform. Lonzo, the photographer, is homosexual; Nowell's wife has left him; Stevenson has no wife and does not seem to need or want one; the Dummy cannot escape his isolation; and the turnkey's wife talks incessantly. Luty Pearl, the natural, is fitted with a chastity belt because she plays with herself in church. Religious expression, too, is unsatisfying. It is not Beulah's ecstasy, nor is it praise that grows naturally out of heightened experience, unaffected by prejudices, by the opinions of others, or by religious clichés. Although the fictional world is filled with signs and objects that take on heightened, symbolic value, the moderns are still not able to see themselves in a religious, mythical context—even Eustis, who is most devoted to religious slogans and to the visible expressions of what could be taken for grace. Bristol may have deep need for the reenactment of the sacrifice of the scapegoat, but Nowell prevents it. To Percy, Foote declared himself to be an "anthropologist of Jordan County," and *Follow Me Down* shows rather emphatically that, indeed, he had adopted the major anthropological themes of the modern novel.

Love in a Dry Season

After completing *Follow Me Down,* Foote turned immediately to his next novel, *Love in a Dry Season.* The themes—the isolation of twentieth-century man from his neighbors and from himself, his separation, dissociation, from his historical and traditional antecedents—Foote treats in a modern, but somewhat earlier, segment of Jordan County history. In this novel the outlook for humankind is, if anything, bleaker, for however duplicitous Parker Nowell may have been in his dealings with Bristol, there is Nowell who "knows well" and can identify much of what is wrong with the community, even though he and most of the other characters are like Gowan—"gone on" in that they do not act on such insight as they may have.

The immediate historical setting becomes more prominent in *Love in a Dry Season;* the events begin during the depression years and conclude in 1941 with the entry of the United States into World War II.

The dramatic situation in *Love in a Dry Season* is to some extent borrowed from Henry James's *Washington Square.* James's Morris Tounsend, an adventurer and man of the world, comes to New York City and begins courting Catherine Sloper, daughter of a prominent pre-Civil War physician, a man of ample though not lavish means. Dr. Sloper, believing on rather solid grounds that Tounsend does not love his daughter, opposes the engagement and successfully insures that the none-too-clever and rather plain Catherine will become an old maid. Harley Drew, the principal figure in *Love in a Dry Season,* arrives in Bristol to discover Amanda

Barcroft, the not particularly attractive younger daughter of Major Malcolm Barcroft, one of the most substantial cotton factors in town. Foote's
major, like James's doctor, opposes the marriage, especially after he discovers that Drew cannot recall the color of Amanda's eyes. But Drew
thinks he has found a good place to invest his time; he resigns his position
as a representative of St. Louis cotton interests and accepts a position in
Lawrence Tilden's bank in Bristol to wait out the major who dies some
eleven years later, long after Drew has discovered Amy Carruthers. In
Amy and in his success in Tilden's bank, he finds advantages that much
outweigh Amanda, and besides Amanda's value is substantially reduced by
the major's decision to leave the bulk of his diminished estate to the
military school he attended as a boy. These events are quite different from
the events in *Washington Square* but the basic plot is similar.

Foote also found *Washington Square* to have a congenial narrative pattern and a flashback technique that James employs with great effectiveness.
Chapter three of *Washington Square* displays the pattern of development
that Foote followed: opening the section with a sentence describing an
event near the chronological end of the narrative, then reviewing the
events that preceded, and finally adding a sentence or so to the culmina-
tion of the event with which the chapter opened. He begins near the end
and then immediately reverts to an earlier point in the narrative which he
develops up to the point of beginning and pushes, then, a little past.
Chapter three of *Washington Square* opens with a description of Catherine
told largely from her father's point of view. The first paragraph concludes
with the announcement that Catherine is to attend "a little entertainment
given by her aunt" and that "Mrs. Almond's party was the beginning of
something very important." We then learn a good deal about the history of
Dr. Sloper's family in New York, and the conclusion of the chapter returns
to the party and the reason for the occasion, which is the engagement of
Mrs. Almond's daughter to "a stout young stockbroker." This same pattern Foote uses to advantage in *Love in a Dry Season*. The book opens, with
the announcement that "Major Malcolm Barcroft was sixty-seven when he
died," and then for the next twenty-five pages, Foote surveys the history of
the Barcrofts and their position in Bristol. In the same narrative fashion,
we learn about other characters in *Love in a Dry Season*—Harley Drew and
Amy and Jeff Carruthers.

The presence of William Faulkner, Balzac, James, and Proust in *Love in
a Dry Season* contributes pointedly to the context in which Amanda

Barcroft might have recognized something of her own condition. She reads about "Eugenie Grandet, Catherine Sloper, Emily Grierson" but seems not to discover that keeping her father's corpse in her house for two days after his death has its antecedents. The isolation that the Barcroft house provides Florence, Amanda's asthmatic older sister, is not as complete as that provided Emily in "A Rose for Emily," but there is more than coincidental similarity in Florence's and Emily's situations. More important than similarity of incident is the similarity of narrative interest. The narrator of "A Rose for Emily" is an accepted member of the community in Jefferson, a party to its gossip. The narrator of *Love in a Dry Season,* though not a familiar figure about town, places himself among the townspeople in Bristol and reports their views, providing a significant perspective on the main characters. The multiple narrators that Foote used in *Shiloh* and *Follow Me Down,* based on Browning and Faulkner, are here replaced by a single narrative voice. Obviously, the narrator is a man of learning and intelligence who, like Parker Nowell, has listened carefully to music—Baroque dance, Brahms, and jazz, and who, like Russel Stevenson, has read widely.

Bristol is one of the central characters whose consciousness the narrator explores; with qualified omniscience he examines the feelings and ideas of the major characters and makes clear that the problems faced by these troubled consciousnesses are no different in any fundamental way from those the community itself faces. Modern Bristol suffers from its inability to care deeply for fellow human beings. The season is too dry for love to grow and the cultural ground is infertile. Perhaps if it could articulate its need, it could understand and find a cure, but Bristol is a world of watchers, observers,[5] who know they have a deep need. But they are inhabitants of a modern world and are reduced to looking out at the world around the barriers that their loss of nerve has built.

Modern Bristol clearly needs love, and in the development of the novel, the narrator suggests that this love is by no means a hollow abstraction. Love is a condition of being that is shaped by art, nature, and history and expressed in manners, rites, and tradition. Foote's position here is close to that of two fellow southerners, Allen Tate and John Crowe Ransom, and, of course, T. S. Eliot and Proust. Bristol in many ways resembles the "dehumanized" and "secular" modern world that Tate deplored in his essay "The Man of Letters in the Modern World."[6] Because of their inability to love, Bristolites, in Tate's words, "may communicate, but they cannot live in full communion," the "end of social man is communion in time through love, which is beyond time." Communion can take place through the arts, particularly the "literary arts." "By these arts," Tate declares, "one means the arts without which men can live, but without which they cannot live well, or live as men." "Communion" fails in Bristol and those characters, and the community itself, are "dehumanized" and mechanical, moving in rhythm to a bubbling juke box and surrounded by "iron trees" (lamp posts) growing from concrete—an image Foote repeats from *Follow Me Down*. Likewise, in his essay "Forms and Citizens,"[7] Ransom asserts his preference for "a program going something like this: In manners, aristocratic; in religion, ritualistic; in art, traditional." Ransom, as he makes clear, has created a variation on Eliot's theme: "In politics, royalism; in religion, Anglo-Catholic; in literature, classical." The failure of characters in *Love in a Dry Season* can be defined, in Ransom's terms, as the failure to insist on the primacy of "aesthetic" forms over "economic" forms. By insistence on the aristocratic, "ritualistic," and "traditional," character can be elevated above the "instinctive." In a world dominated by economic forms, men and women are simply things, objects, means. Love in such a world is reduced to what one selfishly can accomplish by it. "The object of a proper society," Ransom declares, "is to instruct its members how to transform instinctive experience into aesthetic experience." This, of course, is Proust's theme as well. It is only through art, Proust says, that we learn to understand another human being.

Immersion in art and in the religious experience derived from man's dependence on nature (a dependence expressed in the metaphor of the liturgical calendar and ritual) makes love possible, and love would have saved Amanda Barcroft from wretchedness. The inability of Bristol to articulate its need is its fundamental failure. The novel includes no characters who gain insight into their condition; there are no epiphanies. These characters simply endure. If they change at all, the change involves accommodation to existing conditions; there is no deepening sense of fulfillment or even a recognition of what might contribute to it. Amanda Barcroft becomes a "watcher," one of the many frustrated Bristolites who are unable to define or understand the sources of their unhappiness and are unable even to recognize clearly what they are watching for. The failure to discover some humanizing spark of life, together with the necessity of the narrative to suggest what they do not see, gives the narrator a crucial role and, at the same time, gives the novel traces of allegory. Amanda Barcroft, the allegorical modern Everywoman in *Love in a Dry Season,* in her attempt to lead a fulfilled life, is frustrated not simply by Harley Drew, who returns her affection only with insincerity, but by the larger context of her southern community, whose time-honored rituals have become simply the repetition of empty forms. Amanda, Harley, and the other characters, thus, are shut away from the means of understanding what love might be.

Foote has arranged his plot so that ten sections focus on Drew and five on Amanda, making them numerically the most important figures in the novel. Four sections focus on Amy Carruthers, three on Jeff Carruthers, two on Bristol, and one each on Major Barcroft, the clerk in his cotton office, and Florence Barcroft. The count, though, fails to show the relative importance of the community. The narrator frequently reports what characters thought of Bristol and what Bristol said about them.

Foote introduces the reader first to Major Malcolm Barcroft, who has a strong sense of history, perhaps a limited understanding of art, but no sensitivity at all to the natural world. The major had wanted a military career for himself but at every turn he was frustrated. Instead of entering the army after graduation from military school, or perhaps attending West Point, he was forced by the failure of the family's fortunes to return "to Bristol to enter his bachelor uncle's cotton office" (5).[8] The Spanish-American War ended before he could leave Tampa, and a heart murmur prevented his having even a desk assignment during World War I. His reverence for the military tradition, so important to his part of the country, lent him "a courteous old-world manner," which, together with his position in the business community, made him, the narrator says, "an institution in Bristol," but at the same time he was "one of the final representatives of what the town had progressed beyond" (3). Instead of lending life to the major's character, his reverence for military tradition, and his failure to follow the tradition as he would like, isolated him. He was never a member of his community. The town was "hostile" toward him; "'Punch him with something sharp,' they said; 'what would run out? Ice water'" (25).

The major was devoted to formula, to ritual; he had to succeed according to the plan. Had he been less rigid and more human, the world for those dependent on him might have been more pleasant. Had he been more responsive to art and nature, he might have been equipped to "put his lands in order." The plan demanded, however, a male heir. After his first two children, both girls, Florence and Amanda, were born, the doctor warned against another pregnancy. After his wife's third, agonizing labor, she died, but the child, a boy, was saved. His wife had wanted to name a boy Hezekiah, but, dead, what did she matter? "He called him Malcolm, the name of the firstborn male Barcroft for five generations now" (7), the narrator explains.

Against the major's rituals, hollow because he had no feeling, almost nothing in his household could have much abundance of being. Malcolm needed to fit the plan; he must have been a soldier, but he was effeminate. He rejected the pony the major bought him and had almost no interest in toy soldiers. Finally, in July, after his eleventh birthday, Malcolm is accidentally killed by a companion with the 410-gauge shotgun Barcroft had given him. With that the Barcroft military tradition came to an end.

Just as the history that is embodied in the southern military tradition fails the isolated Barcroft household, so art and nature fail to sustain it. The elder daughter, Florence, is representative. Named for the city that is one of the most important centers of Western Renaissance art, Florence was, nevertheless, cut off from the world. The art that she represented had nothing to say; it was dumb, incommunicative. Florence developed asthma and was confined to the downstairs living room, where she slept in a Morris chair, never leaving the room even to bathe. "The room was made airtight for her fumigations, calked with folded newspapers at jambs and sashes, the narrator says. Yet even above the reek of camphor and burning sulphur there was a rancid odor of unwashed female flesh" (14). To pass time Florence made "flower designs on quilted satin," which she gave each year at Christmas to former friends whose addresses she found in an old phone book. The friends, finding the gift "too fine for a tea cozy and too thick for framing," would eventually consign it to a cedar chest, from which it might be removed years later for puzzled children and grandchildren to examine and identified only as "something poor Florry Barcroft sent . . . years ago" (21). Florence's artistry, such as it was, was practically useless in a community that obviously was much in need of it.

The patterns that might have given dimension and substance to Florence's art, the deeper rhythms of nature, were likewise lost in the isolation. Even though she read the Memphis newspaper "with the grim unflagging headlong perseverence of a mole burrowing the loose earth" (20), what fertility the "loose earth" might have was never hers. Her long yellow hair, which "had the rich sheen of cornsilk when the ears begin to tassel" (15), represents something of an attachment to the natural world, but when she suggested that its length made her uncomfortably hot, the major arranged for Sam Marino, his regular barber, to cut it, and afterward to make his visits to the asthmatic invalid four times a year. From his first visit, Sam Marino "felt that something was wrong about this house" (18). Florence's symbolic contact with the natural world and its growing and planting rhythms was quite literally cut away.

In ritual, though, in the Holy Eucharist, a metaphor of man's dependence on the natural world, Florence found at least a distant reflection of the natural world. Mr. Clinkscales, the Episcopal rector, visited the first Sunday of each month, "bearing under his arm a calfskin case containing the utensils and the bread and wine for Communion" (21). Communion became, thus, the most important event for Florence: "she remembered the half-naked man nailed to the wall of the church beside the altar, and she fed on him in her heart and drank his blood." After this ecstasy Amanda "always found her sister sitting with her hands folded in her lap and her eyes would be filled with tears of happiness" (22). Living one's life vicariously by metaphor lacks considerable substance, the narrator implies, but it was all Florence had, the dried out remains of what tradition and art Bristol could claim.

From this failed world Amanda had to face her life and from its narrowness find what she could. The people of modern Bristol gave her little hope as they watched her walking, as was her ritual, with her father after supper. Young men watching would tease each other: "There's your chance." "My chance at what?" "At a million dollars, man. What else?" "Hm. No thanks. It's not enough considering what goes with it" (25).

Three people in addition to her immediate family were especially important to Amanda's life—Harley Drew and Jeff and Amy Carruthers. While the natives of Bristol are not particularly hopeful, or even very interested in Amanda's success, the narrator assures us that "there was someone who thought [the Barcroft fortune] was enough, who weighed it carefully, point against point, made his decision quickly, and believed himself fortunate that no one had done so before him. There was a suitor on the way" (25). The suitor was Harley Drew, but Foote's narrator introduces us first to Amy and Jeff.

Amy and Jeff Carruthers were cousins, but because their marriage was barren, the incestuous relationship was in itself of little consequence. Their marriage was not based on a deep affection for each other, certainly not love, but rather on a variety of what the narrator might identify as perversions. Jeff was a voyeur, and Amy suggested that he might even be homosexual. Amy, "whose nature is essential[ly] promiscuous," loved to dominate and manipulate her sexual partners, whom Jeff, before he was blind, would be content to watch.

Amy's interest in Jordan County developed after she inherited Briartree, a large plantation house her great-grandfather had built on the shores of Lake Jordan in 1857. Returning there "appealed to her as a sort of pilgrimage to hallowed ground, the blind seed returning home" (32). But any resemblance between the pilgrimage of the devout and Amy's "blind" pilgrimage is simply a haunting reminder of how far the modern world has changed. The true meaning of pilgrimage probably did not even occur to Amy, just as their playing at sex is a haunting reminder that love in a saner, more elemental world might actually have something to do with marriage.

Jeff and Amy, who was three years older than he, grew up spending summers together at the family home near Myrtle Beach. The family's substantial fortune came from tobacco. Amy and Jeff were, then, New Southerners, children of economic commercial development. At thirteen Jeff, who had already been thrown out of one fashionable prep school because of his affection for pornography, spent his summers watching Amy and her boyfriends perform on the front-porch swing at the country house. Then, once, he had his chance in the swing, where he, to the tune of Amy's laughter, failed. "He had studied well, watching the others. . . . Then at the critical moment he panicked; he was terrified; he even began to weep; 'Hold me! Hold me!' he cried. Then it was over and he was amazed: Was that all there was to it? Then gradually he became conscious of a sort of animal chuckling near his ear. She was laughing at him: had been laughing all along, he realized. And he was horribly ashamed" (36–37). Amy's manner with Jeff "had been more that of a riding instructor than a lover, let alone a maiden in submission." As a result, Jeff, the narrator assures us, "looked forward to a time when he could repay her, could laugh at her or strike her as he saw fit. Thus marriage was already in his mind" (38).

Driven by her laughter, his shame, and the pleasant memory of watching others, he "proved himself" on the football field at Chapel Hill. Here before large crowds he could, in a narrow but symbolic way, escape the careful rules of a politely superficial world. A more dynamic tournament was simply not available for Jeff, the modern man. "Every September he brought the memory of all this to Chapel Hill and tried to work if off on the football field, to take it out on the opposing team, both in the weekday scrimmages and in the Saturday games," Foote's narrator explains. "What he lacked in weight (it was not until his senior year that he reached a hundred and fifty pounds) he made up for in fury and a nonregard for injuries." After Chapel Hill, Jeff spent a year at Harvard, and after that he made the customary trip to Europe and had the customary affair, this with a debutante from New England. Then it was marriage to Amy. His father objected ("Dammit, boy, she's your cousin"), but then the elder Carruthers went on to other matters of his own.

From the beginning the marriage was stormy. One night after Amy had been too cozy at the Winston-Salem country club with a man named Perkins, Jeff drove his roadster into an oncoming bus and was blinded by a shard of glass from the windshield. What little sex had meant to them before was nothing now, though it was Amy who seemed to care more than he. "She did what she could; she had never been half this tender, and in bed now it was she who made the advances. But there was no response, no resurrection of the flesh. 'It's not any fun in the dark,' he said, and she saw his eyes brimming with tears that glistened in the moonlight. She really felt sorry for him—even she. For what could be more pitiful than a voyeur in the dark?" (45).

The word *resurrection* crops up in the text to bring to mind what Jeff's world lacked. His sensibilities had lost their moorings in both history and the natural world, and there was nothing to restore them, not even the jazz that Jeff had come to love. Jeff retreated with Amy to Bristol and from there into a comfortable isolation. "He would turn his eyes from speaker to speaker twitching his absurdly small, fat mouth; then suddenly he would retreat into himself, almost as if he had thrown a switch or had sound-proof flaps on his ears like a bat, and the voices would be left addressing emptiness; they would trail off and the people would look at one another, embarrassed, ill at ease" (52).

Amy moved to Briartree partly because, for the first time in her life, she had something she could call her inheritance and because she had developed an even deeper "enmity" for Jeff after he killed, with his bare hands, a seeing-eye dog that had become more attached to Amy than to him. Amy had married Jeff to avoid any serious "change in her life," but "the death of the dog made a change" and she "truly resented" Jeff. Originally Jeff had "operated by plan, by calculation, subterfuge," while "Amy went solely by instinct" (48), but after the dog's death, "for the first time she began to plan ahead, to calculate" (49). Briartree became part of her calculation.

Inheritance implies heritage, but in restoring Briartree, Amy and Jeff missed the fundamental. They had a fancy, expensive shell in which the past could exist, at best, as mere sentiment, not as a deeply felt part of life. At Briartree, Amy, like Hugh Bart's wife at Solitaire before her, became "the mistress, the chatelaine," but those women who had come to Lake Jordan almost a century before her had run the house "with efficiency at hand like a muleskinner's whip." At the same time they managed "to be willowy and tender" and to rear "large numbers of children and raise them according to a formula whereby life was simple because indecision did not cloud it." These women "wore clothes that gave inch for inch as much cover as armor," but they also bore the Western tradition that the armor suggests. In a former time, Amy would have been "Old Miss," and Jeff would have been "Mars Jeff," taking his place among those farmers who lived "their lives with a singleness of purpose . . . like priests whose cult was cotton" (50). Amy's and Jeff's lives were not those of planters, though; after all there were only eighty acres of the Tarfeller inheritance left. Without moorings in time or art, their lives became increasingly violent. First, there was the dog, then there was the man whom Jeff tried to shoot in a hotel near Nice, and then there was Harley Drew whom Jeff tried to kill in the bedroom at Briartree.

Harley Drew was as devoted as any character in Foote's novels to Ransom's "economic forms" and he had an "eye for the main chance." Drew, the son of Josef Drubashevski, a Youngstown steel worker, was the youngest of five sons, and he played carpetbagger to Jeff's New Southern-er. World War I had opened doors for Drew; he returned to the country a highly decorated officer, much admired by a wide circle of friends. Proceeds from poker games enabled Drew to make a grand tour of the East and Midwest after the war. It was a search for the right job and location, and at the end of it, he found himself in the employ of the Anson-Grimm cotton trust or, more specifically, in the employ of Leo Anson, the father of young Leo who had a member of Drew's company in the war for the few days before he was killed. Drew filled the elder Leo's ears with tales of his son's exploits, but his employment was not simply for the pleasure of Leo Anson because the affable Harley Drew made his own way among the cotton merchants. There is, of course, no question about his ego or about his motives. "The natural friendliness behind the sheen suggested that behind the façade of high finance the company also had a heart of gold—

as indeed it had, though in another sense" (55). Drew, like his employers, was a man of appearances, and underneath the facade lay the man looking for the "main chance." In the interests of the cotton trust, he had come to Bristol to meet Major Barcroft; in his own interests, after meeting the major and Amanda, he had decided to stay there.

Drew arrived in Bristol on a Friday afternoon in late November 1928. One week later he had Amanda's promise to marry, and on the following Sunday, he made his trip to ask the major for her hand. He had absolutely no illusions; his dream was measured in dollars, and because the money he believed Amanda would inherit was of such importance to him, he would do what no one in Bristol would do. "It aint worth it," the major's book-keeper had told him. "I suppose not," Drew seemed to agree, but he believed otherwise. By Tuesday night just before he had the bellboy bring him a prostitute, he was able to tell himself that even Florence might be "worth it." "But this was just talk, bravado: he was goading himself, accusing himself of a greater enormity in order that the lesser would appear that much the lesser, even to himself" (69), the narrator explains.

On the Sunday evening visit to see the major, Drew suffered the worst defeat of his career. He "faltered, perhaps for the first time in his adult life" (76), the narrator explains in a phrase that echoes Henry James's description of his heroine. His affability and confidence abandoned him, and he stammered "like a schoolboy caught with a crib." He could not remember the color Amanda's eyes when the major, who had no illusions about Drew's motives, asked. Maybe Drew had never known.

He would not give up, however. The major, he believed, would change his mind. At first, he and Amanda planned an elopement, but Major Barcroft sensed this and threatened to disinherit her. Drew gave the eight-dollar nightgown he had bought for Amanda to a prostitute and began his wait. If the major should die before Florence, then the way would be clear, he believed. Amanda, the narrator affirms, was not particularly shocked or surprised to find Drew waiting for her at their usual place and time after their plans had been thwarted. "It was as if she had lost all capacity for surprise, being involved already in events so far outside her experience or hope: as if, after the initial shock of finding herself loved—or, at any rate, loving—all other surprises were bound to be anticlimax" (102). Amanda's emotions were real enough for her, and Drew knew how to play his games on her confidence. "'I couldnt go,' he said. 'I couldnt leave you'" (102), and he painted a picture for her of a Harley Drew fighting with himself,

alone in his hotel room, listening to the lonesome sound of the Drewless
train rushing south in the night. "They walked, and at first his voice was
only a murmur as he told her how he had missed her, how he had tried to
steel himself to catch the train, and then how he had lain in bed and heard
the whistle. Such a lonesome sound, he said, and he had lain there, alone
and lonesome, hearing it" (103). So the pair settled in to wait for two
deaths in the Barcroft family. "It would be necessary," Drew concluded,
"to stay, to protect his investment" (96).

From the employ of the father of one of his war-time associates, Drew
went into the employ of another associate—Lawrence Tilden, the son of
the founder and now the principal owner of the Planters Bank and Trust
Company. What better place for a man with Drew's interests than a bank?
Lawrence, "Aunt Tilly," Tilden "had been adjutant of Drew's regiment"
and, like most of Drew's companions, had developed a considerable admiration for him. Now Tilden had become a typical figure in post-war
Bristol, a town where at night, in 1928 (as later in Luther Eustis's time),
the "street lamps burned in ordered rows down both curbs of the avenue,
the posts like iron trees growing out of concrete, each with a pool of gold
about its trunk, and bearing incandescent globes for fruit" (88). Tilden
"was married, had been married more than eight years now, but there had
been no children; 'Not yet,' he said in the tone of a man repeating a hope
he has long since ceased to believe in" (95). Tilden's family tree did not
bear even artificial fruit, but Lawrence had a plan for Drew. Most things in
Bristol are like the iron forest growing in concrete; they are neat, according
to plan.

Drew would, in Tilden's plan, "begin as a teller. . . . After six months of
this he would move back to the general bookkeeping department," and
from there he would become assistant cashier and then assistant vice
president. Tilden would delight in having someone with Drew's "sales-
manship" and "personality," and for his part, Drew needed Tilden "to
protect his investment." This was not what he told Tilden, however; he
told the banker that it seemed he "never was meant" to be a traveler and
that he had "fallen in love" with Bristol. Drew, of course, was ever a man of
his own schemes, but the words sounded fine to Drew, so in his letter of
resignation to Leo Anson he repeated them. "I have fallen in love with this
sleepy little Southern town" (100). Later Foote's narrator explains that the
phrase was simply untrue. Drew, he tells us, "hardly noticed" Bristol.
"Besides, the statement needed some translating: for when he said 'Bristol'

he meant Amanda, and when he said 'love' he meant something else as well" (105).

Drew moved from the hotel into a two-room apartment owned by a Mrs. Pentecost, about whom Bristol had plenty of gossip. She had come from a aristocratic family, married beneath her, and then drove her husband to alcoholism and a miserable death in the city jail. "And yet to look at her youd never know it," the narrator assures us, "never imagine the nights she had waited for the husband she herself had driven to drink because of her inveterate pretension and because marriage had not measured up to the dreams her people had taught her in her youth" (104). Bristol knew all there was to know about Mrs. Pentecost. "Drew heard her story soon after moving in, yet he was not surprised. By then he had heard many such stories; Bristol was full of such people. Maybe every town was, he thought, but in Bristol everyone knew about everyone else—as if God, an enormous Eye in the sky, were telling secrets" (104).

Harley Drew waited, and meanwhile he moved up Tilden's ladder, not only in the bank, but in the town with its enormous eye. He joined the Kiwanis Club (Tilden assured him that Rotary was just around the corner), the Elks Club (a "sterile, clicking hades" where Drew played hearts instead of poker), and then the Country Club. He learned to play golf and became "quite good at it." His success was characteristic. "He simply would never have taken it up in the first place if he had not intended being serious" (109). His golf was like his "courtship of Amanda Barcroft;" because "no diversion remained merely a diversion in his hands, and thus he never really had one." It was not the money that mattered, it was time. "He had come a long way" after his first year in Bristol, "still with far to go, and Time's chariot always rumbled at his back" (109). At the club's parties he watched dance steps that the more sophisticated East had long since abandoned, and he listened to the jazz. At the club, a little over a year after his visit to the major, he met Jeff and Amy Carruthers, but "it was almost six years before he knew them by more than name" (111).

For nine years Harley Drew waited—"waiting was one of his specialties" (133). At first, under Bristol's watchful eye, he visited Amanda for the regular evening walks. Bristol "had begun to gossip before Drew was in town a week: 'Amanda Barcroft's got herself a beau. She slips out to meet him. Yes. They walk together every night, by the dark of the moon'" (142). But over the next nine years the visits grew less frequent. "In the beginning those meetings had been once-a-week affairs; later they were reduced to alternate weeks, and at last to once a month" (140). This was sufficient for Amanda, though. "During all their years of waiting, these walks were what sustained her. . . . Drew was no less attentive, no less affectionate, and he always said he was waiting" (142). Then after almost ten years of walking and waiting, Florence died, and "Major Barcroft had won the monstrous horse-race" (150). During those years Drew had told himself that if that should happen, he would leave town by the next train, but when it did happen, he could not leave. By then he was extremely successful at the bank and had reason to believe that he might be its president when Tilden retired, and he had "fallen in love" (151) with Amy Carruthers. Naturally it is Amy's style that he "loves."

When Amy and Jeff returned to Briartree after spending most of the early years of the Great Depression in Europe, Harley Drew became Jeff's financial advisor and closest friend. Thus Amy and Drew were drawn toward a relationship that then took two-and-a-half years to develop. Drew, the man in waiting, did not rush things, but when he fell, it was speedy. In late winter, the "leafy rain-washed spring" and summer before Florence died in late September, Drew and Amy "averaged better than a meeting a week" at some motel. They even went as far as Memphis and New Orleans.

Florence's death, thus, presented Drew with a delicate problem. "The truth was—like many men who have reason to suspect (without believing) that they are scoundrels—his nature was essentially so kind and conside-rate, he could never bear to inflict an injury face to face, not even when he stood to profit by it" (106), the narrator explains. But his confrontation with Amanda was nothing like he had imagined. At first he tried to find reasons why he could not marry her, but finally, turning and running from her, he simply cried out, "I wont marry you" (167). That was the best he could do after nine years; "he had to face his own cruelty" (164). Earlier in the day, Drew, looking at Amanda's letter to him, had "felt the weight of all those years piled on his back, like a ruined millionaire looking at old stocks and bonds issued by corporations long defunct; this too was an investment that had failed" (161).

A "year and seven months" later, Drew and Amanda were in the Bristol hospital, if not together, at least at the same time. The shock of Major Barcroft's death had brought Amanda there even though he had been the cause of much of her suffering. His first heart attack came "within a week of the anniversary of Amanda's last meeting with Drew" (175) in "late

September." Toward the end of his convalescence, Barcroft had tried to talk to Amanda about Drew: "I want you to tell me that you . . . realize— that you realize I was right" (178). Amanda's silence was her answer and that silence only intensified her isolation. "Formerly he had spoken to her but seldom: now he never spoke to her at all beyond signifying incidental desires with grunts and gestures" (179). Amanda, insofar as the major was concerned, existed only as a part of his plan, a part of the "familiar schedule," which by "mid-October, three weeks after the attack . . . they resumed" (179). He was disappointed at Amanda's being jilted, "angry," in fact, "because a Barcroft had been humbled," not because he cared particularly for Amanda's feelings. Just after Drew left her for the last time, he had come upon Amanda crying. At first, before she realized she was crying, Amanda had thought his features had grown softer and "she had an impulse to hurry to him, to throw herself into his arms for comfort." Then she realized that the softness came from her own tears, not from the major's expression. "Go to your room. Dont sit there crying like that," he told her (172).

Of course, his plan did not mean that Amanda should not marry, so he brought Henry Stubblefield, a new business associate and childless widower with an appropriately lengthy Bristol background, to court Amanda. In late April, on a rainy Sunday afternoon, Amanda rejected Henry's never-uttered proposal: "Dont" (186). In May the major's fatal heart attack struck on a Sunday afternoon, and for two days Amanda sat in the house with her father's corpse.

Harley Drew was in the hospital because Jeff Carruthers had shot him. Harley, the waiter, had grown impatient. "What I dont like is all this waiting" (175), Harley had told Amy. (Amanda standing on a curb beside Drew's car had heard him say this, but she did not know Amy.) Jeff wanted what Amy and Briartree offered—luxury, sex, and wealth. His feeling for Amy "amounted to love, or very nearly love . . . or as near love, at any rate, as Drew was ever to come" (199). Amy, however, understood Drew, saw through his mask of hearty affability. "She had known from the start what he was really after, beyond the flesh." Between Drew and what he wanted fell Jeff, so Drew suggested to Amy that they plan to murder him. What Drew had not understood about Amy from the beginning was that she was no better than he; what he failed to recognize was that it was her "essential promiscuity" that had drawn her to him "in the first place" (211). Amy, tired of Drew before he suggested murdering Jeff, was amused. She had no "intention of going through with it"; however, "she saw possibilities for an amusing interim and she was in command of the situation" (213). Instead of traveling to Memphis, New Orleans, or local motels, Drew and Amy became bolder, making their plans and enjoying their pleasures before Jeff's blind eyes, but they failed to take Jeff's acute hearing into account. He knew what they were doing, and one night in mid-May, he shot Drew with every intention of killing him, and then he smashed Amy's face. He had meant to kill her too, but his courage failed. Jeff's two bullets, shots of a blind man in the dark, only grazed Drew's head, giving him a severe concussion that put him in the Bristol hospital.

Drew and Amanda emerged from the hospital to begin new phases of their lives. Drew, essentially unchanged, moved to Memphis and married a dowager. Bristol sees his picture in the society pages of the Memphis paper. Amanda became a "watcher" with the rest of Bristol. The major had left her with an interest in an office building, four thousand dollars, and the house on Lamar Street. She sold the house and moved to the top floor of the hotel; except for her interest in the Episcopal church and the Red Cross, she would have been cut loose entirely from her moorings. The house was razed and Maxey's Garage replaced it; a single oak tree was left on the property. There had been four oaks, but they had died with the members of the family. The last was called the Barcroft oak, "one of Bristol's landmarks, even after most people no longer remembered how it got its name" (246). Amanda had "learned to live with despair."

Amy and Jeff also remained essentially unchanged. They sold Briartree and moved from place to place—transient but even more glamorous. A Baltimore specialist repaired Amy's smashed face; with his work and the help of Max Factor's pancake makeup, she had a new mask to wear, a new barrier to hid behind.

Observing and waiting obviously dominate the novel. Jeff Carruthers, the blind voyeur, who found that sex was "no fun in the dark," has by the end of the novel come to resemble "a eunuch, or rather the classic conception of a eunuch—as if the knife-sharp sliver of windshield had performed a physical as well as a psychological castration" (219). References to eyes and "seeing" occur frequently in the novel: Drew cannot remember the color of Amanda's eyes, the major wears a pince-nez, Amy and Jeff come to Bristol "in a car considerably longer than any Bristol had ever seen" (219). Drew, after the war, has his "look round," and he, like Hugh Bart in *Tournament*, imitates what he sees; his affability is an acquisition. Amy is, as Simone Vauthier has pointed out,[9] the "most observed" character in the book, but Harley Drew likes to imagine himself being observed with Amy. "He wanted to wear her like a badge, a panache, her and her expensive clothes, her careless, moneyed manner. 'Look what he's got; look at that,' he wanted to hear them murmur as he entered hotel lobbies and restaurants with Amy on his arm" (200).

Bristol, with its enormous eye, is one of the most curious of the observers in the novel. The town had its views about the "highborn" Barcrofts; "Florence was called 'the pretty one' and Amanda was called 'the smart one,' though both adjectives were applied in a sense comparative strictly between the two of them" (10). Bristol watched Amanda and Drew: "They had begun to gossip before Drew was in town a week" (142). Amanda, over the ten-year courtship, was "thrown with the watchers" at church on Sundays, on her trips to the market, and on her walk to Cotton Row. Her pattern itself gave her the protection of isolation. "There was hardly any change in her beyond a certain fixity of expression which the watchers were hard put to identify as either hope or despair. . . . Her own face at these times was blank, like an empty page inviting them to read into it whatever they chose, and they were quick to do so, there were almost as many versions of the affair as there were tellers" (143). Bristol's gossip, its enormous eye, had a "field day" over Jeff's attempt to kill Drew. Some of Bristol's watchers "shook their heads with mock-serious regret: 'All I got to say is he certainly missed a chance for a lovely death.'" The attempted murder was the most important event the watchers had witnessed in decades. These are the interests that reflect into, and thus are reflected by, Bristol's enormous eye.

> Besides, it provided a sort of counterpoint to the outrage on Lamar Street. Try as they might they could find no humor in that occurrence, only horror. So they swung from topic to topic with the agility of trapeze artists. When they grew weary of brooding they could laugh, and when they grew weary of laughing they could brood: Bristol had not been so fortunate since 1911 when Hector Sturgis, son of old Mrs. Sturgis, hung himself in his mother's attic after his wife was found asphyxiated in a hotel room with a drummer. Gossip had a field day—a field week. By the end of that time, however, distortion had made its inroads; the smallest fact in either event was taken as a theme for variations, until finally by the end of the week the original themes had disappeared, as happens in certain stretches of Brahms. People

no longer believed anything they heard or told. In each case they had killed it, talked it to death. [227]

Of course, Bristol could be wrong, as its people were wrong in their judgment of Henry Stubblefield's first wife; they believed mistakenly that she was pregnant when the handle of the lawn mower struck her, crushing her skull (181–82), but accuracy hardly matters, because what the town looks for and fails to find, while it gives shape to day-to-day events, is far from permanent and fundamental. Bristol's field is full of stubble when what it needs to feel are the roots that run deep in the earth and into time.

Gradually Amanda herself became one of the watchers in Bristol, but from the beginning, she seemed destined to be an observer, conditioned as she was by the major's cold pride and formality, by Florence's isolation and failed art, and by Drew's duplicity. Dreams, newspapers, books, and, finally, the eye of Bristol itself were the limits of Amanda's experience. In her dream, sometimes "carried over into the daylight world as fantasies," her sexual frustrations are revealed; she pictures herself in the garden where Florence and Harley Drew, unreal in painted masks, are making love on a park bench. Florence does not want Amanda to interfere. "'Is he hurting you, Florence?' Amanda cries; she stands there, wringing her hands. But Florence only broadens her painted smile. 'I like it, I like it,' she says" (189). A Negro guard who is wearing a mask of Major Barcroft's face takes Amanda to a large gate and turns her out from the garden. Florence had loved to read the gossip columns in the Memphis papers, and Amanda comes to like the papers too, but it is her reading of novels that most clearly expresses her need. The librarians supply her with Jane Austen, Thackeray, Proust, Dickens, Faulkner, James, and Balzac, among others, and she, on several occasions, "read her own story without recognition." Through the vicarious experiences in her reading, Amanda "lived. Nothing *there* applied to anything outside, and she preferred it so. If some author, up to the tricks of his trade, attempted to increase the verisimilitude of his book by having the narrator insist that the story was 'true,' had really occurred, Amanda was not impressed." Books, she felt, were quite different from one's experience in the "real" world. "Reality was mostly numbness (and in ratio; the deeper the tragedy, the deeper the numbness), whereas in books the characters actually understood—the deeper the experience, the deeper the perception; they suffered or exalted on a comprehensive scale, and the proper emotion was always there, on tap" (241).

After the major's death, Amanda found herself frequently among the watchers. This contact began with her increased interest in the church, particularly in the Altar Guild. She found that what "she enjoyed most was the sense of belonging, of making one among those who kneeled . . . then rose all together like some many-legged animal to murmur the responses or confess their manifold sins and wickedness" (234–35). Soon, coincident with the entry of the United States into World War II, the animal developed eyes as well as legs for Amanda. She joined the "bandage folders" who gathered around the long tables set up in the armory. "This was Amanda's first real contact with gossip as a participant, or at any rate a listener, rather than as a subject," and it was not long before Amanda became a conduit for the stories she heard at the armory. The women of the Altar Guild would bring stories home to their husbands: "Amanda Barcroft was telling me today . . . " (243).

After she had sold the house on Lamar Street and moved into "a room on the top floor of the new hotel, a towering eight-story building twice as tall as any other in Bristol," Amanda would look out on the town below, particularly in the late afternoons, and "absorbed" into the enormous eye, "she too became a watcher." "Best of all she liked the closing hour of every day, when she sat in the Morris chair at her high window and saw the town spread out beneath, with people moving along its checkerboard pattern on the way from work. She sat there while the light failed, watching them; she identified their small, foreshortened figures one by one, gave each its name, recalled its history, and traced its path along the sidewalk to its home. It was as if, brooding there like a gargoyle, her image had been imprinted on the public retina so long that now, at last, she had been absorbed by it, had now herself become a part of the enormous eye, and was looking out as all those others had done" (248).

What she found spread out below was Bristol, a character only somewhat older than herself. Like Amanda the town watched and failed to find the language that would enable it to understand the sources of its frustrations. Bristol, in the eyes of larger Western history, was a new place, but it had already grown in its failed traditions. Soon after his arrival, Harley Drew learned the facts of Bristol's past, how it grew from a landing for river boats, grew "rapidly during the post-Reconstruction building boom," and then expanded eastward beyond the railroad tracks "where old Mrs.

Wingate, 'the Mother of Bristol,' was subdividing her father's plantation. By 1930 the town numbered fifteen thousand inhabitants and called itself 'The Queen City of the Delta'" (105). The "Queen City" suffered from modernity, however, and Bristol changed in the area around the aging Barcroft house on Lamar Street so that the houses set amid grocery stores and filling stations became "a reminder, like the Major, of an era that was gone" (175).

> Workers houses were just beyond it and a new cotton-seed oil mill took up half of the second block; it made a constant crunching sound through the long autumnal nights, like a beast grinding its teeth in pain, and filled the air with a smell of frying ham. Radios and phonographs belonging to the workers' wives shattered the quiet of other seasons with dance music, the blues, dramas consisting mostly of shouts and screams, the bland commercial voices of young men selling soap and breakfast foods, and the shrill, desperate laughter of sponsored comedians. Against this background Amanda followed her daily rounds, leading a sort of posthumous existence in a world reduced to a population of two. [175]

Modernity, not particularly pretty even under the most favorable conditions, is even uglier where tradition is at best a reminder of what has been lost. Bristolites, at their country club, heard tales of an English king's giving up "his throne for a woman"; they thrilled to the vibrations of romance: "Even in their time such things could happen—and they were on hand, almost a part of it, leaning toward the loudspeakers." Nevertheless, they were still "dissatisfied," unhappy, feeling "something weak and sordid about the affair" because they knew "it would not have been so in their fathers' and grandfathers' time" (128). Jordan County's failure of nerve had begun much earlier, however. The failure could be traced at least to Amy Carruthers's grandfather, Cass Tarfeller, who died in a duel and in, as the narrator makes clear, "his belated assumption of a heritage for which he had never been fit" (27).

Scattered around Bristol's dry landscape are hints of the richer past, remnants of a Western heritage that Bristol seems unable to grasp. Particularly noticeable among the fragments are the many references to the religion that seems to have lost its influence. In addition to the Episcopal communion, there is the name Mrs. Pentecost. Workers swarm around the Barcroft house bringing modernity "with the disinterested rapacity of locusts in a Biblical curse" (13). Harley Drew's story "was the Joseph story all over again" (73). The Barcroft house under the watchers "disappeared like the fulfillment of a prophecy out of Isaiah" (245). Blind, and unable to enjoy sex with Amy, Jeff has no "resurrection of the flesh" (45); Amanda, in frustration at her father's insistence that she not leave him to care for Florence, "leaned against the panel, arms extended in a pose of crucifixion" (84–85). Nothing, it seems, can unite the Bristolites into the family of man as children of God. Eating the flesh of God and drinking His blood provide Bristol no access or understanding of its inner being. Except in isolated instances, communion is an abstract art, and even in those instances, it is the sexual ramifications of the sacrament that count, not as metaphor for the union of the family of God in its deepest human need, but as temporary relief from frustration.

History and nature, and along with nature both religion and sex, have failed in modern Bristol, but the arts also have failed. Allen Tate thought that through the literary arts men could deal with each other in "communion" and find "love which is beyond time." In this sense, or any other sense in which modern artists insist on the usefulness of the arts to modern man, the arts have failed in Bristol. Florence's needlework disappears into cedar chests, and Amanda reads without recognition because "reality was mostly numbness." Only the characters in her books could experience deeply and perceive deeply, and books, through that numbed artistic perception, had no bearing on Bristol or its life. Self-knowledge, the province of the arts, according to Tate, lay beyond Bristol's use. "Bristol's one artist," the son of the Barcroft's cook, Nora, was condemned for murder and executed.

The jazz that Duff Conway, the "one artist," once performed is an expression of the needs, the emptiness, Bristol feels, but as an avenue for understanding, jazz is not available because of the general numbness and insensitivity of the age and because it is black. While Jeff carries out his plan for murder, a Bessie Smith record is playing in the background, "My new man had left me / just a room and a empty bed." Blacks in Bristol would serve quite well in kitchens or cotton fields, but Bessie Smith herself, just two years before Jeff tried to kill Drew, had died on the steps of a Delta hospital. "She died after an automobile accident fifty miles from Briartree; they got her to a hospital in time but the authorities couldnt let her in— her color wasnt right and she bled to death" (218).

Foote, as Simone Vauthier observed, is very conscious in *Love in a Dry Season* of the artistry of the novel. By describing Amanda's reading, he draws attention to the art of fiction. Bristol and the characters in the novel are all "watchers," and Amanda "watches" the plots of the novels. The narrator of *Love in a Dry Season* is conscious, too, that the reader of his work is in a position analogous to Amanda's, but in the very act of writing, he seems to hope that the reader/observer is perhaps less benumbed than the other watchers. The narrator often draws attention to his consciousness of the reader's role, and there are occasionally general observations established from a reader's perspective. For example, an "uniformed observer" might have thought Jeff was leading Amy up to Briartree on their first visit (32). Barcroft's tears at his son's birth and wife's death "appeared to be not so much tears of grieving as of triumph" (7). A "person looking back" at Bristol at "the tail end of the jazz age" would have concluded, perhaps, that "they had foreseen the depression" (51). The awareness on other occasions, however, is far more direct. On one occasion we are invited to "observe her [Amy], then, as she sat on an evening in late February beside a log fire in the living room at Briartree" (129). Sometimes the narrator invites the reader to conjecture along with him: Drew, receiving Amanda's letter after Florence has died, toys with his mustache— "This was an accustomed gesture with him lately, almost a tic—though it would have been difficult to identify as troubled or exalted, decisive or indecisive" (162). Occasionally, though, he leaves no room for conjecture. Bristol, in its speculation about Jeff's shooting Drew, was "wrong"; the watchers "were utterly and ironically wrong" (198). On other occasions the narrator seems to converse with the reader. The watchers crowd into the Barcroft house following Florence's death; people came who had seldom if ever set foot inside before. "Here human cruelty was displayed at its worst, youd say," the narrator observes assuming the reader's opinion, "until you considered the reverse of the medal and saw the possibility of a worse cruelty still: an absence of concern, that is, or even curiosity" (148).

One can infer from the narrator's consciousness of his relationship with the reader that *Love in a Dry Season,* the novel itself, can be an art form observed. Perhaps, for this observer and participant, there is at least some scrap of hope.

This book pleased Foote. After a particularly good day, he wrote Percy about it. At the time his working title was "The Arms You Bear" and Harley Drew was Charley Drew.

Something happened to me this week. I approached work sluggishly Monday morning and all of a sudden something took me by the hair: I had to hold back to keep from covering reams of paper with gouts of words. By yesterday afternoon (Thursday) I had produced 5000 of the best words I ever wrote: Amanda Barcroft finding her sister dead, and yearning for Charley to come take her away. It really went well: just the right balance between "inspiration" and objectivity. Unquestionably this is the best sustained writing Ive ever done (the whole book, I mean): it has a technical virtuosity that holds my interest—shifting point-of-view, intensive analysis, and a series of outrageous events that call for underwriting; characters who live in their own right, each with a contrasting personality, and not a "type" in the lot; counterpointed symbolism that can be taken or let alone, but which yet (I hope) gives the book a higher importance, places it in the stream of human experience—and all in all I feel very good about it. (22Dec50)

Jordan County: A Landscape in Narrative

Foote finished *Love in a Dry Season* believing that he was set to launch the major phase of his writing career. In July 1951 he could report to Walker Percy little progress on "Two Gates to the City," his "big novel," though he was excited over his plans for it. He had made extensive notes, "filled fifteen pages of a ledger with notes on the interrelationships," and had made refinements on his themes. The novel would deal with the trials of modern characters and juxtapose them against the past, as he explained: "Nowadays a man is picked to pieces bit by bit, where formerly he was consumed by inner and outward forces too big for him to handle. If I hold to my notion, the big story is to make no progress, solve no problems, be not in the least Dramatic, be in fact a sort of arid (but brilliant) exposition. The conversations will sparkle about nothing; there will be furious entrances and exits amounting to nothing—a sense of constant motion and excitement without progress. If I do it well enough, the reader will know each character just by the pitch of his voice, the individualities of his syntax. I am going to get the Delta into it as the Delta has never been got before." (5July51)

By getting "the Delta into it," "Two Gates," he made clear to Percy, would be firmly grounded in the history and anthropology that was lacking in much modern literature, particularly in Hemingway.

I tell you what writing needs, and badly. It absolutely needs a sense of Place.
A book like The Sun Also Rises (I'm deliberately taking the best of the lot)

is a goddam total loss in every way except for entertainment and psychological observation. What the novel needs is a sense of proceeding from
generations of knowledge. This may come from my being Southern, I guess
it does, but I know that good work has a sense of permanance. I dont mean
the Family novel, certainly not in the old sense; but there does have to be a
family and a past, or else the book is like a free-flying balloon being carried
whichever way the wind blows. This, or something like it, is what I'm trying
to get away from—Two Gates is going to be planted solid as a rock. Not a
bloody damned Incident, for God sake: rather a permanent thing that it
took eighty years to live. The time is the present: yes, it must be: but all the
past is behind it, you know it's there. (11Dec51)

But then, in December 1951, Foote's creative gates were slammed shut
with Peggy's leaving, and "Child by Fever," which he had slated to be Part
IV of "Two Gates," became the central story in *Jordan County: A Landscape
in Narrative*, which the Dial Press published in 1954.

The stories in *Jordan County*[10] trace the history of Foote's county from
the years just after World War II, in "Rain Down Home," back through its
history to the white man's arrival in the eighteenth century, in "The Sacred
Mound." "A Marriage Portion," set in the 1920s, and "The Freedom
Kick," set just after the Civil War, are similar to "Rain Down Home" and
"The Sacred Mound" in that they are brief stories limited to one section.
Two longer tales, "Ride Out," set in the 1920s and 1930s, and "Pillar of
Fire," which is about antebellum Jordan County, have three sections each,
the sum of which corresponds in length to the four one-section tales.
"Child by Fever" is a novel-length tale of late nineteenth- and early twentieth-century Bristol, the time of its rapid expansion. The structure of
"Child by Fever" is an abbreviated form of *Love in a Dry Season*—three
sections, each of which is in turn sub-divided into three sections. Foote had
worked on "Child by Fever" for several years and had incorporated into it
material from his earliest stories published in Chapel Hill. As a whole, the
stories constitute a loosely structured novel about the rise and spiritual
decline of Foote's county, a scope much broader than any of his previous
novels. *"Jordan County*, if it is a novel, is a novel which has place for its
hero and time for its plot," Foote explained to John Carr. *"It* is the main
character in the novel—the land itself. And you go backwards through
time to find out what made it what it is."[11]

Pauly Green, a veteran returning to Bristol soon after the close of World
War II, is the central figure in the opening story, "Rain Down Home." He

encounters Parker Nowell who fails to recognize his former paper boy, but Pauly reaches a conclusion, similar to Nowell's, that love has failed in the modern world. Nowell's response is to isolate himself from Bristol; Pauly turns to violence after he has encountered three instances of failed human relationships.

Walking toward downtown Bristol on a cold, rainy fall morning, Pauly finds a letter that a school girl has dropped. He reads that "Alice" is trying to make her "letters more interesting" for Norma Jean to read and senses the boredom and loneliness that underlie the text. "Why doesnt everybody love each other?" he asks the waitress at the cafe. Of course, she does not understand what he means. Later, in Wingate Park, he encounters a little girl whose mother has warned her against speaking to strangers, and then he meets an old man who has given up trying to make sense of the suffering people endure. "Why wont people be happy?" Pauly asks the old man, "*Not* cant: wont." Back at the cafe, Pauly removes his army pistol from his suitcase and, while he is eating pie and laughing, he shoots "four loaded clips" and wounds the Greek proprietor. Pauly Green's name— Green for nature, Paul for the apostle—and the rain that falls heavily at times, together with the action of the story, imply that modern Bristol is the child parented by feverish economic development, and it is a child that has abandoned its formative aesthetic and religious traditions.

"Ride Out," a revision of "Tell Them Good By," which Foote published in the *Saturday Evening Post* (15 February 1947), explores the life of "Bristol's one artist," as the narrator of *Love in a Dry Season* calls him.

Most of the revisions that Foote made are related to strengthening his style; a few of the additions, however, are more fundamental, pointing up themes and reinforcing ideas that were perhaps inherent in the earlier text but had become matters of more concern in 1952–53. The basic ironic notion on which the story is built, that the apparent means of success contain the flaws that lead to failure, is in both versions of the story, but the emphasis on the formlessness of jazz and on primitive human need, if not entirely new to the revision, are given a prominence they did not have in the 1947 text.

The cornet is Duff's means of success; it also is the source of his failure. This theme resembles Hugh Bart's shooting skill or Palmer Metcalf's battle plan—both examples from Foote's early fiction. Duff grew up surrounded by the Delta blues. As a drummer in a band made up of small boys, then as a cornetist with the "Noxubee High Hat Rhythm Kings" in reform school, Duff learned his art. As a young boy he listened outside a window of the Mansion House where Blind Bailey played "the old river boat and New Orleans classics," and after reform school he became a member of Bailey's group.

It was at the Mansion House that Pearly Jefferson, leader of a band playing on a river boat, heard him. From Jefferson, Duff obtained the only education in music he was to have, playing with Jefferson's band in New Orleans for four years. "They were the years that made him what he was when, later, musicians who were supposed to know called him the best horn man of his time" (41). From New Orleans, Duff went to New York where he met Harry Van, a young composer who became his closest friend. In August 1939 Duff discovered that he had tuberculosis and would have to give up his cornet until he was cured. For a time, at home in Bristol, Duff tried to follow the doctor's orders, but gradually, as spring came to the Delta, Duff felt the need to play at the Mansion House with Bailey. There he met Julia Kinship, and it was because of Julia that he killed Chance Jackson. Awaiting execution in October, he blew the last of his failing lungs into his cornet, making music the town gathered around the jail to hear.

The warden at the reformatory school had given Duff Conway his first cornet; it had belonged to another prisoner who had died of tuberculosis, the disease that would have killed Duff had not executioner Luke Jeffcoat's "old shocking chair" come first. Foote has said that the "symbolism" of Duff's walking away from the warden clutching his cornet to his chest was not purposive: "Now the symbolism of taking this horn, filled with tuber-culosis germs, and holding it against his chest, where the tuberculosis is going to take seat and kill him, is fairly obvious, but I was not at all aware of it when I wrote it. He hugged the horn to his chest because he consid-ered it a precious thing; it seemed natural for someone who had hold of something he considered precious to hold it to his chest. It was only later on, when some critic pointed out the symbolism of it, that I perceived it. And that is, if I may say so, how symbolism should occur, not being supplied by the writer, but being discovered by the writer."[12] In a sense both symbolic and ironic, the cornet, the means of producing art, is also the means, or would have been, of Duff's death.

While Duff is "Bristol's one artist," he is not the towering elemental hero that Bristol needs for him to be. Again, in "Ride Out" as in most of his other tales, Foote examines the theme of the failure of art, for work as he might, Duff's art cannot save him from violence and death. Changes that Foote made in the text of the story suggest that the problem lies in the formlessness of Delta blues as Duff plays it, even though the music itself conveys intense emotional depth.

The form of jazz rises from the land and its people. Duff did not learn by careful study but by imitating. He was already a recognized artist before he had anything resembling formal training. The feeling, the emotion, that is integral to all musical expression, important as it is, is not complete in itself. It fails to provide for the more elemental needs; rhythm and melody without form or musical line are insufficient to convey, in Nowell's words, "the impulse that brought [the music] into being."

The original version of "Ride Out" does not give emphasis to the notion that there is weakness in the formlessness of the musical style. In both versions Foote describes in some detail the growing artistic relationship between Duff and Harry Van. Harry listened day after day to Duff's improvisations; against the advice of his fellow students, Van "was composing things like those he formerly had believed were without melody or harmony or sometimes even rhythm." In the revision Foote added the explanation that later, after Duff's death, Van's work subsumed the jazz influence to become something jazz itself could not be. Jazz is an "inferior art," but one that is capable of giving Van "an approach" to his own work. Foote added the following explanation in revising:

> Later he was to abandon this. Indeed, the jazz influence is hardly apparent in his work today. But he had got what he wanted by then; he had made the breakthrough, and the influence remained, if not the signs. What he wanted was an approach, and jazz had shown him that. An inferior art by virtue of its limitations, it involved great drive and marvelous technique and little else; but jazz men—anyhow the good ones, and where the emotions were so naked, thrown out in such a spendthrift fashion, it was obvious from the outset which were good and which were not—never let technique be anything but a means to an end. This was what he mainly got; this was what had struck him that first night in Harlem (though he did not know it then, or at least could not identify it) and this was what stayed with him after he left jazz behind. [48–49]

As attractive as jazz is, it is nevertheless incapable of sustaining the community that forces of the modern world have undermined.

In another revision, Foote added a description of the changes that Van noticed in Duff when he came to visit him at the Bristol jail. The changes emphasize the notion that it is those primitive, constant needs that art addresses. Tuberculosis had had its effect and made Duff's face resemble that of a primitive African carving. "The skin did indeed fit close; the face was like one of those African masks, the lines of suffering and sickness grooved deep into the wood with all the exaggeration of the primitive, wherein the carver pits the force of his emotion against his lack of tools and training" (67). Duff's appearance, of course, represents his art and identifies the relationship between emotion and training. Duff, in his way, was aware of his break with historical pattern and design, that by taking his jazz to New York, he had lost touch with the resources that made his art what it was. "It's just I ought not ever have left home," he tells Van. "Going off like that I lost touch with everything I was born to be with" (67).

The short vignette, "A Marriage Portion," which follows "Ride Out," is a monologue of a worn-out flapper who seeks happiness and fulfillment in random sexuality, but she is also something of a shrew. She married Snooky for his money and his looks, and she knew that Bristol expected Snooky to tame her. Both sides of this marriage failed, however. She was terrified of her marriage bed, and Snooky, unable to teach her, turned to alcohol for solace. There is only superficial feeling between them; the rest is loneliness and despair.

In 1952 Foote revised "Child by Fever," which at one point the *Atlantic* had rejected, into a 75,000-word novelette that his agent sent to the *New Yorker*. Foote's view was that the shorter version contained the "anthropological and historical implications" of the original. The short version found a publisher, as a part of Signet's series *New American Writing,* and the longer version became the centerpiece of Jordan County. The title of "Child by Fever" encapsulates a great deal of the thematic material in the tale and, for that matter, in all of Foote's fiction. The child is Hector Sturgis and the fever is the yellow fever that struck the Mississippi Valley in 1878, the year Hector was born. The metaphor expands; Hector remains a child, and the fever runs deeper in the veins of Jordan County history than the virus that caused the yellow fever. Time itself is infected with a virus called progress; the symptoms of the disease include restlessness, unhappiness, and suicide. The cure for the disease is art, and the artist must produce a compound made up of history, religion, myth, and tradition to be shaped into a form that can be applied to the disease, and that is difficult work at best.

Discussing his work with Evans Harrington, Foote explained his fascination with the year 1910, to him a "watershed year."[13] In 1910 the agrarian ideal that had guided the development of the South before the twentieth century collapsed, and in its place, sometimes mingled with the remains, came the bourgeois ethos along with technological progress. But the historical foundations of the new ethos were shallow, ever shifting, leaving the people of Jordan County insecure and unhappy with themselves.

The history of the development of Greenville provides the basis for "Child by Fever." The original county seat of Washington County, a town named Princeton, lay along the Mississippi River in what became the extreme southern part of the county when Issaquena was separated from Washington County in 1844. In 1846 old Greenville became the county seat, but this town, like Princeton, became a victim of fire and the caving banks of the river. In 1865 Mrs. Harriet Blanton Theobald gave a portion of her Blantonia Plantation as a site for a new Greenville, and Major Richard O'Hea, who had been responsible for planning the Confederate fortifications at Vicksburg, surveyed and laid out the plans. Mrs. Theobald became known as the "Mother of Greenville;" Foote once published a photograph of Mrs. Theobald in the *Pica,* sitting proudly in a wooden wheelchair.[14]

Mrs. Theobald's first husband, William Whittaker Blanton, died in 1838, about ten years after the couple had moved to Washington County. Harriet Blanton then married Dr. Sam Theobald; she died in Greenville, 23 January 1888, failing by about two months to celebrate her eighty-ninth birthday. Her children, however, were not as long-lived as she; only two of the twelve survived childhood.

Foote's fictional Mrs. Hector Wingate has fewer offspring and only one husband. It is her daughter, Mrs. Sturgis, married to the once-enterprising son of an Irish bartender, who becomes the "Mother of Bristol," and her picture appears regularly on her birthday in the town's newspaper. The original "Mother of Bristol" is, thus, in Foote's fictional presentation, divided into mother and daughter. Their function, however, is quite similar to that of the historical source.

Foote's Bristol of 1910 is the synthesis of a dialectical process that pits an agrarian ideal, which Mrs. Wingate and her daughter represent, against the bourgeoisie; it is a synthesis that does not result from the strengths of either of the antitheses, however, but rather from the weaknesses and failures of both. Bristol, born out of the failure of the agrarian ideal and the inability of the middle class to come to terms with itself, has failed; Foote finds no cultural forces operating which give either the town or its individual citizens purpose, no sense of adhering faithfully to a cultural pattern of fulfilling a historical destiny. The town, during the first decades of the twentieth century, has an ambivalent uneasiness about its past, it has no idea of what it wants to become, and it is decidedly unhappy with what it is at present. The middle class fails to use the inherent strengths that could provide an ethos to replace the lost source of collective regional security. Hector Sturgis, Foote's heir to the short-lived agrarian ideal, belongs to the landed gentry that, in the antebellum agrarian society, provided social, political, and economic leadership for many parts of the South. If one were to be a leader, one had to have the requisite possessions, and they, in turn, give one a public role in the community. In his biography of Stonewall Jackson, Allen Tate describes the relationship between the agrarian aristocrat and his community: "Without possessions a man did not morally exist. The idea of the 'inner life,' held by the Calvinist people in far-off New England, had no meaning. In the South, the man as he appeared in public was the man: his public appearance was his moral life. The nearest equivalent of the 'inner life' was 'private affairs.' The New Englander was mystical, religious; the Southerner, practical, materialistic. Private affairs were not enquired into and they had no public value. A man's property was his character."[15]

Hector's downfall actually began before his time; it began with his grandfather. His great-grandfather, the first Hector Wingate, had come to Jordan County in 1835, one of the first settlers. This Hector subdued a large tract of Jordan County jungle and completed, just months before his death in the Mexican War in 1845, the large plantation house that was the visible symbol of his public character. The second Hector Wingate inherited both land and house in 1845, but by not assuming the role of military leadership in the Civil War sixteen years later, he failed to live up to his own and the county's expectations. This Hector "felt that he had failed his heritage," and after the southern defeat, he "turned bitter" (78–79). In bitterness he began to neglect the wife he had married in 1858 and the daughter born in 1860, so Mrs. Wingate turned to her daughter, Esther, for the attention her husband did not provide. Esther endured her mother's affection for eighteen years, and then, just two months after her embittered father "was killed by a negro tenant following a disagreement over settlement for the '77 crop" (84), Esther announced to Mrs. Wingate that she had to marry the Irish tenor in the Episcopal church choir whom she had managed to seduce. Esther married John Sturgis in March 1878, and in September, Hector was born during the height of the yellow fever epidemic.

Mrs. Wingate had to surrender to inevitable defeat at the hands of her daughter—at the wedding she bore herself "like a general at a surrender following a battle lost to guile and superior numbers" (89)—but the grandson would be hers. Hector Sturgis's mother had little to say about her son's upbringing, and his father had nothing to say at all. For the first fifteen years of his life, that is from 1878 until 1893, when Mrs. Wingate died of yellow fever, the grandmother dominated the boy.

Mrs. Wingate made Hector into an effeminate monster, unfit for either a public or a private role, even though she thought that she was preparing him for the highborn role to which his property entitled him. She did not dress him like other children. Hector wore "tight serge knee-breeches," "hightop button shoes and ribbed black stockings," and a "wide satin bow tie that rode up under his chin" (99). On a typical occasion, Mrs. Wingate refused Hector the wiener and lady finger the butcher and baker offered him when he went shopping with her. "How do we know what they use to stuff those things? Wait till we get home where we grind our own" (101), she said of the wiener. "Don't you know they make those things with the leavings?" (101), she said of the baker's lady finger. Naturally, both butcher and baker regarded her with "cold hostility," but Hector realized that "they were afraid of her," and "it made him proud that she was his grandmother" (101).

Having found public school unacceptable for Hector, Mrs. Wingate had him tutored at home, then she sent him to a "boarding school in Virginia." Hector's acceptance among his classmates there was more a result of their impression of Mrs. Wingate than it was their admiration for Hector. In 1892, when two of the boys spent the Christmas holidays with Hector, they described the Wingate plantation as "something out of the Middle Ages" and Mrs. Wingate as "a lady of the old school" (120).

A year and a half after the boys' visit, Mrs. Wingate died of yellow fever. When Hector finally was allowed to return home, he discovered that his mother had not only assumed Mrs. Wingate's role but had tried to assimilate as nearly as possible Mrs. Wingate's personality: "she began to wear the dead woman's clothes; she even held her mouth awry, irked and bitter-looking" (124). Hector was no more able to rebel against Esther Sturgis than he had been able to rebel against Mrs. Wingate. He simply had no interest in independence, so he too failed his heritage. When Hector tried to join Captain Barcroft's Bristol volunteers in 1898, Esther Sturgis simply would not allow the third Hector to march off to the Spanish-American War. When he insisted that he would be sworn in, she simply said "I reckon not" and rested her unchallenged case on the value of Hector's "fifteen thousand dollar education" (126).

Marriage had been an act of defiance for Esther Sturgis, but when Hector eloped with Ella Lowery, he brought his bride-of-an-hour to the Wingate-Sturgis mansion to introduce her to his mother. In marriage, as in everything else, Hector failed. He could not admit to himself that homo sapiens was a mortal animal that was heir to the pains and pleasures of animalhood. Fear of strange animals had been one of his childhood traumas, but as a young adult, the horror of the three-day labor attendant upon Ella's giving birth to an eighteen-pound baby made him forever incapable of playing the sexual role of husband. When the child died six months later, the end of the Wingate-Sturgis line was reached for Ella, who, "recovered from both the birth and death of her child, turned to Hector with the old urgency . . . and found no resurection of the flesh" (154–55), just as Amy Carruthers had found none with Jeff. Hector had peered through the bedroom door at Ella in labor, and the memory was a "reproach" to him "for having been the cause" of her "animal agony" (155). Ella gave him six months, then returned to the life of promiscuity she had enjoyed before she married Hector. In the winter of 1910, they found her dead in the Bristol hotel, the victim of an apparent accident. The gas fumes also killed the salesman who had rented the room.

After Ella's death Hector retreated into the final isolation of insanity and imagined that Ella's ghost had returned to him. The Sturgis servants told tales of what happened in his room, of his talking to himself and doing strange things. Neighbors also told tales of the strange behavior they observed, his talking to animals on the road and going to the woods to feed the birds. The attic of the Sturgis mansion had been his escape in early childhood, his private play-time kingdom, the only world he could command. From one of the rafters in that attic, in 1911, Hector Sturgis, at the insistence of Ella's ghost, hanged himself.

Hector was an utter failure as the agrarian aristocrat and as a human being, but his mother and grandmother had tried to shape a public role for

him. After he had failed at public school, Mrs. Wingate lectured him about
his role.

> "Now listen," she said. . . . "There are really only two classes of people in
> this world, those who have and those who wish they had. . . . When those
> of the second class begin to realize that they will never catch up with those
> of the first, they jeer. . . . Those of the first class (which includes you . . .)
> must realize that the jeering goes with the having. Besides, when you are
> older and able to strike back at them, by foreclosing their mortgages or
> causing them to be dismissed from their places of employment, they will
> not jeer where you can hear them. . . . And what is said behind your back
> cannot matter, first because you cannot hear it and second because it is a
> sort of underhanded compliment in the first place. It's a certain sign that
> they acknowledge your position, a proof of membership. You understand?"
> "Yessum," he said. . . . But he did not. [116]

When he returned home from the University of Virginia, his mother
tried to make a gentleman farmer out of him, but he was neither interested
nor able. Finally Esther tried to establish him as a kind of patriarch of
Bristol. The town had grown rapidly during the 1880s and 1890s, and Mrs.
Sturgis began to subdivide and develop her Wingate inheritance. Hector
had always been interested in mechanical drawing, so Mrs. Sturgis decided
that his talent might be useful to her real estate projects. Hector's maps,
according to Mr. Clinkscales, the Episcopalian rector, were the ground-
work for "an Athens of the South" (145). Hector enthusiastically threw
himself into his work, but as his insanity grew, his drawings became more
rigid. In his last years Hector "began to add colors, green for trees and
lawns, blue for water in drainage ditches and artificial ponds, red for
underground installations, mains and sewers. By then black was reserved
for details such as carriage blocks and arc lights, streetcars and delivery
wagons, and finally the people themselves, as seen from above, going
about their work and their pleasures. . . at last the sheets resembled a
futuristic painting, a bird's-eye view of Utopia, one to one hundred" (146–
47). Later Mrs. Sturgis had the maps "bound in tooled morocco" and
presented them to the mayor, who arranged for them to be displayed
under glass in the courthouse. They remained there twenty years, "the
crowded, multi-colored sheets that had begun as maps and wound up
resembling work done by a latter-day amateur Bruegel or Bosch looking
down from a seat in the clouds" (147). After Mrs. Sturgis's death they were
removed to the belfry. In the early 1950s an art critic from Memphis wrote

in his column, "The Last Romantic," in the *Commercial Appeal* that Hector Sturgis was "an undiscovered genius" (223). But Hector was no undiscovered genius; he was not equipped to be anything, and in a society where one's public self is one's self, the failure is fundamental. If Mrs. Sturgis was the "mother of Bristol," as the Bristol newspaper for years greeted her on her birthdays, then modern Bristol was the child of incest and failure, for Mrs. Sturgis insisted that Hector's drawings be carefully followed in developing East Bristol.

Foote devotes considerable attention to the people who inhabited Hector's Utopia, people who did not find their situation as idyllic as Hector had drawn it. The narrative voice in the story often repeats what "people were saying," so the community of Bristol, the collective view, becomes a major dramatic force in the story, as it does in *Love in a Dry Season* and, in a more distanced way, in the first and last sections of *Follow Me Down*. Foote's narrator treats Bristol in the third person plural; Bristol is always "they" not "we." This distancing allows the narrator to comment and judge, but the town's views and reactions to the highborn Wingates and Sturgises are far more important to the narrator than they ever were to Hector.

The town could be narrow and hypocritical. Ella's promiscuity was certainly scandalous; the Baptist women, after all, had warned Ella's mother that some dire event lay in Ella's crooked path, but in judging Hector Sturgis, Bristol was not judging him as a private citizen. By its very judgment, it limited his freedom by imposing unnatural restraints. Hector was highborn; his designated role as agrarian leader was a public one. If Bristol were to pass into the twentieth century with its agrarian ideal intact, Hector's position would give the town the security of a social order that was sanctioned and defended in the historical romances Hector had read. That was the public folkway, and a public interest in Hector was the natural outcome. "Not many people nowadays ever heard of [Hector Sturgis]," the narrator explains at the beginning of the tale. "Even fewer ever saw him, and no one at all ever knew him. But there were those who claimed to know his story, know it so well, they said, that between the time when Mrs. Sturgis died and six months later, when the house was razed, they could take you into the attic and point out the rafter beneath which he had brought it to a close: or so they claimed" (76–77).

Hector's failure reveals a conflict between Bristol's need for leadership and its refusal to accept an unworthy but natural heir to the role. The town's ambivalence was apparent in its reception of him in 1898 on his return from Charlottesville. "Those who stood on street corners in Bristol that summer after his graduation and saw him drive past—always in a hurry but going no place, an outlander, rakish and modern . . . watched him with amusement and even admiration, but with hardly any envy. . . . They sniggered as he drove past. They nudged each other. They said, 'It's that Sturgis boy, home from college, a dude. I bet you he's hell with the ladies.'" (127). By one set of standards they condemn Hector, but being "hell with the ladies" was something Bristol could admire.

The town's response to Ella's death was a clear sign of its rejection of the House of Sturgis-Wingate and of its heir. As might be expected, her death was the talk of the town, but only the family, the minister, and the undertaker dared to attend the funeral. Others rode by and looked. "It was Ella—and, by inference, the Sturgis family with her—who held the lime-light. . . . 'If thats blue-blood,' the night clerk had said, 'I'm glad I didnt have any to pass on to my kids. If a man wants his wife to stay home, he by God ought to nail her down. You see what I mean?'. . . For thirty-six hours the talk had been of little else—where she had been, whom she had been seen with, her partiality for traveling men—and when the thirty-six hours were up, they formed a parade out past the cemetery, just short of the lip of the grave" (182).

Had Bristol looked to its own strengths, it might have shaped more appropriate and effective public standards. There were three innate strengths that middle-class Bristol might have developed. The first was a basic regard for life and, growing out of that, the second—vigorous sexuality. The third was its middle-class heritage to which, in its own interests, it might have been stubbornly loyal.

Bristol's basic regard for life was evident in its gossip about Ella's death. They condemned her on narrow, conventional grounds, but ringing through their talk was the realization that her death was a waste. "People . . . passed [the news of Ella's death] along with an air of having foretold it. Women discussed it in grocery stores and over backyard fences. . . . 'Have you heard about Ella Sturgis?' 'Did you *ever*?' Men gathered on street corners and reviewed her life over bars and cafe count-ers, philosophizing on morality and the sanctity of marriage . . . in de-fense and condemnation, alternately saturnine and sardonic. This death seemed such a waste. 'They say you cant take it with you. Ha. By golly, she took it with her'" (178–79).

The community condemned Ella's violation of its sexual taboos, but it was also keenly aware of its hypocrisy, for it had more than a secret admiration for her. Until she married Hector and allied herself with the weakness of the Wingates and Sturgises, she was potentially a figure through which Bristol could redeem itself because she had no regard for narrow standards of judgment. She simply refused to consider what she was doing to be wrong and would not let contrary views interfere with her pleasure. As a young woman "her only concern had been young men . . . and thus she had acquired a reputation. When she was fourteen the watchers downtown would see her pass the barber shop or pool hall window, legs wobbly on high heels and wearing the flimsy, violet-flowered dresses she persuaded her mother to make for her— . . . and returning, out of the tail of her eye, the stares of all the watchers. She not only seemed not to care what they thought, she seemed to go out of her way to make sure they understood that she did not care: so that, in the end, she showed how much she did care after all (but in reverse) and they responded with the frank, lickerish stares and the gossip she not only provoked but invited; it was reciprocal" (136). It was indeed reciprocal. The men of the town envied the salesman and wished they could "go that way," if they had to go at all. Ella was a mother-earth figure who had missed her calling, her potential resembling that of Beulah in *Follow Me Down*.

The character of John Sturgis represents Bristol's third basic strength— its middle-class, bourgeois ethos. Before Esther Wingate seduced him, Sturgis, the son of the Irish barkeeper Barney Sturgis, was on his way to becoming a substantial figure in Bristol—the sort of a fellow a town could admire and its sons could emulate. "Finishing high school he went to work for one of his father's customers. . . . The boy did well, first in the [feed and grain merchant's] warehouse and then on the road. He was liked and even admired, and now in his middle twenties after six years in the business world he was being pointed to as a man on the way to success, an example of what could be done in the world by a young man who would apply himself, keep cheerful, and not grouse about salary or overtime" (86). The community approved of him, but John Sturgis failed the middle-class ideal and whatever virtues it may have had. In the Wingate mansion, where he had a room on the second floor, he listened to Mrs. Wingate's condescending views about the Irish without so much as a whimper of protest. It is no surprise that his son could not later even remember what he looked like.

Bristol entered the twentieth century guided more by its weaknesses, ambivalent feelings about the leadership of the highborn and hypocritical standards, than by its strengths, the exercise of a physical and economic vitality. The town was unprepared for rapid change; it did not have the security of knowing its place and its role in the overall nature of things— some tradition made permanent by the practices of generation after gener- ation. Bristol was not a European town fifteen-hundred years old. It was a new town that did not know what it wanted to become and lacked the leadership to find out. Bristol's condemnation of Ella at her death was based more on insecurity than on firmly held convictions about the sancti- ty of marriage. The twentieth century had brought changes that had made Bristol uncomfortable. In the nineteenth century "the trees, the war, the Negroes, [and] the river" had dominated Bristol and given it its character. In 1910 the movies, the automobile, and the telephone were among the new dominants; products of technological development had replaced the forces of history and nature. "These were the things which the preach- ers . . . railed . . . against, quoting the eschatology of Jeremiah and Isaiah and Jesus—to no effect: for the people sat in their Sunday clothes, soberly nodding agreement with all the preachers said about impending doom on earth and searing flame hereafter, and came out Monday morning as before. . . . Yet they were new to these involvements. These devices that saved labor agitated their brains, and there was an increasing dichotomy between the Business life and the Christian life; they began to have ner- vous stomachs" (181).

Overrunning and swelling are symptoms of failure. Bristol engulfed the Wingate lands; Ella swelled with an eighteen-pound fetus. Mrs. Lowry was prevented from chasing after her husband when he ran away to Texas because her legs swelled; in 1910 the president of the country was a fat man; at the seminary in New Orleans, Esther spoke of Bristol with a "glut of useless knowledge"; Hector returned from Charlottesville a "plump" young man. The list could go on, but Foote's point is clear. Glut, swelling, and boundless growth for modern Bristol have no purpose and no direc- tion, just swelling.

Foote has described "Child by Fever" as a "modern gothic novella," but he goes on to point out that the story "was also a second attempt ('Ride Out' was the first) to deal with the juxtaposition of the artist against the backdrop of society. You'll notice they both lost."[16] Of course, Hector does not compare favorably with Duff Conway as an artist, and his vision of developing Bristol is inadequate. Hector Sturgis, "the last Romantic" as the critic labeled him, is ill-equipped by training, experience, and understanding to be the artist that Bristol needs. His drawings are the result of his growing insanity, the imposition of an abstract form rather than an art that grows naturally from the relationship between artist, time, land, and people. When Mrs. Sturgis insists that his plans be followed, the engineers complain that it is impractical to do so.

The wages of the failed artist and the failed ideal are "nervous stomachs" and loneliness. Art fails to communicate; Duff Conway, Foote says, "is very close to his mother. But they never communicate."[17] The same condition prevails for Hector. His grandmother and mother have made it impossible for him to communicate with others; the last months of his life he spent alone in his room talking with what he believed to be Ella's ghost.

Between "Pillar of Fire," the final three-section story, and "Child by Fever" comes a short one-section story about life in Jordan County immediately following the Civil War. The story, "The Freedom Kick," is narrated by a black photographer who has inherited his "art" from his father, and the focus of his tale is on his mother who has received her "freedom kick" from the Bristol police. The theme of the story is the accommodation of blacks to resurgent white interests after the Civil War, and the photographer, who identifies himself as an artist, gives the bare historical facts a human dimension.

The artist's mother, Esmy, the daughter of a barber who was proud to be a descendant of "African chiefs," married a former slave who became a photographer, "a kind of artist, high-strung and determined." He failed to come home one evening only to appear the next morning "with a lump beside one eye." When Esmy learned that the lump had come from a police officer and that her husband's only offense was not displaying proper obeisance to the officer, she determined to take matters into her own hands. Esmy went to the jail "looking for damages," and the constable "thought it was some kind of joke," but then she grew angry "and started to yell in a loud voice about freedom and justice" (228). Even after they had knocked her down, she continued to yell, and one of the officers "kicked her full in the mouth, twice, cut both her lips and knocked several of her teeth right down her throat" (228). The next day she fished the teeth out of the slop jar and "put them on the mantel to remember freedom by" (229). Even with her sunken cheek, she was proud of her fight for freedom.

The artist claims that race relations worked in two directions. "You think we didn't laugh at those white men cutting head-holes in their wives' best sheets and eye-holes in the pillow cases?" he asks rhetorically. At the same time, the narrator comments that, even though he now is able to vote, and in a technical sense has what his mother lost her teeth seeking, it does not mean very much to him: "it seems like they dont mean so much as they did back then with the Kluxers riding the roads to take them from you" (229). If anyone in Foote's fictional world is to give meaning to freedom, then it is the artist, but this one, like most of Foote's artists, has failed to see beyond the surfaces of what his photographs record. He inherited his father's art, his equipment, and his clothes, but now he has grown fat. The black artist, unlike Hector, has children—"one on Beale, one in Detroit, one in New Orleans, and one to help my wife keep house" (230)—and there is room to hope that the proud spirit of the African chief will in time reappear. There is a suggestion from the names of the cities to which his children have fled that they, too, are artists, possibly musicians like Duff Conway.

"Pillar of Fire" has as its central figure a man in whom the original fire still burns; at least it burned until he was near death at age eighty-six when he had seen the plantation he carved from the virgin Delta swamp destroyed by the northern invader whose cause, in general, he had originally supported. Isaac Jameson, already forty years old in 1818, the year Mississippi was admitted to the Union, was one of the first white settlers in Jordan County. His original fire is that same "spark" that made Hugh Bart, who farmed the same plantation after Isaac, the man he was. In contrast to Hector Sturgis of "Child by Fever," Isaac enjoyed a harmonious relationship with both time and nature; his will coincided with the forces of history and the more mysterious anthropological forces of the physical world. His energy together with that harmony provided the spark that propelled him almost inevitably to success. It made him not simply an able manager of resources but also gave him that inner fullness of being that Foote's modern characters often seek. Thus, Isaac Jameson himself became a part of the myth-making process, playing the role of the American frontiersman who was confronting the primeval forest. At the same time, over the last years of his long life, Isaac believed that he was falling victim to those same historical forces that were later, during the first years of the twentieth century, to bring about what Foote has called a "failure of nerve." The story of Isaac's rise and demise is set in a framework narrative, a first-person account presented by Lieutenant Lundy of the Federal unit that burned the original Jameson mansion.

The actual history of Washington County is again an important source for Foote's story. As Bern Keating has explained, the records of early settlement of Washington County are not at all clear. As early as 1822 there were apparently several plantations in the area, and by 1828 settlement had begun on the eastern shore of Lake Washington. The records, according to Keating, list only two families in the county when, on 29 January 1827, it was officially designated Washington County. "The county was allowed one delegate to the legislature and was named a senatorial district. The legislature even called the Washington County unit of the state militia the 24th Regiment." This, Keating observes, was "not bad for a two-family county."[18]

Foote's fictional version of the settling of Lake Jordan follows what was probably the actual history of the development of the rich Delta farmland around Lake Washington. Isaac Jameson's father had been a Loyalist and had moved to Natchez "to escape the Revolution." Isaac was born "in a wilderness shack beside the Trace," and his father attributed the wildness in Isaac's personality to the conditions of his birth. As a young man he held his own against the flatboatmen in Natchez-under-the-Hill and was an embarrassment to his father who had become a respectable and prosperous merchant. After a fifteen-year absence from Natchez, during which time his father, who rejoiced considerably at his son's leaving, heard reports of Isaac's having been seen with Lafitte, the pirate, and his having fought "against the Creeks at Burnt Corn." Isaac was brought home unconscious from wounds he had received at the Battle of New Orleans. "He was a year mending," and then, after a brief resumption of his old ways, on a trip with two others through the Delta, "he found what he had been seeking from the start" (241).

From his father, who "considered it a down-right bargain," Isaac obtained his legacy—ten slaves and five thousand dollars. With these he moved to Lake Jordan and began in 1820 developing the plantation he named Solitaire. In 1826, the year before "Jordan County was formed," Isaac owned "thirty-two hundred" acres of prime Delta land, and two years later he married the daughter of the innkeeper in Ithaca, a settlement at the southern end of the lake. By the 1860s Isaac had prospered.

Isaac's pillar of fire resembles the one that led Moses from Egypt to the Promised Land in that Isaac, too, is on a journey to a new land that he will help settle and build. Like Moses, Isaac serves a historical purpose, but the source of the purpose is more abstract than Moses's God of Israel; the source of Isaac's strength is represented by the fire itself.

To his father there was little evidence that Isaac would become a pillar of almost mythical strength in the southern Delta. The first manifestation of that spark was undirected or, at best, misdirected energy. Isaac had grown to be a large-framed, big man and seemed, as his family feared, to have inherited "some goading spark of rebellion, some fierce, hot distillate of the jungle itself" (240). It is hardly inappropriate that he would associate with other heroic figures of the river valley—Jean Lafitte, Dominique You, and Andrew Jackson; and it would perhaps have been appropriate for him to have associated, as his father feared he had, with Burr or the outlaws along the Natchez Trace—"Murrel and the Harps." Isaac grew to be man of that dimension among the nation's builders, but the spark, that "hot distillate of the jungle," led Isaac in directions his father had not foreseen.

Traveling with two trappers through the Delta, Isaac had a dream about the settlement of the land and what he was to become.

> He dreamed an army of blacks marching upon the jungle, not halting to chop but walking steadily forward, swinging axes against the retreating green wall. Behind them the level fields lay stumpless and serene in watery sunlight, motionless until in the distance clanking trace chains and clacking singletrees announced the coming of the plowmen. Enormous lop-eared mules drew bulltongue ploughs across the green, and the long brown furrows of earth unrolled like threads off spools. What had been jungle became cultivated fields, and now the fields began to be striped with the pale green lines of plants soon burdened with squares, then purple-and-white dotted, then deep red with blooms, then shimmering white in the summer heat. In a long irregular line (they resembled skirmishers except for the singing; their sacks trailed from their shoulders like limp flags) the pickers passed over the fields, leaving them brown and desolate in the rain, and the stalks dissolved, going down into bottomless mud. Then in the dream there was quiet, autumnal death until the spring returned and the plowmen, and the dream began again. This was repeated three times, with a mystical clarity. [243–44]

Isaac had found the place in history for which he had spent the better part of forty years seeking "though he did not know he was looking for it until some time after he found it" (241). For Isaac, dream and history harmonize.

He named the ten-square-mile plantation, which following his dream he had carved out of the jungle, Solitaire because he intended to remain a bachelor. But then, in 1828, he married the innkeeper's daughter Katy, and she matched Isaac strength for strength. To a frontier country where the chief entertainment was watching a slave named Memsy "butt heads with the bull till the animal bellered with pain," Katy brought such refinement as was to be had. In a flurry after the marriage, she bought new furnishings for the house, which was enlarged and cleaned top to bottom. Isaac "had been in much the same position as a man watching what he thought was a spring breeze develop into a tornado, then back into a breeze again as soon as the holocaust was done" (247). The natural image, the tornado, is as appropriate to Katy as the "hot distillate of the jungle" is to Isaac.

From such a union it is natural that an exceptional heir would be born. Clive, the only child to survive, became "one of the sainted names of the Confederacy," for he had some of his father's "spark." His fame "began when he came out of Donelson with Forrest. . . . Then he distinguished himself at Shiloh. . . . By the time of Vicksburg, in the summer of '63, newspapers were beginning to print the story of his life" (260–61). Clive's fame might have been foretold, for he, too, achieved a harmony with those deeper forces of time which the stars control. "Southern accounts [of his life] always mentioned his having been born the year the stars fell; Starborn, one called him, and the others took it up." Verses that "Poetesses laureate" wrote for newspapers all across the South described how "he had streamed down to earth like a meteor to save the South; they made much of the flaming wake" (261).

Ironically, flames have a great deal to do not only with the spark that gave heat to Isaac's jungle distillate but also with consuming his spirit and with it the spirit of his civilization. Clive was baked hard in the "furnace of war," but the war also destroyed his father.

After the fall of Vicksburg, there was little the Confederates could do to defend the Delta against the Federal troops. In August 1864 a Federal platoon camped in Isaac's pasture and burned the slave quarters. Isaac and the three slaves who remained on the plantation—Edward Postoak, the deaf butler; a lame cook; and a "half-witted woman"—watched as the roofs caved in, sending sparks "upward in a fiery column that stood steadily upright for a long moment, substantial as a glittering pillar of jeweled brass supporting the black overhang of smoke, before it paled and faded and was gone" (267). To those watching, the fire burned with a "roaring sound like the rush of something passing at great speed." Civilization itself, born of a pillar of fire and guided by the brilliance of the fiery stars, was consumed, destroyed by the very forces that had given it strength. The fire resembles Duff Conway's trumpet and Metcalf's battle plan in that what seemed to be a source of strength becomes the means of failure.

Soon after the burning of the slave quarters, Isaac joined the three handicapped slaves by becoming afflicted with "motor aphasia," like M. de Charlus in *Remembrance of Things Past,* which meant that he mixed his words and could not make them follow the order that he wished. Civilization had lost its means of communication; life at Solitaire was indeed solitary and lonely for its owner. When he meant to ask the cook "Is breakfast ready?" it came out as "Is heck us riding?" (267).

Forced into loneliness, confined, enclosed within himself, Isaac engaged in "abstract thinking." At first he meditated as he walked across his wasted plantation, but then "he gave up the walks and spent his days in a big armchair in the parlor, keeping the curtains drawn" (270). In the destruction, he thought, there might be the judgment of God against those who had committed "the double sin of slavery and mistreatment of the land," but then he returned to an earlier conviction: "It's the sun and we go back there, back to fire" (270). Fire, Isaac saw, was the source of strength and the means of destruction, the visible sign of natural and historical sources beyond his control.

> He remembered the land as it was when he first came, a great endless green expanse of trees, motionless under the press of summer or tossing and groaning in the winds of spring and fall. He ringed them, felled them, dragged them out; he fired the stumps so that the air was hazed with the blue smoke of their burning, and then he had made his lakeside dream a reality; the plowmen came, the cotton sprouted and he prospered; until now. The earth, he thought, the earth endures. He groped for the answer, dealing with such abstract simplicities for the first time since childhood, back before memory. The earth, he thought, and the earth goes back to the sun; that was where it began. There is no law, no reason except the sun, and the sun doesnt care. Its only concern is its brightness; we feed that brightness like straws dropped into its flame. Fire! he thought suddenly. It all goes back to fire! [267–70]

Lieutenant Lundy, second in command of the gunboat *Starlight* and of the troops who burned Isaac's house, developed a respect for Isaac as though he seemed to recognize after only a few minutes that there was something very special and unusual about him. Lundy narrates the frame that encloses the general narrative of Isaac's career. Commanded by Colonel Nathan Frisbee, the mission of the *Starlight* was reprisal against the partisans, the few remains of Confederate resistance in the Delta.

Lundy, too, is something of a hero. He went back into Isaac's burning house to rescue the half-witted woman who had remained behind, but was not particularly impressed by his own courage; rather, what he remembers, what haunts him, is his memory of the fire reflected in Isaac's eyes. Isaac had been carried from the house in his armchair, and sitting on the lawn as his house was being burned, he suffered the stroke or heart attack that killed him. Lundy "saw in the dead eyes a stereoscopic reflection of the burning house repeated in double miniature" (279). Lundy saw that Isaac had not created a civilization that could outlast his own life. A profound, historical loneliness had at last entrapped Isaac, and his fire was no longer a living flame. It had become a source of destruction and death, not of strength. The half-witted woman was right when she shouted the words that continued to ring in Lundy's ears: " 'Calling yourself soldiers,' she said. 'Burners is all you is' " (281).

It was a conscious part of Foote's plan for "Pillar of Fire" to suggest the cultural significance of the Old Testament pattern that Isaac, in some measure, followed in settling the Delta, for such recognition of recurring patterns in history contributes to the fullness of human experience. Another pattern that the text suggests is that of the *Odyssey*. It is no mistake that the man who established the Ithaca Inn and became Isaac Jameson's father-in-law, was a professor of Greek. Isaac's role resembles that of Odysseus in several respects. Just as Odysseus was King of Ithaca, father of Telemachus, and husband of Penelope, so Isaac is a husband, father, and a founder of a civilization. Isaac also resembles Odysseus in the time and effort that he invested in discovering his cultural role.

The last story in *Jordan County*, "The Sacred Mound," is the story of John Postoak, the Indian forebear of Isaac Jameson's butler, Edward Postoak. To prevent the encroachment of white settlers in the Delta, Choctaws sacrificed two white trappers to the corn god at a fall full moon. One of the trappers had smallpox, but the Indians attributed the outbreak of the disease and the resulting deaths to the anger of the white men's god.

When Postoak recovered from the disease, the chiefs sent him to Natchez as a sacrifice to the white man's "slain god." There John encountered a priest, who, over the course of a year, explained Christianity and converted him. Still, John felt his obligation to the Choctaws and so he explained his mission to the Spanish civil authorities who agreed to return him to his people.

The central theme of the story is the clash of cultures and the traditions that the white and Indian cultures represent. The Indians had difficulty understanding why anyone would want to own land. All men, they said, were brothers and, "No man owns the land" (287). The rites of the corn god no doubt bear some resemblance to Christian ceremonies, but, hidden under centuries of tradition, the roots of belief do not reveal themselves.

The issues that Foote treats in his Jordan County stories are obviously not far removed from the issues that consumed a somewhat older observer of another Mississippi county in the clay hills somewhat to the east of Jordan County. The history of Faulkner's Yoknapatawpha County bears a strong resemblance to the history of Jordan County; after all, the historical facts of the development of Mississippi are facts and cannot be reasonably altered. The Indians were removed from the land by a series of treaties, the white men did take and abuse the land by overfarming, and they did abuse their own kind by making some of them slaves. Foote, like Faulkner, found deeper forces operating in history and nature. Both of them sought out those primitive, mystical, ritualistic underpinnings that modern man, to his own destruction, often forgets. Isaac Jameson's "distillation of the jungle" is not markedly different from those primitive spirits "concentrated and distilled" in the whiskey that Isaac McCaslin drinks with the other hunters, and both Isaacs have their own big woods.

Of course, there are many parallels between Foote's work and Faulkner's. Faulkner is said to have told Foote that he must escape the spell of Yoknapatawpha. In many ways Foote did escape, and to read Foote with Faulkner always in mind does as much injustice to the reader's imagination as it does to Foote's artistry, for Foote is an artist seriously interested in the organic whole, in the total form of his fiction.

Foote believed, as he explained on a number of occasions to Walker Percy, that with *Love in a Dry Season* his apprenticeship had come to an end. He felt, one may assume, that he had assimilated all of his models, all of the imaginative and creative forces that he needed to shape his own art.

His letters to Percy at that time expressed an outright joy at approaching a major novel that was to cover four generations of life in the Delta, a novel to be titled "Two Gates to the City." It was an accident of time that many of those skills and much of that enthusiasm would go in another direction—*The Civil War: A Narrative.*

Chapter IV

Form and *The Civil War:*

A Narrative

Hugh Bart helped bury Major Dubose, Foote's Civil War veteran in "Flood Burial," the veteran who had devoted years and thousands of pages of manuscript to a history of the war. Bart gave him temporary burial in the iron-bound wooden chest that also contained the pulpy remains of his flood-ruined manuscript. It is a telling Proustian image of a modern world that has lost touch with its past and makes even more fitting Foote's acceptance in 1954 of an offer from Random House to write a history himself. He did not realize in 1954 that he would spend twenty years, the very heart of his career as a writer, writing a three-volume history, but he could explain to Percy at the end of those two decades, as Major Dubose could not, that he wanted "everybody everywhere to read it so they can learn to love their country."

Almost from the beginning of his career, Foote had been interested in writing about the Civil War, projecting three novels and actually publishing one of them. The audience he addresses in *The Civil War* is one that is increasingly removed from the events that, more clearly than any other events in the history of the United States, established its character. "What a war," Foote declared to Percy in 1956, almost two years into his book, "Everything we are or will be goes right back to that period (29Nov56)." Foote stands at the transition; he knew veterans of the war and watched them die away until there were no more. He watched a generation grow up in the South which was removed from the great tragedy of defeat and inclined increasingly toward the national optimism. In such a context it was time to take stock of a war that was for the southern consciousness until lately, The War.

Mastery of Form

Random House had wanted a short history of the war, and Foote, as he explained to Helen White and Redding Sugg, believed that a 200,000-word history would provide him with a pleasant interlude. "I figured that I could write about twice as much history per year as I did fiction per year—fiction is hard work," he explained. About a week into the project, he knew that he had miscalculated. "I saw that it was no part of my makeup, that nothing about me would be happy writing a little summary of the war. . . . And then it began to open out for me and I was able to outline all three volumes."[1] The result was an agreement with Random House for a much larger work, one that would take him not a year but two decades to complete, and at the end of his work, he could look back with great satisfaction on what he had accomplished, pleased with "how beautifully it's structured (30Dec74)." "Open out," "outline," and "structured" are operative terms for Foote because meaning may lie not so much in the events or on the actors but in the form of the work, the narrative plan. Over and over in his letters to Percy, in his interviews, and in his essay on writing history, "The Novelist's View of History,"[2] Foote reiterates his conviction that the writer cannot tell anyone anything, but he can, if he is lucky, show the reader something. For example, writing to Percy in 1963, he comments that people who think that writers write to deliver a message are incorrect in their expectations. "If I knew what I wanted to say I wouldn't write at all. What for? Why do it, if you already know the answers? Writing is the search for the answers, and the answer is in the form, the method of telling, the exploration of self, which is our only clew to reality (13Aug63)."

Approaching *The Civil War* with a knowledge of Foote's conviction about writing from a thesis,[3] one is often surprised to find an abundance of judgments. When, for example, the narrator comments that General Hooker, at Chancellorsville, had "the tactical disadvantage of not knowing he had been surprised" (II, 298), he is rendering a judgment about Hooker's perspicacity. Or when he comments that the "tone" of Charles Francis Adams, Jr., "was exceptionally high, which made him something less than tolerant of the weaknesses of others—particularly the weaknesses of the flesh, from which he himself apparently was exempt" (II, 234), one cannot escape the feeling that this narrator has reached a conclusion about Adams. Judgments such as these abound in *The Civil War*, but these are judgments in relatively insignificant matters, and there is often the narrator's more or less playful suggestion that there may be other possible and plausible conclusions to be reached. The judgments about which Foote the artist is concerned are not casual but are concerned with the conception of form; they lie in the relationship between the narrator and his subject. This interest in form was, of course, hardly new to Foote as he began writing *The Civil War: A Narrative*.

In mid-November 1951 Foote missed several days of work, the result of a cold, and this occasioned a letter to Percy. Foote had attended a concert given by a pianist who "played mostly Chopin, along with a passel of Debussy, and wound up with Liszt's 'Mephisto's Waltz.'" The music must have brought on the illness. "I think this last was what did it," he wrote, "for that was when I began sneezing, though doubtless the Chopin and Debussy hadn't helped matters; anyhow next morning my head was stuffed tight as an egg and I've been going through old billy hell ever since (15Nov51)." The problem, no doubt, for Foote, who was given to Mozart, Beethoven, and Schubert, was that these romantic composers were un-healthily free with form.

The interruption in his schedule, however, gave him time to plan out still another novel, so he said. Setting, character, and point of view would be important, but the most important, and hence the most difficult consid-eration, was the shape of the plot.

Scene: a small Southern town (I'll draw on Greenville for this, for I dont think a writer ought to pretend to know about anything except what he's seen firsthand). Time: the present, shunting back to Indian days (1778)— thats where the symbolism first works in: red skins, white skins, whereas in the future sections of the book (2090) all the characters will be Pink (no Marxian connection, though the critics doubtless will try to read it in). Well, there are four main characters: two men and two women—they will be handled contrapuntally, with a shifting point-of-view (Jamesean in fact); I'm planning on a 1-2-3-4-3-2-1 construction, but there's nothing definite yet; I may decide to do it 1-3-2-3-1 even though it leads to some confusion among the reprint people. What the hell: I can get along, I can always put in for a Guggenheim—tax-exempt, too. (15Nov51)

The settings would be a roller rink and an Indian mound; the connection between the two would be established through the four characters as they went "round and round." The connection Foote says, is "subtle" and the "general reader" will not see it at first reading. There will be a calliope playing, and Foote will "quote musical notation from the various tunes the calliope plays (15Nov51)."

Foote is satirizing himself, but the spoof identifies what is important to him as a writer. The construction might be "1-2-3-4-3-2-1" or "1-3-2-3-1," and musical notation will accompany the whole. Neither Foote's public statements, nor his comments to Percy treat the matter of form systematically, but they provide a basis for the speculation that Foote has a classical conception of form that, his objections to Liszt and Chopin notwithstanding, is subsumed into a somewhat romantic belief about the value of art and the role of the artist, derived, in part, from Proust. To use the paradoxical terminology of W. K. Wimsatt, Jr., the "concrete universal" in Foote's work can be found in symbol, but it is more significantly present in the form of the artifact. The form of Foote's work, whether fiction or history, is a concrete structure, but its correspondence with the forms in earlier writing and in musical composition suggests a broader historical significance, and that, in turn, leads to speculation that form is based upon a more abstract metaphysical dimension.

Some of what Foote has said about form seems to imply that he sees it as a conscious pattern that the artist imposes on his subject, an arbitrary creation of his own. At Memphis State University, he spoke of the artist's giving the work "order so that he can encompass it," thus enabling him to "understand what he is writing about." In the same lecture (20Feb67),[4] he said that in writing he has to give his work "a form that satisfies" him. But even these comments imply that form is more than an arbitrary pattern created at the moment for the work at hand. It may have its antecedents in the artist's study of history, particularly his study of the way in which previous artists have discovered form, or form may lie in the artist's own independent discoveries as he contemplates the object of his art. Men may have created form over a long period of time, or form may lie altogether outside of history and have to do with the very nature of the universe. In either case, form for Foote transcends the particular moment of creation; it has, instead, its antecedents in the experience of all men on earth.

Although Foote occasionally mistrusted the New Critics or "formalists"—on one occasion he told Percy that they were "a bunch of clowns

(11Dec51)"—he nevertheless considers John Crowe Ransom his favorite modern poet, a congeniality that lies in a shared interest in form. Ransom explained the importance of form in his 1933 essay "A Poem Nearly Anonymous: The Poet and His Formal Tradition" (later reprinted as "Forms and Citizens").[5] Ransom identified two kinds of form, economic and aesthetic. Economic form allows us to obtain what we need to survive; aesthetic form, in the context of history, is the substance of manners, religion, and art. Observing an object through an aesthetic form, Ransom argues, provides one with a "new kind of knowledge." In "The Novelist's View of History," Foote gives emphasis to plot, which for practical purposes in the novel he identifies with form. He observes, "In the *Poetics,* Aristotle called the management of *plot* the most important element in dramatic composition," and then he explains that he sees plot as much more than an arrangement of sequences. "It includes, as well, the amount of space and stress each of these events is to be accorded—and because of this, by combination of them all, it gives the book its larger rhythms and provides it with narrative drive, the force that makes it move under its own power" (223). For Foote, as with Ransom, the "larger rhythms" are the substance of manners, ritual, and art, and he seems to agree with Ransom that observing experience through aesthetic form provides a special "knowledge."

For Ransom's purposes in "Forms and Citizens," it is sufficient to consider form itself as historical. "Tradition is the handing down of a thing by society," Ransom writes, "and the thing handed down is just a formula, a form" (59). Whether, for Shelby Foote, the achievement of form has a teleological reference of universal, romantic dimension, or whether the idea of form has developed from thousands of years of human experience, both historical and even prehistorical, and is passed on from generation to generation, is not altogether clear in his novels. Whether, in Allen Tate's terminology, the forms develop from the "religious imagination" or from the "historical imagination" is, from Foote's comments, impossible to determine; both are possible and, given the functions of form, perhaps the consideration of ultimate source is unimportant. Foote has preached to Walker Percy and reminded almost every interviewer that his fiction is speculative; it is a search for answers and not a declaration of answers found. The reader's response to Foote's texts, he says in effect, should not be agreement with a position but a questioning, perhaps an extension, of the author's speculations.

Whatever the origins of form may be, it is only through experience and not abstract thought that the artist captures it. The artist, Foote explained to Percy "comprehends [experience] with his soul, his artistic perception, and in this his socalled 'brain' has very little share. No good writer trusts anything but experience; he least of all trusts 'thought' or dogma, and he never takes anyone's word for anything. He trusts intuition, using his style to transform experience into laws, unrecognizable even to himself until he has done so (20Jul52)." Over three years later Foote, as he so often did, drew Percy's attention to Proust, who was seeking art of a very high order, one having to do with an "inner reality."

> For Proust, every work of art is a harmonization, a kind of metaphor. It can be understood only in relation to something else, for it is always in harmony with something of a quite different nature which exists only in the author's mind. For him, a work of art is not an aspiration; it is not a fulfillment of desire or an expression of faith; it is not a means to any end whatever; nor is it a discovery of something new, since it only reveals a discovery which necessarily precedes it. It is none of these things. It is the concrete equivalent of a reality belonging to another order: an order perceived because it confers upon things the enigma of a new and autonomous beauty. What he discovers is what all artists are seeking: inner reality. Without it there can be no esthetic beauty, for it is itself the source of beauty. Artistic sense (so called) is inseparable from submission to that inner reality (29Oct55).

"[R]eality belonging to another order," comprehending reality with the "soul," and a reliance on "intuition" suggest that Foote sees form in art as reflecting form in a much broader dimension.

Much of the aesthetic theory that Foote expounds to Percy must be understood in terms of Proust's *Remembrance of Things Past*. Not content simply to explain Proust's conception of the quality of art, Foote on "5Aug70" typed out for Percy a paragraph that occurs in the seventh volume of the English translation. Proust's hero and narrator, Marcel, discovers his literary vocation in the articulation of an aesthetic that will provide the foundation for his art. The revelation occurs as Marcel is waiting for a musical piece to be completed so that he can join a party in progress in the drawing room. He suddenly discovers that his art must convey the relationship between sensations in the present and the memories those sensations evoke. "An image presented to us by life brings with it, in a single moment, sensations which are in fact multiple and heterogeneous," the passage begins. Proust identifies "what we call reality" as "a certain connection between these immediate sensations and the memories which envelop us simultaneously with them—a connection that is suppressed in a simple cinematographic vision, which just because it professes to confine itself to the truth in fact departs widely from it." Reality, for Foote as well as for Proust, lies not in the concrete description of people and place (what W. D. Howells identified as the real as opposed to the artificial grasshopper) but in the connections between the perception of the present, material world and memory. The literary artist draws "a unique connection which the writer has to rediscover in order to link forever in his phrase the two sets of phenomena which reality joins together." "Truth" and "life" lie in the "essence," the connection revealed by the artist. The artist "can describe a scene by describing one after another the innumerable objects which at a given moment are present at a particular place, but truth will be attained by him only when he takes two different objects, states the connection between them—a connection analogous in the world of art to the unique connection which in the world of science is provided by the law of causality—encloses them in the necessary links of a well-wrought style; truth—and life too—can be attained by us only when, by comparing a quality common to two sensations, we succeed in extracting their common essence and in reuniting them to each other, liberated from the contingencies of time, within a metaphor (5Aug70)."

Pointing out the influence of Proust that is evident in *Tournament,* referring to the same passage that Foote mailed to Percy, Louis D. Rubin, Jr., explains succinctly the aesthetic that Foote admires. "It is only through art—time regained—that the relationships between our otherwise perishable moments of existence in time can be recognized and joined together into a reality that may endure free of chronology."[6] This art for Foote, as for Proust, enables one to establish links with what is not limited by time and to establish links as well with other human beings. "Real life," says Proust, "life at last laid bare and illuminated—the only life in consequence which can be said to be really lived—is literature, and life thus defined is in a sense all the time immanent in ordinary men no less than in the artist" (151–52).

Self-knowledge achieved through art, perhaps through enscripting oneself in such language as Proust used in his novel, or even in the vocabulary of an imaginative response and appreciation of it, conveys the lives of others: "But art, if it means also awareness of our own life, means also awareness of the lives of other people—for style for the writer, no less

than color for the painter, is a question not of technique but of vision. . . .
Through art alone are we able to emerge from ourselves, to know what
another person sees of a universe which is not the same as our own and of
which, without art, the landscapes would remain as unknown to us as those
that may exist in the moon" (152).[7] A world without art is a world of
enormous, haunting isolation—the isolation that defeats character after
character in Foote's novels. "I can always read Proust," Foote told William
C. Carter. "If I even want to read anything, I'll go get a volume of Proust
down and I'm absorbed right away. It's always been that way."[8]

Whether form in art lies in deep, universal rhythms or is, on a narrower
level, constructed from man's experience of nature and time, it nevertheless relies on resources that transcend the writer's immediate experience.
Form transcends rules, dogma; it is something realized in the work of art,
the skeleton that the light reveals shining through the fingers. The artist
concentrates on his own experience and on the concrete world, but the
result of his concentration goes far beyond narrow mimesis. Form is a
more unintentional achievement of the work of art for Foote than it
appears to be for Ransom. It can be recalled, revealed, however, as naturally as the essence Proust identifies.

While the writer must write from his own experience, while form in art,
just as the form of the bones in the artist's hand, may have its origins in
what lies beyond time, it is equally important that form has its evolution in
history and time. Form, after all, is not reflected in the current moment
only; it has been reflected in art and ritual from the time man began to
shape his own experience by them. "What the novel needs is a sense of
proceeding from generations of knowledge," Foote told Percy (11Dec51).

Whatever sources of form may be foremost, may exact the largest
influence at the moment of creation, the artist must always rely on himself,
Foote feels, for only then can the pure force exert itself unimpaired. The
artist must be willing to make and accept responsibility for his mistakes as
Hugh Bart in *Tournament* was unable to do. On 18 February 1952 Foote
wrote Percy one of his most thoughtful letters. Apparently editors had
suggested that Percy make changes in one of his novels, and Foote warned
against it. "A good writer *never* makes a mistake in the basic sense: not
when he is writing of things that matter to him—and when he is not doing
that, no amount of editing can correct it; the fault will be so intrinsic that
no amount of editing can correct it. All an editor can do is make it
'readable' (for Godsake!) . . . . Don't you see?"

"Art is my religion if I have one," Foote reported to Evans Harrington,[9] a very demanding religion. "The real answers," he told Percy, "can only be found in art." The price the artist pays in loneliness alone is "so severe that no one ever chooses this vocation any more than a priest chooses his (20Jul52)." Through the artist's work flow forms more permanent than his own creations, and the artist, as agent or priest, provides in the achievement of form a body of knowledge that includes a sense of history, an awareness of one's place in time, and a means for a more intense and sensitive understanding of the self. The artist's role, Foote seems to argue, is to restore the usefulness of the past by drawing upon the form of the arts to find order in the present and to shape, or discover the inherent shape, in both the past and present so that they can be useful to the readers' consciousness. Form, in Foote's conception of it, probably does not encompass precisely what Proust meant by "essence," but it is integral to the artistry of literature.

While the emphasis on form suggests the influence of a number of modern writers in addition to Proust and Ransom, Foote possibly arrived at his beliefs through a variety of literary sources and an intensive study of musical form which began, perhaps, because of Proust's interest. He embarked on his study of music soon after he returned to Greenville after World War II, so the form of *The Civil War: A Narrative* results from many years of thought and experiment. The metaphor of enclosure that is central to *Tournament* is reflected in the form of the novel. Asa's narrative surrounds and encloses the story of Hugh Bart, providing a framework, set apart on pages numbered in Roman numerals. The framework thus extends the themes of separation, isolation, and the metaphor of enclosure in that it falls between the reader and Bart, giving the impression that we see Bart through Asa's narrative eyes. The games and pattern into which Bart fits begin to enclose his life. His forty-room house, Solitaire, walls him in physically and spiritually, and, finally, his own "grossness of the flesh" insulates "his mind's quick." *Shiloh*, likewise, demonstrates a framing device. Palmer Metcalf, a lieutenant on Johnston's staff, opens and closes the narrative, and, again, the form suggests closure, distance, and separation. The same framework appears in "Pillar of Fire," in which Lieutenant Lundy provides the framework for the tale of Isaac Jameson, founder of civilization in Lake Jordan and a Promethean fire-giver. Isaac dies while his plantation burns, and he is literally unable to speak coherently; communication between Lundy and Jameson can occur only in the reflection Lundy sees in Isaac's eyes of the house burning.

The form in these tales bears some of the weight of meaning both by extending the central metaphor beyond character or sequence of events, and by separating the reader from those events, distancing the reader by an elaboration in narrative structure. In these tales of the nineteenth century, form may imply that the past is closed and not accessible to the modern reader, but the opposite seems more likely, in view of Foote's conviction about the value of art and his love of Proust. By giving shape to the past, art makes it available, but art is difficult and takes the devotion not only of the artist but of the reader as well. If Hugh Bart, Isaac Jameson, and A. S. Johnson's army lose touch with the spark that gave them purpose and a sense of direction, if Foote believes that there is something "horribly wrong" with modern civilization in the Mississippi Delta, then one might reasonably assume that the artist explores and analyzes these conditions in the hope, even if that hope is faint, that his work will help make right the wrong, will supply some of the understanding that is missing.

Form in Foote's third novel, *Follow Me Down*, becomes much more complex. The concern for form and the attention he had devoted to it are reflected in his disappointment that the reviewers did not recognize this as "the best-constructed American novel since Gatsby." The immediate source for this form, as has been observed above, is Browning's *The Ring and the Book*. The different narrators provided a flexibility that Foote found useful; "The form," he said, "makes it possible to heighten interest by the use of nine different styles (May Day 1948)." It also allowed him to use the basic framework he had used in *Tournament* and *Shiloh* and, at the same time, introduce formal elements derived from classical music and from Greek tragedy.

The reviewers did not understand Foote's interest in form, and that irritated him, but what irritated him even more was that Walker Percy did not like the book. Percy thought it lacked unity, that it was prurient and crude, and Foote wrote several letters defending his artistry. One such letter, "7April50," begins with a diagram of the form, one that resembles diagrams Foote would have encountered in critical discussions of Dante or Milton. In one letter Foote reminds Percy that the original title was to be *The Vortex* and demonstrates with a diagram the meaning of the original title. Each narrator is a little closer to the central event in the novel, just as

STYLE: SPEAKER:

                                                    pages:
1. Vernacular ---- Circuit Clerk (19)

PART
ONE   2. Professional -- Reporter   (36)

       3. Lyric --------- Dummy   (17)

       4. Eustis -------- Eustis   (48)

PART   5. Lyric --------- Beulah   (21)
TWO

       6. Eustis -------- Eustis   (48)

       7. Lyric --------- Wife   (20)

PART   8. Professional -- Lawyer   (38)
THREE

       9. Vernacular ---- Turnkey   (17)

Browning's narrators are in *The Ring and the Book*. Beulah's narrative is the "keystone of the arch," Eustis's narrative frames Beulah's, the reporter and the lawyer frame the narratives of the two central figures, and the narratives of the two public officials provide the more distant and disinterested framework. Foote offered his explanation as a defense against Percy's charge that *Follow Me Down* failed to fulfill Aquinas's criterion that a work of art must have "'wholeness' or 'unity.'" Not only does the book have "wholeness," Foote argues, it also "has something Aquinas also deemed necessary: 'claritas.'"

Foote's attention to symmetry, his careful balancing of the parts of his narrative, derives from his interest in classical form. In his diagram he lists the number of pages in each section of narrative; he does not, however, explain to Percy that the balance has its antecedents in the Greeks and in classical music. In his correspondence he often urges Percy to listen to particular recordings, and at least once he suggested that Percy read Aeschylus. Perhaps he hoped that Walker would discover the resemblance without help.

Periodically during the late 1940s and early 1950s, Foote worked on

"Child by Fever," which finally became the centerpiece of *Jordan County* in 1954. This novelette shows the developing interest in classical form that contributed so forcefully to *Follow Me Down*. Aristotle's *Poetics* had long been influential on Foote's work, as his comments in "The Novelist's View of History" explain, but perhaps more fundamental to his conception of form was the Aeschylus trilogy. He probably encountered the *Agamemnon* originally in school, but it became an interest to which he returned on several occasions. In writing to Percy on "25Jan79," Foote explains that he is at work once again on his major novel and at work on a "framework that . . . will bear any and everything I want it to support." His reading he felt contributed to the effort: "Dante, Joyce, and perhaps most of all the *Oresteia*, which," he said, "I just finished studying to the dregs for about the tenth time in the past twenty years." Actually he had been studying it for more than twenty years. In a letter dated "8Nov51," writing to Percy about the first version of "Two Gates to the City," he said, "In conception . . . it's the greatest thing since Aesculus' Orestia."

The many allusions to Greek literature in "Child by Fever" cannot escape notice of even the casual reader. The name of the principal character is Hector, and the name of his wife, Ella, is a derivative of Helen and is related to Electra. Hector's grandfather is an Irish bartender who listens to "dythrambic confidences" and looks like an "Olympian deity." Hector, according to the Reverend Mr. Clinkscales, draws plans for developing Bristol into "an Athens of the South." Even Hector's hanging himself in an attic is probably intentional irony.

More significant, however, are the thematic parallels and the most striking of these is the reversal of traditional male-female roles. In the *Agamemnon*, Clytemnestra took upon herself the obligation, according to ancient law, to kill Agamemnon upon his return from Troy, avenging his sacrifice of Iphigeneia, their daughter, in the interest of the war. The chorus in the *Choephoroe* declared Clytemnestra's act "unwomanly." Clytemnestra's accomplice, Aegisthis, according to Orestes, "wears a woman's heart." Mrs. Wingate and her daughter, Mrs. Sturgis, in "Child by Fever" played the man's role. Both ran the Delta plantation they owned; both were so overbearing that Hector, Mrs. Sturgis's son, was incapable of a traditional male role.

The theme of Greek tragedy is the fall of the elevated hero. Agamemnon was murdered; and Orestes, his son, after avenging his father's murder, was pursued by furies until Athena intervened. Citizens of Foote's

Bristol conceded that the Sturgises and Wingates were highborn, but these highborn, at best, were caricatures of aristocracy. The pursuit of furies is a third parallel between the *Oresteia* and "Child by Fever." Clytemnestra's ghost appeared in the *Eumenides,* the third part of the *Oresteia,* to urge her furies, her "vengeful hounds of hell," in pursuit of Orestes. The ghost of Ella Sturgis is both ghost and fury in "Child by Fever"; the effect is similar in that the ghost drives Hector mad. In addition, in "Child by Fever," the community's interest in Hector resembles the chorus of Greek tragedy.

The allusions and the parallels in theme also reinforce the notion that the *Oresteia* had much to do with Foote's conception of form. The events that occur within that structure are sometimes similar, but parallels in plot are far from exact, for Foote is treating the history of Jordan County and Bristol, and that history cannot be made to fit event for event the Greek model. In the *Agaememnon* the hero returned home to his death. The first third of "Child by Fever" treats the birth of Hector Sturgis, the history of the Wingate-Sturgis family, and Hector's early life and education. The first section closes with Hector's return from the University of Virginia and his symbolic death at his mother's hands when she refused to allow him to fulfill his heritage by joining the Bristol volunteers for the Spanish-American War. The second section of "Child by Fever" concerns Hector's marriage to Ella Lowry, the birth and death of their son, Hector's subsequent failure as a husband, and Ella's death by gas in a Bristol hotel in the arms of a lover. In the second section of the *Oresteia,* the *Choephoroe,* Orestes returned to Argos and avenged the death of Agamemnon. In the third section of the *Oresteia,* the *Eumenides,* and the third section of "Child by Fever," both Orestes and Hector Sturgis are pursued by their ghosts and furies. "The Greeks knew better than anybody," Foote told John Carr. "A man's own character is his demon."[10] So it was for Orestes and for Hector Sturgis.

In 1948 Foote sent a draft of the novelette to Percy, who apparently did not like it. It is particularly apropros that Foote comments that he intended Hector to be a "tragic cipher;" the structure was to be "contrapuntal." "Your letter on the Child came today. Both your objections are indeed valid. I intended Hector to be a cipher (which he is) but I intended him to be a tragic cipher (which he is not). And your second objection—too much blood and cunt—is even righter. However, behind that there is also an idea which did not come off. The idea was that this poor spook, who never accomplished anything, was nevertheless surrounded by blood and thunder. The two were intended to be contrapuntal, pointing each other up. I see now that I failed at both ends and resultantly in the middle too. But I still believe the conception was right. Execution, however; thats another matter (30Jul48)."

Hector, though, is a would-be artist. He draws plans for the subdivision and development of the Wingate-Sturgis estate, and the critic from the Memphis paper labeled him "the last Romantic." Among the many flaws in Hector's work was the artificiality of form. He attempted to impose his ideas, abstract as they were, on the terrain, and when the engineers complained to his mother that his plans were impractical, she insisted that they be followed anyway. The difference between Hector's application of the abstract form and Foote's notion that form derives from the artist's intense awareness of his own experience is fundamental to the meaning of Foote's artistry. The three-part form here is not artificial, imposed form but, rather, it echoes the rhythms of time itself. Unless the artist can make these rhythms available for modern man, then the happy conclusion of the *Oresteia,* the taming of the furies at Athena's bidding, is not possible for Bristol. And if the form is artificial, then the writing fails to measure up to Proust's criteria for artistry.

Music of the classical period, particularly the chamber music of Mozart, Beethoven, and Schubert, also gave substance to Foote's conception of form. "I always think everything I do is a miracle of organization and exposition—at least while I'm writing it or typing it for the printer; later on it's a different matter," he wrote Percy in July 1948. "All art is an organization of experience, whatever the form. . . . 'Child by Fever', for instance, might have been a string quartet—and a damn bad one, too (30Jul48)." The term "form" here is applied to the distinction between music or drama or novel, and "form" in that sense can be "unimportant," but the shape of a particular work is not "unimportant." "Child by Fever" could have been by this reasoning "a string quartet," but the form of the quartet has a direct bearing in its meaning.

Foote began his study of music almost casually and very likely under the tutelage of Proust, but soon he was immersed in it, listening to recordings and discussing them with his friends (especially Kenneth Haxton, a composer who helped found the Greenville Symphony), learning to read musical notation, studying the scores of the compositions that interested him, and reading the history and criticism of music. To his audience at Memphis State University in his lecture on "Creative Writing," he commented on his study of music: "I listened to music for years and would not learn musical notation or study music because I was afraid it would interfere with my understanding and pleasure. . . . I then persuaded myself that maybe I was wrong and began to study music hard. And I could not have been wronger than I was. The more you know about a subject, the more fascinating it is."[11]

At times Foote recommended particular works or particular recordings in his correspondence with Percy. Later, in the 1970s, he copied measures from scores in his letters, just as he did in Parker Nowell's narrative in *Follow Me Down*. "As for myself," he told Percy, "I long ago confined myself to chamber music—I found that I returned to it most often. Mozart, Beethoven, Schubert—these three; and the greatest of these is Mozart (25Nov49)." Almost thirty years later he was again writing to Percy about Mozart, in particular about the Quartet in D Major, K 499, and the Quintet in D Major, K 593. Although the correspondence, beginning in winter 1979, comes over thirty years after Foote began his study of music, the letters reveal how intensive and serious his study was. In February 1979 Foote had sent a cassette of the two Mozart chamber pieces to Percy and commented on their structure and history.

> The quartet (K. 499, written a year before Don Giovanni) is a miracle of making something out of almost nothing. The first movement, for example, has almost no second theme, yet never slacks in interest—and the other three movements grow out of it in a wonderfully logical way. It used to bother me that M's last movements seemed to me basically lightweight; but I was never wronger. The clew is in what almost all his serious pieces seem to say to us when they have ended: "How sad life is, and how brief. Let us enjoy it!" Then too, I began to see, these last movements are the most "learned" of all: fuges, canons, inversions, etc. The more his genial spirits rise, the more he calls on all his ingenuity. . . . I began to see this, really, when I started following the scores; my eye taught my ear to hear things it did not hear on its own, that is until it "saw" them—then it heard them in all their glory.

The quintet is Foote's "favorite;" its "perfection" reaches to "forces far beyond us." Foote had obviously found Mozart's music, seen in the classical commitment to order and reason, charged with transcendent magic.

> The quintet (K.593, from the last year of his life) is, as Ive told you often, perhaps my favorite of all his chamber pieces. Like the quartet, written five years earlier, (five years is a tremendous span in Mozart) it has a melodious

beauty that can truly be called Schubertian, but beneath the surface beauty there are things poor Schubert never knew existed. You listen and you listen and they come over you in a kind of exultant way. Perfection is the strangest of all things to encounter, not just because it is so rare, but because it has some quality of being in touch with forces far beyond us. The adagio really is other-wordly; Ive had some strange sensations listening to it down the years. (21Feb79)

About three weeks later, Foote sent Percy a cassette recording of Beethoven's Fourteenth and Fifteenth String Quartets. The Fifteenth, particularly important to Proust, has one of Foote's favorites, the *Heiliger Dankgesang,* "for the middle of its five movements," but the Fourteenth he finds to be "the most beautiful piece of music ever written."

It is in seven movements, with no break between any of them, but it boils down to a true four-movement quartet with certain embellishments. Like so:
1. A long fugue-introduction.
2. Actual first movement (ABA, "arch" form).
3. A bridge passage.
4. Actual second movement; theme and seven variations, plus coda.
5. Third movement: Scherzo.
6. Bridge-introduction to the finale.
7. Fourth movement—Finale. (Sonata form) (10Mar79)

The division of his work into distinctive parts that resemble musical form characterize Foote's work after *Shiloh.* When he speaks of a "1-2-3-4-3-2-1" or "1-3-2-3-1," the model is musical form.

Parker Nowell, his lawyer-narrator in *Follow Me Down,* like his author, knows music well—"highbrow music" the circuit clerk called it. Nowell, the master of musical form, organizes the summation of his defense of Eustis accordingly. "I gave it to them straight, sonata-form: Exposition, Development, Recapitulation," he says (253). Nowell's artistry, his composition of "the busy little symphony of Time," enables him to sway the jury. The artist plays upon their reactions to gain his ends. Just as Foote found that Mozart's quintet "has some quality of being in touch with forces beyond us," so Nowell, listening to the Fortieth Symphony felt himself "frightened by it, not so much hearing the melody, the music itself, as experiencing the impulse that brought it into being" (243). The artist's effectiveness depends upon his ability to perceive the essential and when he is able to lay before his reader a "symphony of Time," then he has done his best. Nowell was "sour" and cynical, and his artistry was limited to making a jury do his bidding, but the relationship between Nowell and his jury parallels the relationship between the artist (the writer) and the audience (the reader). "'Child by Fever' might have been a string quartet" because the aim of the various arts if for the listener or reader to experience what Parker Nowell and Shelby Foote experience when listening to Mozart.

Foote's fourth novel, *Love in a Dry Season,* has the same formal interests that appeared in *Follow Me Down* although his principal source, James's *Washington Square,* did not contribute to the form as Browning's *Ring* had to *Follow Me Down.* The book had, he explained to Percy, "counterpointed symbolism that can be taken or let alone, but which yet (I hope) gives the book a higher importance, places it in the stream of human experience." Again "Time" is a major consideration. "The historical background (the 30s) pinpoints the plot, locates it in Time, and I hope is interesting on its own account (22Dec50)." The plan for *Love in a Dry Season* is an elaborate structure—the three major sections divided into three sections and each of these further divided into three sections. Foote devised an elaborate schema of his plot. As Calvin Brown has observed, it is difficult to impose the forms of one art on another,[12] but in this instance form reflects both the form of the *Oresteia* and the form of the ternary musical composition. In terms of events it is difficult to identify clearly exposition, development, and recapitulation, but in the themes that underlie the events and give them meaning, one finds the external form more directly reflected.

Simone Vauthier, writing in the Shelby Foote issue of the *Mississippi Quarterly,* has found a "ternary pattern" in the novel: "The narration proceeds from a state of relative order, previous to the arrival of Harley Drew, to the various disorders caused by the actions of the outsider, and then to the new order into which people settle after his departure" (387).[13] The ternary "rhythm" supports the series of triangles on which the plot develops. "In the enormous Bristol eye, there is inscribed as in a circle the triangle of what happens to three sets of people, the Barcrofts, the Carruthers and the loner, Harley Drew, whose lives may only touch in 'the public retina' that encompasses all." Vauthier goes on to point out that the delta sign, a triangle that Foote has used as a printer's mark to mark the separation of sections, is "emblematic of the triadic pattern of the novel" (380–81). Set against the ternary pattern is "a different pattern of reversal that is dualistic," reflected in the series of reversals that the charac-

PLOT	POINT OF VIEW	TIME SPAN
1. THE BARCROFTS. Major B and his daughters; the shotgun death of his son.	Maj B	1873-1911
Florence and Amanda -- asthma; major supervises haircut.	Amanda	1911-1918
Florence's nightmare; bad heart; a suitor on the way.	Flo	1918-1928
2. JEFF AND AMY. Briartree: Jeff and Amy arrive; restoration begun.	Amy	Apr. 1928
Life in NC, early infatuation; marriage, auto smash-up.	Jeff	1903-1928
Why they came to Delta; Amy's boredom; someone coming.	Amy	Nov. 1928
3. CHARLEY DREW. Appearance, recent history; he first sees Amanda.	Drew	1895-1928
Courtship begun: "I love you," "Speak to papa."	Drew	Nov. 1928
Interview with major; Florence; plans for elopement.	Drew	"
4. CITIZEN BACHELOR. Drew waits with tickets; note; waiting for different deaths.	Drew	"
Alma & bride-bed gown; accepts teller's job at bank.	Drew	"
Settling in Bristol -- rising; joins country club.	Drew	1928-1930
5. ANOTHER COURTSHIP. The Carruthers inheritance; life on European tour.	Jeff	1930-1935
Home to Briartree; first contact with Charley Drew.	Amy	1935-1938
Drew lays siege to Amy; his hopes and his plans.	Drew	Feb. 1938
6. A RENOUNCEMENT. Amanda finds Flo dead; says so in note to Drew.	Amanda	Sep. 1938
Drew & Amy, backtrack; liaison; furthering plans.	Drew	Feb-Sep38
Receives Amanda's note; says he wont marry her.	Drew	Oct. 1938

7. DEATH OF A SOLDIER.		
Her reaction -- grief; Major B has first heart attack.	Amanda	Oct38-Sep39
Major encourages cotton clerk, but Amanda rejects him.	Amanda	Dec39-Apr40
Clerk suspicious, finds body in house on Lamar St.	Clerk	May 1940
8. SHOTS IN THE DARK.		
The plot; ignominy in Arkansas; resolves' on murder.	Drew	Oct38-Sep39
Amy's reaction; tiring of Drew; wants a change.	Amy	Sep39-May40
The blind man turns the tables; shoots Drew, smashes Amy.	Jeff	May 1940
9. MISS AMANDA.		
Major's funeral; Bristol talks of shooting -- ironical.	Bristol	"
Drew Memphis, JeffAmy Baltimore; the marriage photo.	Bristol	May40-Dec41
Amanda hotel, JeffAmy Santa Fe; Drew at ball, Colonel THG.	Amanda	Dec41--1945

ters experience and in the central metaphors of the text, especially in "the polarity of seer-seen" (392). Finally Vauthier observes that within the elaborate patterns of the novel "echoes play not a little part." "The repetitions and variations of verbal patterns," she concludes, "will catch the ear of even the unsophisticated reader, and will make him aware of some of the echoes that sound throughout the novel" (399). Without identifying the musical forms on which the structure of *Love in a Dry Season* is based, Vauthier has drawn attention to the rhythmic, auditory quality of the novel.

In 1964 the Dial Press issued, appropriately enough, three of Foote's books bound in one volume. *Three Novels* attests to Foote's contention to Percy that "all my novels are one novel anyway," and he arranged the three novels in a way that strengthens the ternary patterns in the single novels and adds another compositional dimension. *Follow Me Down* comes first, and *Love in a Dry Season* is third; between them is the 1954 collection *Jordan County: A Landscape in Narrative,* which is structurally a great deal more than simply a collection of stories arranged in counter-chronological order. As was pointed out above, the book includes much that Foote might have used in the original "Two Gates to the City." The table of contents is integral to Foote's three later novels, and here too it provides the first hint of the formal structure of the texts.

The indented titles in the table of contents are one-section, brief sketches. "Ride Out" and "Pillar of Fire" are made up of three sections, each section set apart by Foote's emblematic delta. In "Child by Fever" with three sections of three parts each, Foote again employs the delta sign to set off the sections. The form is balanced in *Jordan County,* and that balance is maintained by the novels on either side—the 271 pages of *Follow Me Down* that are bound before *Jordan County* in the 1964 edition and the 250 pages of *Love in a Dry Season* that follow it.[14] Foote may not have planned the second half of his "apprenticeship" with such an eye for form, but that is the way it evolved.

If Foote's work is an investigation, a search for answers, and if the artist invites the reader to extend his speculation, then that extension must take place for the reader much as it took place for Foote in combining his books into *Three Novels*. That is, the reader is not left to speculate on what may become of a character as James's readers speculate about what will happen to Isabel Archer or Lambert Strether. Foote's form is a closed form, the action is complete.

Vauthier found, "*Love in a Dry Season* requires, on the part of the reader, an active involvement in the structural aspects." The characters, she says "disappear behind the extensive network of correspondence and transformations that constitute the story" (399–400). What Vauthier has observed in *Love in a Dry Season* is true as well for *Follow Me Down* and much of *Jordan County*. The reader becomes involved with the characters, "they have great fictional presence," as Vauthier says, but they experience no epiphanies except perhaps for Beulah. They never seem to break through to some new understanding about themselves although, particularly in Amanda Barcroft's case, the means for doing so are plentiful because she reads Faulkner, Balzac, and Henry James—but all "without recognition."

Over and over she reads about herself but does not make the connection. For Foote the novel is a completed form, a completed event, of which the reader is an observer. The reader is not invited to grow with the character as James's readers might be invited to grow with Lambert or Isabel. Foote's carefully constructed form is closed, and the reader-observer is invited to feel the force of the totality of the form realized. The reader experiences not so much growth through the development of character as understanding through form. The emotional experience is more restrained while the intellectual experience is heightened. What the reader feels is the repetition of timeless form, an experience that lies outside the fictional world and is, instead, found between the reader and the text. Vauthier has pointed out that the events in *Love in a Dry Season* are the stock events of the Western novel and that, by mentioning what Amanda reads, Foote calls attention to the fact. The result is, she says, that we are drawn "to the design of the story" (379).

While the classical style is built on the repetition of form, the style of modern, popular music is not. This music, referred to frequently in Foote's tales of modern failure, represents the longing, the inarticulate need, that his characters feel for some truth by which they can understand themselves. While Hector's form fails because it is inflexible, the opposite is true for popular music. When Luther Eustis returns to Bristol after he has drowned Beulah, he enters a cafe where the first thing he hears from the juke box is *"Take me where that concrete grows."* A little later the machine plays a song about moving to the outskirts of town and another called "Civilization." The music is background for Eustis's restlessness, his relationship to civilization. He has been away from civilization and now he is back where the "concrete grows." Eustis is a microcosm for modern Bristol; its music represents a welter of conflicting notions of what is pleasurable and good, but the Proustian metaphor that would reveal "essence" is absent.

Jeff Carruthers listens to jazz. His collection of records is one of the finest anywhere, and it accompanies him on his travels. But jazz, like the songs Eustis hears, cannot provide for the more thorough and complete experience of art; it may have in it the "quality of being in touch with forces far beyond us," but the form is not developed to the extent that the "quality" is accessible to us. In *Love in a Dry Season* and *Follow Me Down*, popular music, blues, and jazz provide a backdrop for the action, representing the restless uncertainty of the age. Foote's revisions in "Ride Out" explain this view. At first, according to revisions Foote made in the early 1950s, composer Harry Van is influenced strongly by Duff Conway, a jazz trumpet player, but soon Van becomes a more mature artist. Jazz, the narrator of the story says, is "an inferior art by virtue of its limitations." Its appeal depends not on intricacy of form but in "great drive and marvelous technique and little else."[15] The blues and lyrics in jazz express frustration, longing for love, failure in the modern world; jazz is emotion cut loose from formal moorings in a deeper historical context. If Van is to be a true artist, that context must be given emphasis. Van's lesson is one that Foote has learned.

The Civil War: A Narrative

Hector's plan was too inflexible, too rigid; Duff Conway's jazz was too ahistorical, too improvisational. Both failures are found in *The Civil War*. The men who are successful as generals or simply as men are those who fit intuitively into the patterned flow of time; those who in some degree fulfill Proust's idea of artistry.

The form that "opened out" for Foote, and by which he was able to outline all three volumes in 1954, developed from the form that had given shape to his fiction. The history develops from and subsumes the earlier efforts. It is not surprising that the reviewers of the volumes as they appeared—Volume I, *Fort Sumter to Perryville*, in 1958; Volume II, *Fredericksburg to Meridian*, in 1963; and Volume III, *Red River to Appomattox*, in 1974—particularly the professional historians reviewing the first two volumes, were not particularly pleased with Foote's nonacademic, apparently nonscholarly approach.[16] Quite naturally his approach was consciously that of the narrative artist, but the work was solidly based on research, as he explained to Percy: "I have been engaged in the hardest, or at least the most tedious, occupation of my writing life," he wrote. "That doesn't mean I don't enjoy it; I do indeed. What I have to do is learn everything possible from all possible sources about a certain phase or campaign, then digest it so that it's clear in my own mind, then reproduce it even clearer than it has been to me until I actually began writing about it (29Nov56)." What Foote seems to explain is that, in the actual process of composition, the form develops, and out of the act of writing, the creation of the artifact touches upon the deepest resources of history and individual experience—the wellsprings of form. Foote goes on to explain parenthetically to Percy that "the right words will invariably do that ('reproduce it even clearer'), if they're arranged so as to bring out the essential meaning and drama." Then, characteristically, he adds, "Drama *is* meaning, just as character is action, provided it is clear."

In Volume III after Grant has driven deep into Virginia, after the bloodshed at Cold Harbor, Foote's narrator says that it was time "for taking stock." Grant had accepted, "as a condition of the tournament that there would be heavy casualties" (III, 299). Earlier, near the opening of Volume I, he had made a similar comment. The people, he said, had accepted Davis and Lincoln, the leaders, "as a condition of the tournament" (I, 164). These reminders, these echoes, from the earlier novels, point up the continuity in Foote's work. Writing history was no real departure from his vocation as a novelist. The form that had developed in the first two novels appeared again as a shaping force in the history, the "spark" that guided Bart in *Tournament* might well be what guides Lincoln or Lee, and the predictions that Judge Wiltner made to Bart seem very close to those that Sherman made for the South. Framing devices surrounded the central narrative in Foote's first two novels—*Tournament* and *Shiloh*—as well as in the story "Pillar of Fire," and the framework appears again in *The Civil War: A Narrative*. The history opens and closes with a narrow focus on Jefferson Davis, just as Asa had opened and closed *Tournament,* as Metcalf had done in *Shiloh,* and Lundy in "Pillar of Fire." Apparently Walker Percy raised questions about the ending. "I think if you go back youll see that it balances the antebellum biography that opens Vol. I, no more sympathetic and with the same narrow focused point of view," Foote explained and then commented further:

> There, though, it was offset by the antebellum biography of Lincoln, and originally I intended to do two things I dropped at the end—one, a contrapuntal treatment of L's funeral, the train winding north and west while Davis fled southward; the other, an account of the growth of L's postwar reputation, interwoven with Davis's postwar life at Beauvoir. But once I had written Lincoln's death scene in such detail, once he had drawn that last long breath, I found I couldnt come back to him; it would be wrong for him to be anything but *gone* once the doctor put those half-dollars on his eyes— except, that is, the two closing touches: when the thieves attempt to steal his body for ransom, then when I re-quote him on the war as "philosophy to learn wisdom from," a final touch of the Lincoln music Davis couldnt match or even catch. I may have done wrong to drop my early plan for coming

back to him, thereby offsetting the total concentration on Davis, but I dont
think so. He's gone, man, gone—"like a turkey through the cawn," as
Leadbelly says. Sometimes (and often they are the best of times) writing has
to be done by instinct, and this was one of them. You get these instinctive
reactions, and if you dont trust them youre not going with your talent.
(11Jul74)

Apparently the framework was to have been more elaborate than it is in
the final version, more "contrapuntal" and "balanced."

Parker Nowell's narrative in sonata form is more fundamental to the
composition of the history than the framework—the balanced three parts,
each with three parts, and each of these subdivided again into carefully
balanced sections. To emphasize the significance of form in *The Civil War*,
Foote has included a "Comprehensive Table of Contents" at the end of
each volume of the paperback Vintage edition. Volumes I and III are
almost identical in structure, but Volume III is longer by two hundred fifty
pages of text, excluding the back matter. In Volume I, *Fort Sumter to
Perryville,* the first chapter of Part I has three sections as does the last
chapter, Chapter 8, of the first volume; Chapters 2 through 7 have four
sections each. In Volume III the three chapters of Part I and the three
chapters of Part III each have four sections, and the middle chapters each
have five sections. A section has been added to each of the eight chapters
in Volume III, *From Red River to Appomattox.* The second volume has nine
chapters; the first and third volumes, eight chapters each. In the center of
Volume II, *Fredericksburg to Meridian,* the "extra" chapter, is the story of
Gettysburg. Just as Beulah's chapter was the "keystone of the arch" in
Follow Me Down, so Gettsyburg is the center in the history. The events
leading up to Gettysburg occupy 1,237 pages; the events after Gettysburg,
1,599 pages.

The outline or form is successful, however, only insofar as it derives
from the substance it contains. By pointing up the structure, Foote may
have made a segment of the past more useful to the reader, but the form
also contains such interpretation of history as he is able to give. In the
"Bibliographical Note" to Volume III, Foote states bluntly that "nowhere
along the line [had he] a 'thesis' to argue or maintain—partly no doubt
because [he] never saw one yet that could not be 'proved,' at least to the
satisfaction of the writer who advanced it" (1064). Thesis lies in the narrow
realm of logic and "proof," but what Foote seems to want to show us is

that history has form and rhythm and that we, as human beings, would be better off to recognize the fact, to feel the flow of time and its rhythms. Though Foote is not about to, the critic may find a theme or make a thesis out of the thrust of the narrative and the many "voices" that contribute to it. Foote believes, one can argue, that the trust of the many and sometimes unwilling participants whose voices weave in and out of the fabric of his text is often betrayed by the ambitious, the greedy, the rigid, or those who, out of simple ignorance, give themselves over to the sound of hollow rhetoric, the formless jazz of the time. He feels that ultimately a leader will emerge who, sometimes consciously but far more often unconsciously, is responsive to the forces in time that are more powerful than those of his own personality, forces that perhaps exert themselves through his personality because he feels what he seldom can explain. It is a leader who, like Foote the writer, is "going with [his] talent" by "instinct." He takes charge and points armies and even politicians along the road that history will take, giving in the process the tone of his leadership and maybe even his name to the event. The narrator of *The Civil War* is a participant in the text, not quite in the sense that the generals, troops, politicians, and presidents are, but as the artist who seeks out the essence of what they are doing and who points the reader's imagination in that direction. The narrator is an artist of history; he is not a philosopher or a historiographer, and except in the creation of the artifact, his carefully crafted narrative, his truth, is not empirical truth. He treats the known in an attempt to "get at" the unknown. Through its form the book brings the reader who participates in the text with an active imagination into proximity with the determinants of his own being and, at the same time, with the experience of others, of mankind. These concerns for the shape and rhythms of time do not, however, seem to imply that we are observers of a linear progress in time toward some utopia; that history involves progress does not seem to be his conviction. Rather the rhythms are those of the day that mankind divided rather arbitrarily into twenty-four equal segments of sixty minutes; and the rhythms are those of the year that falls into four seasons without help from anyone. Mankind has lived with these rhythms for a long time, some since he began to think of himself as mankind, others even longer. Thus Shelby Foote is a romantic, but not a romantic in the sense that Emerson or Thoreau were. "Universal being" and "oversoul" are simply too verbal; abstract as they are, the terms are too solid to be applied to Foote's conception of what is permanent in our experience of time.

The voice of the narrator of *The Civil War* is obviously not the distanced, academic voice of much historical writing; Foote's purpose is to tell a good story, first of all. In tone the narrator's voice resembles that of the voices in Foote's novels, the general narrator in *Love in a Dry Season* and "Child by Fever," and Parker Nowell and Stevenson in *Follow Me Down*, except that he does not have Nowell's cynicism or Stevenson's flippant sarcasm. This narrator has obvious respect for his subject, for many of those who participated in the events, and for the reader.

With respect to the events themselves, the fullness of the narrator's knowledge is apparent. As Foote explained to Percy, he tried to learn all there was to learn about a particular battle, person, or event, to read all that he could find, and then to write about it. The bibliographical notes appended to each of the three volumes make the extent of research clear, but it is the text itself that substantiates the impression of trustworthiness—the inclusion of resources of all kinds, diaries and letters, official reports, reports from periodicals, and the written histories. The narrator reports the events themselves and occasionally comments on how others have viewed them. For example, at Gettysburg, Union General Sickles had his troops occupy a salient in front of the Union lines, and around the salient there were over four thousand Union casualties. "There was to be a great deal of discussion," the narrator reports, "beginning tonight and continuing down the years, as to whether his occupation of the salient, half a mile and more in front of the main Union line, had been a colossal blunder or a tactically sound maneuver" (II, 507). A few pages later, reporting the plans that General Lee and General Meade were making for the third day of the battle, the narrator comments, "In this, the two reacted so literally in accordance with their native predilections—Lee's for daring, Meade's for caution—that afterwards, when their separate decisions were examined down the tunnel of the years—which provides a diminished clarity not unlike that afforded by a reversed telescope—both would be condemned for having been extreme in these two different respects" (II, 520–21). The narrator of *The Civil War* gives every impression of having studied his subject well. He is aware of the judgments that historians have made, judgments that are subsumed into his text as a part of the flow of history rather than as a contribution to some scientifically objective attempt to arrive at an evaluation of what occurred.

The text benefits, moreover, from a much wider reading than simply the records and evaluations of the war. The cultural context into which the narrator sets his drama includes considerably more. Foote has said that the two major influences on *The Civil War* were Proust's *Remembrance of Things Past* and the Lattimore translation of the *Iliad*,[17] but the text also is full of references and allusions to the Bible and to English and American writing—Shakespeare, Milton, Browning, Whitman, Swift, Hemingway, Scott, Byron, Mark Twain, Petroleum V. Nasby, and Bill Arp among others. The narrator also appreciates effective writing in the comments of those less distinguished in literary annals than Milton or Browning. Samuel R. Curtis, a civil engineer who commanded the Union troops at the Battle of Pea Ridge in March 1862, wrote to his wife after the battle: "The vulture and the wolf have now communion, and the dead, friends and foes, sleep in the same lonely grave." The narrator, with obvious appreciation of the quality of Curtis's prose, commented: "So he wrote, this hightly practical and methodical engineer" (I, 293). Deckerd, the provost marshall of Buell's staff, could also write to the narrator's apparent approval: "The whole army is concentrated here, or near here; but nobody knows anything, except that the water is bad, whiskey scarce, dust abundant, and the air loaded with the scent and melody of a thousand mules" (I, 566).

For all its obvious learning, the narrator's tone places him with the men whose language he often admires. He is very much in control of the narrative, but he tells his story with a dignified informality. Grant, for example, had a "nine-division bear hug on Pemberton's beleaguered garrison" at Vicksburg (II, 407). Earlier, in describing Jefferson Davis's expectations of European intervention, Foote's narrator remarks that Davis expected the Confederacy to have at its service "the use of armies that had blasted Napoleon himself clean off the pages of military history" (I, 113). A more formal, academic historian probably would not have written "clean off the pages."

If the studied elimination of any pretentiousness in the narrator's tone gives the story a certain informality, it simultaneously makes possible an immediacy that would not be possible from a more formal pose. The narrator from time to time seems to place himself among the troops whose experiences he seems to share. In July 1864 Forrest was wounded, "his third serious gunshot wound of the war," and rumor had it, particularly among the Yankees who found rumors of Forrest's troubles comforting, that he had lockjaw and had given command over to Chalmers. The narrator, to dispel the rumors, invites us to have a look at Forrest. "It was true that Chalmers was in nominal command, but not that Forrest was dead, either of lockjaw or of any other ailment, although a look at him was enough to show how the rumor got started" (III, 513). To aid the reader's imagination, the narrator adds the comments of "one witness" who described Forrest as "sick-looking, thin as a rail, cheekbones that stuck out like they were trying to come through the skin, skin so yellow it looked greenish" (III, 513). Had we been there we would have seen exactly what "one witness" saw. Much earlier, in the first volume, the narrator tells us, "There was no middle ground for confidence where Stonewall [Jackson] was concerned: you either trusted him blindly, or you judged him absolutely mad" (I, 438).

A sense of immediacy develops also as the narrator often concentrates more generally on the experiences of the troops, elaborating on what they must have felt, what any soldiers in such circumstances would have felt, and what they saw—Proust's communication of "sensation." Such is the case with the soldiers in Meade's command on their way to the April 1863 disaster at Chancellorsville.

> Coming down to the ford at sunset the advance guard plunged across the cold, swift-running Rapidan, chased off the startled pickets on the opposite bank, and set to work building fires to light the way for the rest of the corps approaching the crossing in the dusk. Regiment by regiment the three road-worn divisions entered the foam-flecked, scrotum-tightening water and emerged to toil up the steep south bank, which became increasingly slippery as the slope was churned to gumbo by the passage of nearly 16,000 soldiers, all dripping wet from the armpits down. Once across, they gathered about the fires for warmth, some in good spirits, some in bad, each arriving cluster somewhat muddier than the one before, but all about equally wet and cold. By midnight the last man was over. Low in the east, the late-risen moon, burgeoning toward the full, had the bruised-orange color of old gold, and while all around them the whippoorwills sang plaintively in the moon-drenched woods, the men lay rolled in their blankets, feet to the fire, catching snatches of sleep while awaiting the word to fall back into column. Meade had them on the go again by sunup of the last day of April, still marching southeast, but now through an eerie and seemingly God-forsaken region; the Wilderness, it was called, and they could see why. Mostly a tangle of second-growth scrub oak and pine, choked with vines and brambles that would tear the clothes from a man's back within minutes of the time he left the road, it was interrupted briefly at scattered points by

occasional small clearings whose abandoned cabins and sag-roofed barns
gave proof, if such was needed, that no amount of hard work could scratch a
living from this jungle. [II, 269]

The "swift-running Rapidan," the "foam-flecked, scrotum-tightening
water" is cold. The rising moon "had the bruised-orange color of old gold"
and the "whippoorwills sang plaintively." These details, gleaned from what
those sixteen thousand wet and cold troops said and wrote about their
experience, and from the narrator's own imaginative re-creation, bring the
reader into proximity with the men themselves. Such descriptive details
abound in The Civil War. At Ball's Bluff in 1861, the Mississippi troops
who were firing at the recklessly exposed Yankees "were reminded of
turkey-shoots down home," and when the Confederates advanced, "the
rebel yell quavered above the crash of snapping brush and trampled sap-
lings" (I, 107). At Elkhorn Tavern in 1862, "The sun rose red, then shone
wanly through the haze, like tarnished brass" (I, 289). When the men in
Pickett's division stepped from the shade into the sun, before their charge
at Gettysburg, the sunlight "was not only dazzling to their eyes but also
added to their feeling of elation and release" (II, 552–53). The cumulative
effect of such detailed observation is that the narrator is, in his way, there
among the troops and at the conferences of the generals; he takes the
reader by the arm, steps aside, and talks about what is happening.

This is a narrator who stirs the reader's imagination to see, feel, and
hear—sometimes even to smell and taste—what the men who fought the
war sensed; but in the larger view, he responds to their experience, particularly to the bloody horror of the fighting. Wilson's Creek, fought in
Arkansas in August 1861, was one such bloody affair: "Far from resembling panoplied war," the narrator says, "it was more like reciprocal
murder" (I, 94). The "carnage" at Fredericksburg was "staggering" for the
Federal army—"12,653 casualties." Burnside, the Union general at Fredericksburg, had had nearly 200,000 men in his command in early December
1862 "before the butchering began," the narrator recalls. After the first day
of battle at Murfreesboro on 31 December 1862, "Except for the surgeons
and the men they worked on, blue and gray, where screams broke through
the singing of the bone saw, both sides were bedded down . . . amid the
wreckage and the corpses, preparing to sleep out as best they could the last
night of the year" (II, 95). They expected the battle to resume with fury the
following day, but "New Year's Day saw nothing like the carnival of death

that had been staged on New Year's Eve" (II, 96). Fighting around Port Hudson produced a "grisly harvest" (II, 399); the "butcher's bill for Gettysburg, blue and gray together, exceeded 50,000 men" (II, 578).

Many battles of the war were grim affairs in the eyes of Foote's narrator, but Spotsylvania, fought in May 1864, earned his deepest sense of loss. At a place in the line called "The Bloody Angle," "slaughter became an end in itself," and the men who fought there and survived never forgot it.

> The Bloody Angle. The term had been used before, in other battles elsewhere in the war, but there was no doubt forever after, at least on the part of those who fought there, that here was where the appellation best applied. It soon became apparent to both sides that what they were involved in now was not only fiercer than what had gone before, today, but was in fact more horrendous than what had gone before, ever. This was grimmer than the Wilderness—a way of saying that it was worse than anything at all—not so much in bloodshed, although blood was shed in plenty, as in concentrated terror. These were the red hours of the conflict, hours no man who survived them would forget, even in his sleep, forever after. Fighting thus at arm's length across that parapet, they were caught up in a waking nightmare, although they were mercifully spared the knowledge, at the outset, that it was to last for another sixteen unrelenting hours. [III, 221]

Men under these conditions fought like "blank-faced automatons, as if what they were involved in had driven them beyond madness into imbecility; they fought by the numbers, unrecognizant of comrade in the ultimate loneliness of a horror as profoundly isolating in its effect as bone pain, nausea, or prolonged orgasm, their vacant eyes unlighted by anger or even dulled by fear" (III, 222). The sense of immediacy here brings with it the narrator's sincere concern for the men, often treated by others as mere numbers in some general's division or corps, who were caught up in the bloody drama.

There were others who gave their names to obscure bits of horror. T. B. Smith, at twenty-six the Confederate "army's youngest brigadier," was captured by the Federals near Nashville in December 1864. "While being conducted unarmed to the Union rear he was slashed three times across the head with a saber by the colonel of the Ohio regiment that had captured him, splitting his skull and exposing so much of his mangled brain that the surgeon who examined his wounds pronounced them fatal," but Smith survived to live out his last years in the Tennessee Hospital for the Insane. "This was another face of war," the narrator comments, "by no means unfamiliar on either side, but one unseen when the talk was all of glory" (III, 704).

Concern for the political and economic conditions that affected the lives of the troops appears in the narrative voice as well. There is considerable scorn, for example, for the greed that was driving financial capitalism in the North. In 1970 Foote declared to Percy that "the worst cause won" the Civil War, and the primary reason that the cause was bad was its "Dollar diplomacy" (5Aug70). While recognizing that there was much "solid and even permanent" growth in the North during the war, Foote nevertheless picks up a phrase from the New York *World* and dubs these years the "Age of Shoddy." The manufacturers, lords of industry, who supplied goods to the armies on government contract were growing wealthy, and the politicians and much of the public seemed unconcerned by "the purveyors of tainted beef and weevily grain, the sellers of cardboard haversacks and leaky tents."

> No one was really discomforted by all this—so far, at least, as they could see—except the soldiers, the Union volunteers whose sufferings under bungling leaders in battles such as Fredericksburg and Chickasaw Bluffs were of a nature that made their flop-soled shoes and tattered garments seem relatively unimportant, and the Confederate jackals who stripped the blue-clad corpses after the inevitable retreat. If the generals were un-ashamed, were hailed in fact as heroes after such fiascos, why should anyone else have pangs of conscience? The contractors asked that, meanwhile raking in profits that were as long as they were quick. The only drawback was the money itself, which was in some ways no more real than the sleazy cloth or the imitation leather, being itself the shadow of what had formerly been substance. With prosperity in full swing and gold rising steadily, paper money declined from day to day, sometimes taking sickening drops as it passed from hand to hand. All it seemed good for was spending, and they spent it. Spending, they rose swiftly in the social scale, creating in the process a society which drew upon itself the word that formerly had been used to describe the goods they bartered—"shoddy"—and upon their heads the scorn of those who had made their money earlier and resented the fact that it was being debased. [II, 147–48]

There was nothing "shoddy" about the fine clothes the newly rich afforded themselves, "except," the narrator suggests "possibly what they enclosed." There was protest—workers who were not receiving their share of the new wealth in wages, an occasional journalist like the one who called this the "Age of Shoddy," and the old wealthy who watched the value of their money decline. "In any case, with profits and progress involved, who could oppose the trend except a comparative handful of men and women, maimed or widowed or otherwise made squeamish, if not downright unpatriotic, by hard luck or oversubscription to Christian ethics?" (II, 150). Later in the war, when he describes how the Confederate army under J. E. Johnston saw hope of turning to the offensive against Sherman on his March to Atlanta, the narrator comments that, among the Confederates, "hope soared, anticipating a still greater drop in the pocketbook barometer that best measured northern greed and fears" (III, 341). The "pocketbook barometer" was the price of gold that had plummeted in New York at news of Confederate successes in Virginia and Louisiana.

An "oversubscription to Christian ethics" and a "pocketbook barometer," phrases that give the narrative voice a pointed humor similar to that found in Mark Twain's later writing, occur regularly during the telling of the tale. The narrator's sense of the absurd and his effort to seek out a contrast for the sake of humor emerge through his profound sympathy for those who suffered the horrors of war and who found no profit in it.[18] Frequently the humor in the narrator's voice is less pointed; he shares with the southerners in Richmond "a native inclination toward light-heartedness" (II, 162), no matter how grim surroundings and events may be, but it can be "light-heartedness" with a little bit of a sting in it, much like Mark Twain's early humor.

Leonidas Polk, the Episcopal Bishop of Louisiana, in the eyes of the narrator of *The Civil War*, becomes a "transfer from the Army of the Lord" when he joins the southern army (I, 87). The bishop-general played an important role in the Confederate army until he was killed by a cannon ball at Pine Mountain near Marietta, Georgia, in June 1864. On one occasion, at Perryville in 1862, Polk had the pleasure of capturing a Federal brigade almost single-handedly. "For all his churchly faith in miracles," the narrator remarks, "he could scarcely believe his ears" (I, 736).

The humor lies in the narrator's comment, the unexpected, off-hand juxtaposition. George McClellan, the Union commander in Virginia during the early months of the war, was not particularly successful in dealing with politicians. "Lincoln the politician understood [politics] perfectly," but McClellan had his problems "partly," the narrator asserts, "because he operated under the disadvantage of considering himself a gentleman" (I, 247). Or again, in the Valley of the Shenadoah, Thomas "Stonewall"

Jackson could ignore the Union army under Frémont's command. "He could turn his back on Frémont and walk off, as if dismissing him absolutely from his mind," Foote's narrator reports, and then he adds, "In bullfight terms—or, for that matter, in veterinary jargon—he had 'fixed' him" (I, 426). Olivia Langdon Clemens might have expunged such a remark from a Mark Twain manuscript, but Foote's narrator's comment that Joe Johnston's army in Virginia "had perhaps the greatest number of high-strung troop commanders, per square yard, of any army ever assembled" she might have approved.

The narrator obviously capitalizes on the humor inherent in the events themselves. One such involved Colonel Abel D. Streight, the "New York-born commander of a regiment of Hoosier infantry," who in April 1863 proposed to General Rosecrans that he be allowed to lead a raid into Alabama. About two thousand men, according to Streight's plan, would be mounted on mules; there was a shortage of horses and, besides, Streight believed that mules "were not only more sure-footed, they were also more intelligent." On his march Streight commandeered five hundred mules to add to the nine hundred sick or unbroken mules that Rosecran's quartermaster had provided. At Eastport, Mississippi, Streight learned that about four hundred of his mules "had escaped from their crudely-built corrals and now were scattered about the countryside, disrupting the night and mocking his woes with brays that had the sound of fiendish laughter." The narrator takes some pleasure in assuring us the four hundred were "naturally the most intelligent of the lot" (II, 179–80).

At Vicksburg the Union engineers dug under the Confederate fortifications and exploded mines. In late June the explosion of one of these catapulted a Negro slave named Abraham from the Confederate to the Union lines. "He landed more or less unhurt, though terribly frightened," we are told. "An Iowa outfit claimed him, put him in a tent, and got rich charging five cents a look. Asked how high he had been blown, Abraham always gave the same answer, coached perhaps by some would-be Iowa Barnum. 'Dunno, massa,' he would say, 'but tink bout tree mile" (II, 423). From Vicksburg, Foote moves the narrative to the Gettysburg campaign where, just before crossing the Potomac, Lee wrote to Davis that he had hopes that "all things will end well for us in Vicksburg." The narrator goes on to remark that Lee was "unaware that this was the day Grant exploded the mine that transferred the slave Abraham's allegiance to the Union" (II, 442). As with the mules, the quiet and dignified informality of the prose in which Foote often describes events of grave concern gives way upon occasion to events that fall considerably below the formality and dignity of the tone with which they are presented.

Foote's narrator occasionally quips about the broader issues of his topic, throwing the events into humorous juxtaposition. On the day Lincoln signed the bill making West Virginia a "full-fledged state," 31 December 1862, the states of the Confederacy, because of their rebellion, were naturally not represented. They "had no representation in Congress," he says, "pending the settlement of their claim to have abolished their old ties" (II, 110). A few pages later, describing the Vicksburg campaign, the narrator declares that the onslaughts of riverboat men before the war, who found Vicksburg convenient "for letting off what they called 'a load of steam,'" were quite "mild" in comparison "to what was visited upon them by the blue-clad host sent against them by what had lately been their government" (II, 411).

The closing months of the war, which are the subject of the third volume, were grim months indeed for the troops doing the fighting during the Forty Days in the trenches at Petersburg and Richmond, at Franklin, and in front of Nashville. Even so, the narrator can often find occasion for an off-hand comment. Lee, for example, sick and unable to leave his cot was, we are informed, "betrayed by his entrails" (III, 273); Sigel's retreat to his starting point in western Virginia was "one more trifling readjustment" (III, 250). At Brice's Crossroads, Forrest predicted that the day would "be hot as hell," and Rucker "was to discover" that Forrest had been absolutely right in all of his predictions except, perhaps, for "the temperature estimate, which was open to question in the absence of any thermometer readings from hell" (III, 367).

The occasional comment that crops up in this narrator's text, even among descriptions of the most bloody affairs, derives not at all from an attempt to patronize or to downplay the gravity of the events themselves. Rather, they seem to grow from the general spirit of the troops themselves, from the wit and humor of the American people who play out their history on his pages. As James Cox has observed, *The Civil War* is full of "voices,"[19] the words of those whose names have not often found their way into the histories. Reports from contemporary newspapers and magazines; anecdotes Foote gathered from letters, diaries, and general accounts of the war; and even the lyrics of the songs they sang—these things representing not the plans of the generals or the contrivings of the politicians but, rather, the spirit and humor of the common citizen and soldier—are what, to borrow James Cox's term, make this not a "lively" but a "living" account of the war. The people themselves, not just their leaders, have a significant part to play.

The press contributed much to the popular contemporary account. For example, in the spring of 1862 Stonewall Jackson enjoyed considerable success in the Shenandoah Valley, and at one point, resting near Port Republic just before their victory there, Jackson's men had time to read the newspapers. "Elated by their victories, the editors had broken out their blackest type," Foote's narrator says. "The Charleston *Mercury* called Stonewall 'a true general' and predicted that he would soon be 'leading his unconquerable battalions through Maryland and Pennsylvania.'" Other papers, particularly the Richmond *Whig*, joined in the praise that the troops, "of course, enjoyed." Jackson, however, soon gave up such reading. "Members of his staff observed that from this time on he gave up reading the papers—perhaps for the same reason he had given up drinking whiskey: 'Why, sir, because I like the taste of [it], and when I discovered that to be the case I made up my mind to do without [it] altogether'" (I, 458). These newspapers did not create Stonewall the hero, but they did express what the soldiers and the people felt and celebrated the concensus they helped create.

The same was true for many others, heroes and those who failed, and it was true for Ulysses Grant, especially after Donelson, where he had become "Unconditional Surrender Grant."

People had his message to Buckner by heart, and they read avidly of his life and looks in the papers: the features stern "as if carved from mahogany," the clear blue eyes (or gray, some said) and aquiline nose, the strong jaw "squarely set, but not sensual." One reporter saw three expressions in his face: "deep thought, extreme determination, and great simplicity and calmness." Another saw significance in the way he wore his high-crowned hat: "He neither puts it on behind his ears, nor draws it over his eyes; much less does he cock it on one side, but sets it straight and very hard on his head." People enjoyed reading of that, and also of the way he "would gaze at anyone who approached him with an inquiring air, followed by a glance of recollection and a grave nod of recognition." On horseback, they read, "he sits firmly in the saddle and looks straight ahead, as if only intent on getting to some particular point." The words "square" and "straight" and "firm" were the ones that appeared most often, and people liked them. Best of all, perhaps they enjoyed hearing that Grant was "the concentration of all that is American. He talks bad grammar, but talks it naturally, as much as to say, 'I was so brought up, and if I try fine phrases I shall only appear silly.'" [I, 214]

The attention he received brought about changes that "the veterans saw when he came up to Pittsburg [Landing] to inspect them" before the near disaster at Shiloh. "He was Unconditional S. Grant now, and his picture was on the cover of *Harper's Weekly*" (I, 322).

The newspapers and magazines could lead the cheering or fix the blame, picking and shaping such slogans as suited their purposes. Fighting in Virginia on his way to Richmond, Grant had written in a report that he "purpose[d] to fight it out on this line if it takes all summer." Someone in the press cut it to "I propose to fight it out," and the phrase caught the attention of the public (III, 212), ringing out across the continent in headlines and speeches.

The voices of the troops themselves weigh more heavily, however, than the voices of editors and reporters in *The Civil War*—the stories they tell, the songs they sing, and especially their humor. Anecdotes and comments of the soldiers fill all three volumes. Although politicians elaborated on the many causes of the conflict, elaborate rhetoric meant little to the soldier. The simple, direct explanation was best, and "no soldier in either army gave a better answer . . . than a ragged Virginia private, pounced on by Northerners in a retreat." "'What are you fighting for anyhow?' his captors asked, looking at him. They were genuinely puzzled, for he obviously owned no slaves and seemingly could have little interest in States Rights or even Independence. 'I'm fighting because you're down here,' he said" (I, 65).

The troops, more frequently than the newspapermen and the politicians—and certainly more than either Davis or Lincoln—admired the generals who led them, even those who seemed inept to the general public. There was no more fiery, romantic bungler than Beauregard, and yet, on the retreat from Shiloh, one soldier wrote home: "It is strange Pa how we love that little black Frenchman" (I, 348). Almost everyone, however, admired Jackson. A northern reporter who was caught in the fall of Harpers Ferry declared, upon his first sight of Jackson and his tattered army, that he "in general appearance was in no respect to be distinguished from the mongrel, bare-footed crew who follow his fortunes." This reporter added that he "had heard much of the decayed appearance of the rebel soldiers. . . . Ireland in her worst straights could present no parallel, and yet they glory in the shame." Having presented the newsman's view, Foote then turns to the captured Union troops: "The captive Federals (except perhaps the Irish among them) could scarcely argue with this, but they drew a different conclusion. 'Boys, he isn't much for looks,' one declared, inspecting Jackson, 'but if we'd had him we wouldn't have been caught in this trap'" (I, 680).

The troops, as all troops everywhere in any war, spent much time speculating on the purposes of those who led them, and Foote found an abundance of such speculation among the Federals at Fredericksburg. The Confederates had abandoned the town on the banks of the Rappahannock River and fortified the heights overlooking the river. The northerners, occupying the town, had a "field day" pillaging it. "Gradually, though, the excitement paled and the looters began to speculate as to why the rebs had made no attempt to challenge the crossing today, not even with their artillery." The troops put forward a number of possibilities. "Some guessed it was because they had no ammunition to spare, others that were afraid of retaliation by 'our siege guns.' One man had a psychological theory: 'General Lee thinks he will have a big thing on us about the bombardment of this town. He proposes to rouse the indignation of the civilized world, as they call it. You'll see he won't throw a shell into it. He is playing for the sympathies of Europe.' Still another, a veteran private, had a different idea. 'Shit,' he said, 'They *want* us to get in. Getting out won't be quite so smart and easy. You'll see'" (II, 30).

One of Foote's favorite stories, one he has referred to in interviews, is the story of a slave who was attending his North Carolina master on Lee's march into Pennsylvania in the summer of 1863. "This is a beautiful country," the man told an inquiring Pennsylvania lady, "but it doesn't come up to home in my eyes" (II, 444).

Troops going into battle naturally are fearful, but among the Confederate troops before the last stages at Gettysburg, this fear seemed to be heightened. Foote includes the story of June Kimble as representative of the reactions of the men chosen to fill the ranks for Pickett's charge on the center of the Union line.

The men themselves, though few of them had the chance to examine the terrain over which they would be advancing, knew only too well what lay before them; Lee and Longstreet had directed that they be told, and they had been, in considerable detail. "No disguises were used," one wrote afterwards, "nor was there any underrating of the difficult work at hand." They were told of the opportunities, as well as of the dangers, and it was stressed that the breaking of the Federal line might mean the end of the war. However, there were conflicting reports of their reaction. One declared that the men of Garnett's brigade "were in spendid spirits and confident of sweeping everything before them," while another recalled that when Mayo's troops, who were also Virginians, were informed of their share in the coming attack, "from being unusually merry and hilarious they on a sudden had become as still and thoughtful as Quakers at a love feast." Some managed to steal a look at the ground ahead, and like their officers they were sobered by what they saw. One such, a Tennessee sargeant from Fry's brigade, walked forward to the edge of the woods, looked across the wide open valley at the bluecoats standing toylike in the distance on their ridge, and was so startled by the realization of what was about to be required of him that he spoke aloud, asking himself the question: "June Kimble, are you going to do your duty?" The answer, too, was audible. "I'll do it, so help me God," he told himself. He felt better then. The dread passed from him, he said later. When he returned to his company, friends asked him how it looked out there, and Kimble replied: "Boys, if we have to go it will be hot for us, and we will have to do our best." [II, 537–38]

Posturing, the making of grand gesture, and gaudy rhetoric might do for leaders in public places, but the men themselves were far more skeptical. They were, after all, the men who had "paid in blood for the blasting of a number of overblown reputations," and when Grant was given a third star and made a lieutenant general, they had their questions about his "military worth."

"Who's this Grant that's made a lieutenant general?"
"He's the hero of Vicksburg."
"Well, Vicksburg wasn't much of a fight. The rebs were out of rations and they had to surrender or starve. They had nothing but dead mules and dogs to eat, as I understand."
About the best thing they could say for him was that he was unlikely to be any worse than John Pope, who had also brought a western reputation east, only to lose it at Bull Run. "He cannot be weaker or more inefficient," a jaundiced New York veteran declared, "than the generals who have wasted the lives of our comrades during the past three years." [III, 11]

The generals planned the troop movements and sometimes planned the battles, but the wisdom of the troops was far more likely to be reliable. " 'Say, Johnny,' one of Logan's soldiers called across the breastworks, into the outer darkness. 'How many of you are there left?' " Logan was on his way with Sherman to Atlanta. " 'Oh about enough for another killing,' some butternut replied" (III, 490). There were a few left for "another killing" at that point in the career of the Confederate western army, but some months later, after Hood's defeat at Nashville, there was not even that. " 'Ain't we in a hell of a fix?' one ragged Tennessean groaned. . . . 'Aint we in a hell of a fix: a one-eyed President, a one-legged general, and a one-horse Confederacy?' " (III, 709).

Whenever the troops marched they were likely to sing—*"Hail Columbia, happy land!/ If I don't burn you, I'll be damned"* was what Sherman's soldiers sang after burning a good bit in Georgia (III, 790). Early in the war, the songs had represented the humor, and more often the sentiment, the men felt. "They were sentimental, and their favorite songs were sad ones that answered some deep-seated need: 'The Dew is on the Blossom,' 'Lorena,' 'Aura Lea,' 'The Girl I Left Behind Me,' and the tender 'Home, Sweet Home.' Yet they kept a biting sense of the riduculous, which they directed against anything pompous" (I, 63). As the war drew out and the casualty lists grew longer, the "deep-seated need" continued to find its expression in song. The military units had bands, and the night before battle at Murfreesboro, the bands in Rosecrans's and in Bragg's armies began playing. Men in one army could hear the bands of the other, and soon the men in both armies were singing with the bands. "Finally, though, one group of musicians began to play the familiar 'Home Sweet Home,' and one by one the others took it up, until at last all the bands of both armies were playing the song. Soldiers on both sides of the battle line began to sing the words, swelling the chorus east and west, North and South. As it died away on the final line—'There's no-o place like home'— the words caught in the throats of men, who, blue-coat and butternut alike, would be killing each other tomorrow in what already gave promise of being one of the bloodiest battles in that fratricidal war" (II, 86–87).

The sentiment of the songs was matched, on the other hand, by the humor of the anecdotes the soldiers told and the comments they made. The narrator of *The Civil War* finds the humorous comment when he can, and his talents along that line correspond very clearly with the interests and talents of the common soldier. The most notable in this, however, was the commander-in-chief of the Union forces; Lincoln loved a good story and he excelled at telling them. A group of politicians came to Lincoln to complain about Grant's plan for handling the Confederates that he had captured with the fall of Vicksburg, and Lincoln simply told the group about Sykes's dog.

> "I thought the best way to get rid of them was to tell the story of Sykes's dog. Have you ever heard about Sykes's yellow dog? Well, I must tell you about him. Sykes had a yellow dog he set great store by—" And he went on to explain that this affection was not shared by a group of boys who disliked the beast intensely and spent much of their time "meditating how they could get the best of him." At last they hit upon the notion of wrapping an explosive cartridge in a piece of meat, attaching a long fuze to it, and whistling for the dog. When he came out and bolted the meat, cartridge and all, they touched off the fuze, with spectacular results. Sykes came running out of the house to investigate the explosion. "What's up? Anything busted?" he cried. And then he saw the dog, or what was left of him. He picked up the biggest piece he could find, "a portion of the back with part of the tail still hanging to it," and said mournfully: "Well, I guess he'll never be much account again—as a dog." Lincoln paused, then made his point. "I guess Pemberton's forces will never be much account again as an army." [II, 625]

Sometime later, after Gettysburg, Lincoln had hoped that Meade would pursue Lee and destroy the Army of Northern Virginia before that army could recross the Potomac. When Meade failed, Lincoln, maintaining his control, told the general of the image that came to mind: "I'll be hanged if I could think of anything else than an old woman trying to shoo her geese across a creek" (II, 799).

Lincoln's humor is that of the people, humor that could appear sometimes even under grave circumstances. At Chickamauga, when the battle had turned against the Confederates, a colonel ordered a soldier to pick up the flag that had just fallen. " 'By the holy St. Patrick, Colonel,' a Tennessee private replied when told to pick up the flag that had fluttered down when the color-bearer fell, 'there's so much good shooting around here I haven't a minute's time to waste fooling with that thing'" (II, 718). The flag would naturally have made the man a conspicuous target. On the Richmond-Petersburg line, conditions for the Confederates were dire. " 'General, I'm hongry,' some would reply when Lee rode out and asked them how they were, but through this grim time, a veteran would say, 'I thanked God I had a backbone for my stomach to lean up against'" (III, 629).

The reports of the individual voices, the media that voiced the public view, and the songs are not simply color added to give *The Civil War* incidental appeal; rather, these are the substance of history. This is a history greater than any one man's capacity to affect through the force of his own will unless that will is coupled with those forces that transcend it. Lincoln and Davis offer the most obvious contrasts, and they are the characters who provide the framework. Foote's "counterpoint" is that be-tween Lincoln, a figure intuitively in tune with time's rhythms and largely unconscious of the harmonies that rise from events and the men who play out those events, and Davis, a man of more rigid adherence to less per-vasive and less successful forms. Lincoln's humor is indicative of his identification with the people; Davis had none of this in his character. Lincoln was flexible; he could change with the flow of time. Davis could not.

Foote wrote Percy on 11 December 1973 that he had "killed" Lincoln and that he would miss Lincoln a great deal in the last "seventy-odd" pages of the history. These pages, he said, would be "like *Hamlet* with Hamlet left out." Foote went on to comment on his admiration for Lincoln: "Christ, what a man. It's been a great thing getting to know him as he was, rather than as he has come to be—a sort of TV image of himself, with a ghost alongside." Lincoln, unlike Florence Barcroft in *Love in a Dry Season* or Hector Sturgis in "Child by Fever," was the successful artist. Even when the clerk read Lincoln's December 1862 message to Congress, the tone, rhythm, and melody of his prose prevailed; "through the droning voice of the clerk," the narrator explains, "the Lincoln music sounded in what would someday be known as its full glory" (I, 810). Lincoln is the Parker Nowell of *Follow Me Down,* the man who can shape his prose to the rhythms that Mozart and Aeschylus had heard, except that Lincoln is more than the limited and disillusioned Nowell. Lincoln fulfilled the promise that Nowell abandoned. The Union victory is thus the victory of the artist over lesser men.

In 1862, though, most people did not regard Lincoln's art highly, in fact, most would deny that he had any art. It was only later, and Foote was surely aware of the parallels to Poe and Faulkner, that "critics across the Atlantic, unembarrassed by proximity, called attention to the fact" (I, 804).

Most of Lincoln's "genteel" fellow citizens "had scarcely begun to suspect" that "there was such a thing as the American language, available for literary purposes" (I, 804). They were like Caliban in *The Tempest:* "Lincoln's jogtrot prose, compacted of words and phrases with the bark on, had no music their ears were attuned to; it crept by them" (I, 804).

Lincoln, however, did not take his gifts for granted; he worked hard at his writing, and "he worked with the dedication of the true artist, who, whatever his sense of superiority in other relationships, preserves his humility in this one." At least one visitor sensed more of Lincoln's artistry than others had done. This man found a "'two-fold' Lincoln"—one "slightly humorous but thoroughly practical and sagacious"; the other "the President and statesman . . . seen in those abstract and serious eyes, which seemed withdrawn to an inner sanctuary of thought, sitting in judgment on the scene and feeling its far reach into the future" (I, 804). Foote points out that for Lincoln that "inner sanctuary" was the writer's workshop; it was through his command of language that "he reached out to the future." That, says Foote, is the most essential "clew" to Lincoln's commanding artistry. The first occasion upon which Lincoln read a speech from manuscript, obviously the first time that he entered his "workshop," was when he accepted the nomination of the Illinois Republican Convention. "It was at this point" the narrator says, "that Lincoln's political destiny and the destiny of the nation became one" (I, 30). It was through Lincoln's artistry that the rhythms of prose and the rhythms of history itself were tied together and as finely crafted as a Beethoven string quartet.

Jefferson Davis, Lincoln's full-time companion in the first half of Foote's framing device, could "charm" listeners with "the music of his oratory" (I, 41); his "voice was low, with the warmth of the Deep South in it" (I, 4), but he was no match for Lincoln, whose music could do far more than charm those assembled to hear him. "Davis," Foote points out at the conclusion of the first volume, "in time, like other men before and since, found what it meant to become involved with an adversary whose various talents included those of a craftsman in the use of words" (I, 806). This is a point to which Foote returned at the conclusion of the history. *The Civil War* ends with two quotations—one from Davis, one from Lincoln—and Davis, as Foote points out, comes out second best. Davis's last words in the history, words recorded by a reporter shortly before his death, were: "Tell the world that I only loved America" (III, 1060). Foote's selection from Lincoln's prose came from his remarks at the celebration of his election to a second term. "What has occurred in this case must ever recur in similar cases. Human nature will not change. In any future great national trial, compared with the men of this, we shall have as weak and as strong, as silly and as wise, as bad and as good. Let us therefore study the incidents of this, as philosophy to learn wisdom from, and none of them as wrongs to be revenged" (III, 1060). Foote comments that "Davis could never match that music" and that all that Lincoln "had said or written would be cherished as an imperishable legacy to the nation" (III, 1060).

There were many differences between Davis, the politician and states-man, and Lincoln, the politician, statesman, and artist, but the most notable to Foote's perspective was the flexibility of Lincoln's response to whatever influences and forces presented themselves and Davis's relative inflexibility. Such a contrast had, in fact, been thematic in Foote's writing from the beginning. In *Tournament*, Judge Wiltner, predicting Hugh Bart's ultimate failure, recognized that, as long as Bart could respond flexibly to his "spark," he would continue to grow and his greatness increase, but when he ceased to change, failure would soon follow. Following not only the theme of his first novel but its tone as well, Foote describes the important difference between Davis and Lincoln. Davis, he says, was a man of "iron control" over himself (I, 4); Davis was cerebral, given to thinking through the plan or pattern and then rigidly insisting on it. Lincoln, at the beginning, "had no fixed policy to refer to: not even the negative one of a static defensive, which, whatever its faults, at least had the virtue of offering a position from which to judge almost any combina-tion of events," but this was by no means a weakness in Foote's view. "This lack gave him the flexibility which lay at the core of his greatness, but he had to purchase it dearly in midnight care and day-long fret" (I, 166).

Around these two poles—the flexible and the inflexible, the artist and the plodding—the other major figures of the war play their roles, some of them at times approaching great artistry, some of them continuing to grow and change as conditions present themselves. Robert E. Lee and Ulysses S. Grant play prominently among these figures, and again the measures of heroism that appeared first in *Tournament* come into play. Hugh Bart's exceptional qualities were admired and recognized; they made him a natu-ral leader, though Bart mistook the reasons for this.

Robert E. Lee was perhaps the most admired of all of the Civil War heroes, emerging as the leader of the Army of Northern Virginia after McClellan's failure to take Richmond in the Peninsula Campaign in the spring and early summer of 1862. Lee could count on the respect of his soldiers. Although he had acquired other names with his less-than-spectacular performance during the war's early months, he became the great hero after saving Richmond from McClellan. "Granny Lee, Evacuating Lee, the King of Spades, he had become for his troops what he would remain: Mars Robert. They watched him as he rode among them, the high-colored face above and behind the iron-gray beard, the active, dark-brown eyes, the broad forehead whose upper half showed unexpectedly dazzling white when he removed his wide-brimmed hat to acknowledge their cheers. Distrust had yielded to enthusiasm, which in turn was giving way to awe" (I, 585). Almost a year later came Lee's great triumph at Chancellorsville. There, as Lee rode amid his victorious troops, awe, at least in the eyes of one staff officer, gave way to even greater exaltation. "I thought that it must have been from such a scene that men in ancient times rose to the dignity of gods," this officer wrote (II, 306). Almost a year after Chancellorsville, at the beginning of the Forty Days, a soldier from Alabama felt the same way about Lee, even though Grant was bearing down on Lee's army. Lee had come too close to the front as he spurred his men into battle, and the troops had urged him to find cover. " 'I thought him at that moment the grandest specimen of manhood I ever beheld,' one among them later wrote. 'He looked as though he ought to have been, and was, the monarch of the world'" (III, 170). Foote points out, "Lee's veterans fought less . . . for a cause than they did for a tradition," and later adds: "Mainly, though, Lee's veterans fought for Lee, or at any rate for the pride they felt when they watched him ride among them" (III, 630).[20]

Lee, even in his unsuccessful cause, was an artist of the quality and, very nearly, the magnitude of Lincoln. He often surprised his listeners with highly accurate predictions of his enemy's plans, an intuitive quality, almost mystical. His craft of military intelligence was as highly developed as Lincoln's craft of words, but in Lincoln's case, the artistry was of a higher and more lasting order. To many it seemed that Lee had the power of "divination," but Foote identifies what seems to be the real source, and it is identical to Lincoln's. "Like other artists in other lines of endeavor," Foote says, "Lee produced by hard labor, midnight oil, and infinite pains what seemed possible only by uncluttered inspiration. Quite the opposite of uncanny, his method was in fact so canny that it frequently produced results which only an apparent wizard could achieve" (III, 144).

Grant, in Foote's narrative, was by no means the man Lee was. Men admired Grant, but not as much as they admired Lee, and there were always nagging questions about Grant's habits. There was not as much artistry about Grant as there was an abundance of bloody force and the determination to defeat the rebels no matter what the cost in lives. In a letter to Percy, Foote describes bluntly the differences he found between Lee and Grant. "Ive made the rather amazing discovery that Grant was a son-of-a-bitch of the first water—basically, that is; which doesnt rob him of his fascination by any means," Foote wrote. "In a sense, the whole first two-thirds of my book (Vols. I and II, that is) is a preparation for the meeting of Grant and Lee in the Wilderness and southward: Lee, the representative of the best of the Cavalier tradition, and Grant, the representative of almost the worst of the Puritan tradition, which took over the country about that time . . . and has brought us to where we are, playing second lead to Kruschev because we put the dollar above life itself (15May60)."

If Lee is the flexible hero, divining his opponent's intentions and responding as best he can to his advantage, then Grant is the flawed hero— playing his part mechanically to time's metronome. There was public adulation, of course, beginning when U. S. Grant became "Unconditional Surrender" Grant after his victory at Fort Donelson in February 1862. His victory at Vicksburg added to his stature, and his determination at the beginning of the Forty Days to "fight it out on this line if it takes all summer" ran in the headlines. But always there were questions about his love for barleycorn, and he never seemed to look like a major and then a lieutenant general. The tale at the beginning of Volume III of his registering at the Willard Hotel, unrecognized after his appointment as overall commander, is amusing. The clerk had no idea the man in the rumpled blue uniform was Grant, but after Grant signed the register, things changed. While Lee, in the eyes of his worshipful men, could be a monarch, even a demigod, Grant was Grant, admired surely but not adored. The report of a private at Vicksburg, for example, pictures Grant as a commonsensical man, but a human among common men. " 'Gen. Grant came along the line last night,' an Illinois private wrote home. 'He had on his old clothes and was alone. He sat on the ground and talked with the boys with less reserve than many a little puppy of a lieutenant. He told us that he had got as good a thing as he wanted here'" (II, 407).

There were others who, in various combination, had heroic traits according to Foote's view of heroism. Sherman had some of the artist's qualities in his generalship. Looking at his maps to plan his movement on Atlanta and taking into account the personalities of his subordinates, Sherman, on one occasion, according to Foote, "experienced a surge of joy not unlike that of a poet revising the rejected draft of a poem he now perceives will become the jewel of his collection" (III, 322). Sherman's troops admired him: "Uncle Billy, they called him, with an affection no blue-clad soldiers had shown for a commander, West or East, since Little Mac's [George McClellan] departure from the war" (III, 492). Like Hugh Bart, Sherman was convivial and exuberant, not glamorous and self-assuming. Nathan Bedford Forrest, among the Confederates, also approached the level of intuitive heroism that Bart represented. In the late 1940s Foote had planned to write a novel about the Battle of Brice's Crossroads, which was perhaps Forrest's most brilliant victory. According to one of his troopers, Forrest "looked the very God of War" riding the line of his cavalry just before ordering them into battle. Forrest lacked the elegance of Lincoln's musical rhetoric, but he could fight Brice's Crossroads "as he did all his battles, 'by ear'" (III, 370).

Both armies suffered from inept generalship, but the Union army was especially prone to blundering; "the public's and the army's expectations had been lifted only to be dashed, more often than not amid charges of incredible blundering, all up and down the weak-linked chain of command" (III, 531). Near the end of the war, at Petersburg and Richmond with Grant's hordes pouring into eastern Virginia, there were mistakes, but Lee sorely missed the failed commanders who had preceded Grant. Lee, Foote says, "would miss [Burnside], much as he missed McClellan, now in retirement, and John Pope and Joe Hooker, who had been shunted to outlying regions where their ineptitudes would be less costly to the cause they served" (III, 538). A few pages earlier Foote referred to the "multi-thumbed commanders who were often in need of reassurance, even if they had to express it themselves" (III, 524). The causes of the ineptitude could be traced to any number of sources, pride and ignorance being high on any list. Among the sources that seem particularly significant to Foote's history are the rhetorical posturing, ambition, and inflexibility, all of which inhibit contact with the more basic rhythms of history and a spontaneous response to them.

Early in the war commanders on both sides, seeing war in terms of some preconceived abstract notion of heroism, sought to heighten the significance of their actions through rhetorical embellishments, but later these embellishments disappeared, and men and their leaders settled into the tiresome and bloody business of marching, digging, and seeking each other's annihilation. Many had seen glory in the rhetorical flourishes that bore little resemblance to the natural, elemental quality of Lincoln's "music" although it made a grand but empty sound. Although Beauregard's plan for the defense of middle Tennessee was "built on something more than rhetoric and hope" (he had been sent reinforcements), Foote nevertheless includes a sample of the rhetoric, pointing out that Beauregard did not "neglect the accustomed flourish at the outset." "Soldiers: I assume this day the command of the Army of the Mississippi, for the defense of our homes and liberties, and to resist the subjugation, spoilation, and dishonor of our people. Our mothers and wives, our sisters and children, expect us to do our duty even to the sacrifice of our lives. . . . Our cause is as just and sacred as ever animated men to take up arms, and if we are true to it and to ourselves, with the continued protection of the Almighty, we must and shall triumph" (I, 319).

When Albert Sidney Johnston took command of the troops that Beauregard had addressed and sent them off to fight at Shiloh, he did so with these words ringing through the April blossoms: "Remember the precious stake involved, remember the dependence of your mothers, your wives, your sisters, and your children on the result," and he exhorted them to be "worthy of the women of the South" (I, 327). Each man in Johnston's vision would assume the status of a Lochinvar or a Bayard. Earl Van Dorn reached for even greater heights in his camp in the "bleak western woods." "Soldiers! Behold your leader! He comes to show you the way to glory and immortal renown. . . . Awake, young men of Arkansas, and arm! Beautiful maidens of Louisiana, smile not on the craven youth who may linger by your hearth when the rude blast of war is sounding in your ears! Texas chivalry, to arms!" (I, 279).

Southerners were the chief perpetrators, but they were by no means alone in these excesses, although Van Dorn must surpass most. Colonel Edward D. Baker, senator from Oregon, close friend of Lincoln, and a sometime soldier, went into the Battle of Ball's Bluff singing out quotations from Walter Scott, greeting his fellow officers with lines from *The Lady of the Lake*. When the battle turned decisively in favor of the Confederates,

Baker received a mortal wound, "in the form of a bullet through the brain, which left him not even time for a dying quotation" (I, 106).

Overblown rhetoric, because it represents a superficiality in motives, diminishes the possibilities of the human spirit, as does the Davis-like rigidity of personality and inflexible adherence to a plan. Both A. S. Johnston and Beauregard insisted on the rigid adherence to battle plans, Johnston basing his plan for the attack at Shiloh on Napoleon's battle plan for Waterloo and Beauregard, Foote's "high-spirited Creole," making a career of grand plans. "For three years now the Hero of Sumter had specialized in providing on short notice various blueprints for bold victory, simple in concept, large in scale, and characterized by daring" (III, 259), Foote says of him on the eve of Petersburg. The description might also apply to Hector Sturgis's plans for developing Bristol in "Child by Fever." Braxton Bragg, one of the most unattractive figures in the Confederate high command, suffered from "dyspepsia and migraine [which] had made him short-tempered and disputatious all his life" (I, 567). He suffered also from a strict adherence to the rules, an adherence that at times made him ludicrous, as Foote demonstrates: "In the old army there was a story that in his younger days, as a lieutenant commanding one of several companies at a post where he was also serving as quartermaster, he had submitted a requisition for supplies, then as quartermaster had declined by endorsement to fill it. As company commander he resubmitted the requisition, giving additional reasons for his needs, but as quartermaster he persisted in denial. Having reached this impasse, he referred the matter to the post commandant, who took one look at the correspondence and threw up his hands: 'My God, Mr. Bragg, you have quarreled with every officer in the army, and now you are quarreling with yourself!'" (I, 567).

On Foote's scale of heroes, Stonewall Jackson is a curious mixture. A military genius, he should rank with the greatest heroes, but there was something about Jackson's personality that created a barrier between himself and others. His men respected and admired him, but not with the genuine warmth that Lee and Sherman were admired. After his early successes, "a certain aura was gathering around him, a magnetism definite but impersonal," Foote comments (I, 429). What Jackson might have become had he not been killed at Chancellorsville, we can only speculate, but he likely would have continued to be rigorous in his self-discipline. His victories in the Shenandoah Valley brought him praise in the southern press, but ambition to Jackson was "a spiritual infirmity, unbecoming in a

Christian and a deacon of the Presbyterian church" (I, 458). When the
praise in the newspapers grew to a crescendo, he gave up reading the
papers.

While Jackson controlled his ambitions, many other generals could not.
If admiration of the troops for their leader and comraderie were the only
hallmarks of a hero of Hugh Bart's dimensions then George B. McClellan
would have become the most successful of generals. McClellan's flaw was
that he was too much aware of the opinions of others; he resembled Bart in
that he became too conscious of what others thought of him and thus too
insecure and doubtful of himself. For example, when it became obvious to
him that he had lost the Peninsula Campaign, he began to consider the
consequences. He felt that the soldiers "would understand"; it was others
that caused the concern—"the body politic, the public at large, and especially among the molders of popular opinion the editors, and later the
historians" (I, 492). But McClellan, for all his other failures, was a soldier.
The political generals suffered considerably from uncontrollable ambition,
and the Federal army had an abundance of these in its "weak-linked chain
of command," Frémont, McClernand, and Banks among the most prominent. Frémont had Bart-like qualities; "he had a magnetism that drew men
to him," and "his voice had overtones of music," but Frémont had been the
Republican party's first candidate for the job Lincoln had won, and his
aspirations had received encouragement from the abolitionists. McClernand had practiced law in Springfield, Illinois, "alongside Lincoln." He
was about as short as Grant, Foote reports, "but he *looked* tall, perhaps
because of the height of his aspirations." Foote adds that McClernand
"had a firm belief that the road that led to military glory while the war was
on would lead as swiftly to political advancement when it ended" (I, 198–
99). The lawyer from Illinois who had given up a seat in the House of
Representatives to become a general continued, from the outset of the war
until June 1863 at Vicksburg, to nettle Grant. He had sought advancement
as leader of the campaign against Vicksburg only to have Grant assume
command with Lincoln's blessing. Finally Grant had had enough of Mc-
Clernand and had acquired sufficient evidence to relieve him of his command. The evidence, a "congratulatory order," claimed that the thirteenth
Corps deserved "the lion's share of the credit for the victory he foresaw" at
Vicksburg. Sherman called the order "'a catalogue of nonsense' and 'an
effusion of vain-glory and hypocrisy . . . addressed not to an army, but to
a constituency in Illinois'" (II, 421). Grant sent McClernand packing back

to that constituency, and from Springfield, McClernand protested at length to his former townsman, but to no avail.

Nathaniel P. Banks, a former governor of Massachusetts, like McClernand, had political motives for seeking military advancement. Banks's spring campaign against Shreveport in 1864 bore the marks of comic opera, with the result that Banks was "sneered at by his military inferiors, all the way down to the privates in the ranks" (III, 51). As Banks's army retreated across Louisiana, "a mutinous frame of mind" possessed them, but "presently the company clowns took over," and "they began to ridicule their plight and mock the man who had caused it, inventing new words for old songs which they chanted as they slogged." "Napoleon" P. Banks they called him in the refrain (III, 51–52). For Banks the "road to glory, which led from Shreveport to the White House" (III, 55) had been closed for repairs, the result of his ambition-driven ineptitude.

The cause for which Banks fought continued on its inevitable way even though Banks, McClernand, Frémont, and many others in both armies were left waiting. Sherman had seen in the beginning what the result of war would be. "You are bound to fail," he had told the professor of Greek and Latin at the Louisiana State Military Academy. And so, over the next four years, it happened as Sherman had said it would, and in the end the war and the Confederacy passed into the collective memory. "All things end, and by ending not only find continuance in the whole, but also assure continuance by contributing their droplets, clear or murky, into the stream of history," Foote says in his conclusion (III, 1040), and he quotes the Greek philosopher Anaximander: "It is necessary that things should pass away into that from which they are born. For things must pay one another the penalty and compensation for their injustice according to the ordinance of time" (III, 1040).

In the course of *The Civil War: A Narrative,* Foote occasionally reminds the reader that time is governed by ordinances and that these become visible in the words and actions of men, just as the skeleton of the hand becomes visible when the hand is held up to light. McClellan, for example, entering the Virginia home of the granddaughter of George Washington, Mrs. Robert E. Lee, "gave the youthful commander a feeling of being borne up and on by the stream of history" (I, 418). At Sharpsburg, Burnside stared at the bridge he believed his men must take "with a fascination amounting to downright prescience, as if he knew already that it was to bear his name and be in fact his chief monument, no matter what ornate shafts of marble or bronze a grateful nation might raise elsewhere in his honor" (I, 696). These comments, like the references to "fate" that occur with some frequency, are hints and reminders of theme, but other comments are more direct. For example, Lee's seasoned Confederates near Cold Harbor "flowed onto and into the landscape as if in response to a natural law, like water seeking its own level" (III, 288). This was by no means the only occasion upon which events seemed to take charge of themselves and to make commanders not so much instruments as pawns. That happened at Missionary Ridge and to no less a commander than Grant. " 'Damn the battle!' he was quoted as saying . . . 'I had nothing to do with it' " (II, 859). Indeed Grant did watch "his carefully worked-out plans go by the board, or at any rate, awry" (II, 851). Thomas's attack against the strength of Bragg's defenses was meant to be a diversion, but the men pushed forward on their own, even against orders, until Bragg had been driven from the ridge. There was something almost instinctive about the charge up the mountain that reminded one observer of a "flight of migratory birds" (II, 855).

Stars, the instruments of fate, appear with some frequency in the text of *The Civil War*. Stars in the national flag represent the states of the Union; the Confederate flag, by contrast, is "star-crossed." Beauregard and Grant both believe that they have a "lucky star," but it is in the character of Jefferson Davis to believe that the stars have great influence. History seemed to have "intervened" (I, 10, 14), according to Foote, on a number of occasions in Davis's career, but "the people of the Deep South" were perhaps mistakenly encouraged in their belief that "the providence of history" had given to them, as it "gave every great movement, the leader it deserved" (I, 41). In the eyes of the Unionists, Davis appeared "ambitious as Lucifer" (I, 164) and to a certain extent the identification of Davis with the Unfortunate Miscreant approximates Foote's view. For the title of the final chapter, which includes Lincoln's death, the surrender of the remaining Confederate armies, but focuses chiefly on Davis's capture, imprisonment, and final years, Foote chose the title of a poem by George Meredith, "Lucifer in Starlight." Davis, in the years that followed the war, may not, like the Lucifer of the poem, have "Soar[ed] through wider zones that pricked his scars/ with memory of the old revolt from Awe," but Foote seems to imply that Davis realized, "Around the ancient track, marched rank on rank,/ The army of unalterable law." The fact that the provinces of history are governed by an "unalterable law" and that the "army" marches to the rhythmic cadence we may sometimes hear is what Foote wrote about in *The Civil War.*

Again Proust's comments are appropriate: "The stupidest people, in their gestures, their remarks, the sentiments which they involuntarily express, manifest laws which they do not themselves perceive but which the artist surprises in them."[21] "Stupid" may not apply to most of the major figures in *The Civil War,* but few of them seemed to know of the "laws" that the artist discovers.

Davis and Lincoln occupy the outer framework of Foote's history in the overall three-part structure that Foote so carefully planned. In *Follow Me Down,* Beulah's monologue is at the center of the three parts of the novel. Foote had originally titled the novel "Vortex," and Beulah's monologue was to be the center of the whirlpool. Another metaphor that Foote used to describe the structure of *Follow Me Down* was the arch, Beulah's monologue being the keystone. Both arch and vortex are recognizable in *The Civil War.* Gettysburg, the center and keystone, took three days to fight.

When the Confederates planned an invasion of Pennsylvania in an effort to relieve the pressure on Vicksburg and Tennessee, they hoped to frighten Lincoln into transferring troops to defend Washington. The battle that occurred at Gettysburg, by chance rather than by design, was a disaster for Lee. Here nothing seemed to work for a man who had seemed almost invincible because of his capacity for miracles. "Coincidents refused to mesh for the general who, six weeks ago in Richmond, had cast his vote for the long chance," Foote wrote. "Fortuity itself, as the deadly game unfolded move by move, appeared to conform to a pattern of hard luck; so much so, indeed, that in time men would say of Lee, as Jael had said of Sisera after she drove the tent peg into his temple, that the stars in their courses had fought against him" (II, 461). Hence Lee's encounter with "unalterable law," and hence, also, the title of Foote's centerpiece—"Stars in Their Courses."

The battle simply happened to take place. Lee did not plan it, and Meade had decided to plan his defenses in another place. Missing his cavalry, having allowed Stuart to operate on his own, Lee did not know with certainty where Meade's army could be found. Sunday, 28 June, "had been a day of puzzlement, mounting tension, and frustration" for Lee (II, 455). His army was scattered and he did not know where the enemy's armies were. His first task was to effect a concentration of his forces. General Heth, a division commander in A. P. Hill's corps, had heard that a supply of shoes was to be had at Gettysburg, and it was in an effort to get the shoes, while on his way to rendezvous with the other parts of Lee's forces, that Gettysburg by happenstance became a battlefield. But once Gettysburg had selected itself, or rather that the subordinate commanders had selected it, Lee's fighting spirit overcame whatever caution he may have felt earlier. Lee had heretofore placed great confidence in, and entrusted great responsibility to, his subordinate commanders, but here, in Pennsylvania, his instructions seemed too indecisive, particular to Ewell who had fought under Jackson's firm command. Nor was Lee receptive to the suggestions of his subordinates. Longstreet, whose troops arrived late on the battlefield after most of the first day's fighting had ended, advised a shift to the south to take up defensive positions. Lee's response was firm: "The enemy is there, and I am going to attack him there" (II, 480).

If a lapse in the magic of Lee's leadership occurred at Gettysburg, then the behavior of his subordinates, and even of some of the soldiers in the ranks, was also uncharacteristic. Pickett's famous charge against the Federal line, which ended the third day of battle and also ended Lee's hopes for success in Pennsylvania, differed dramatically from other charges against other Union lines. Foote quotes Harvey Hill's description of the usual rebel attack: "Of shoulder-to-shoulder courage, spirit of drill and discipline, he [the Confederate soldier] knew nothing and cared less. Hence, on the battlefield, he was more of a free-lance than a machine. Whoever saw a Confederate line advancing that was not crooked as ram's horn? Each ragged rebel yelling . . . and aligning on himself" (II, 553). It was different here at Gettysburg on the third day. The natural and instinctive was replaced by rigidity and uniformity. "Forbidden to step up the cadence or fire their rifles or even give the high-pitched yell that served at once to steady their own nerves and jangle their opponents', the marchers concentrated instead on maintaining their alignment, as if this in itself might serve to awe the waiting bluecoats and frighten them into retreat" (II, 553). Foote quotes a "foreign observer" who said that the attackers "seemed impelled by some irresistible force" (II, 553).

Meade did not realize that he had won a battle until a "lieutenant from Gibbon's staff" told him, but Lee realized the depth of his defeat and, much to his credit, took full responsibility. The "survivors" of Pickett's charge "came streaming back . . . like hurt children in instinctive search of solace from a parent: meaning Lee." Lee provided what he could: "All this will come right in the end" (II, 567). In a contest with "unalterable law," even as great a man as Lee will fail, even though he senses history pulsing in the earth and in the lives of voices of those around him.

Chapter V

September September

I t was a bad time in many ways, some of them comprehensible, others not," Foote's narrator begins *September September,* sounding somewhat like Dickens beginning *A Tale of Two Cities.* The time was September 1957, a watershed in the history of the civil rights movement in the United States, for that was the month President Eisenhower sent troops of the 82nd Airborne Division to Little Rock, Arkansas. The conflict between Arkansas governor Orval Faubus and Eisenhower over the integration of Central High School in Little Rock provides the background against which the events of Foote's novel take place.

The final volume of *The Civil War* completed, Foote treated himself to an eighth complete reading of *Remembrance of Things Past* before setting to work on the short novel that would, he hoped, prepare him to begin once again his big family novel—"Two Gates to the City." If he had been measuring his career against the plans he had laid down to Percy in the early fifties, then, excepting twenty years and three volumes of *The Civil War,* this would have been the first novel of his mature phase. However Foote might have felt in the seventies about the shape of his career, *September September* is the work of a practised, sure hand that is fully in control of theme, style, and form. To say, as most reviewers did, that race is the theme is to narrow the novel; the theme is race only insofar as race fits the broader issue of human understanding—the understanding of self and of one's fellow creatures—but understanding had always been Foote's theme, just as form had always been his principal concern. There are two sets of characters in the novel, one white, one black. The black set of characters has a future; the white set, which typically and symbolically leeches the life blood of the blacks, does not.

In *September September* as in his earlier novels, fictional characters are never far removed from major historical events. Major Barcroft in *Love in a Dry Season* keeps up with the battles of World War II; the characters in *Shiloh* take part in a very real battle. Here the three characters who drive into Memphis from Bristol, Mississippi, depend upon Governor Orval Faubus to create the atmosphere of anger and fear which will provide the proper timing for their crime.

Foote had conducted extensive research in the Memphis Public Library for *September September,* and he kept careful notes in two composition books.[1] The headlines from the Memphis papers—the *Commercial Appeal* in the morning and the *Press-Scimitar* in the afternoon—appear in the text of the novel along with the television schedules and weather reports. Events having nothing or little to do with Central High School find their way into the novel from the papers—news of Elvis Presley, Faulkner's birthday (20 September), Ford Motor Company's introduction of the Edsel (4 September), and four days into October, the Soviet's launching of Sputnik.

Foote, in *September September,* has not abandoned his interest in the larger currents of history that in one way or another bring four of his characters from Bristol to Memphis, and three others from Moscow, Tennessee, to Memphis. Leath School, central to the events of the novel, had been built as a school for whites; Abe Fortas, the famous lawyer, had attended school there when it was known as Linden Street School. By 1957 the seventy-year-old building was run-down and had become an elementary school for blacks.

Union Station, "between third and second" had also seen better times. "In its high-rolling prime . . . better than three dozen passenger trains a day pulled in and out" (109),[2] but by 1957 there were few more than a dozen; then "it had one limping decade left, and for three of those last ten years it would sit there trainless, empty as an abandoned barn—or, better, the desanctified cathedral it resembled," Foote's general narrator explains, and he continues making the station emblematic of change: "Union Station, knocked down and hauled away for landfill, would be abolished so completely that not one of its hundred thousand hand-cut stones would remain to signify that the massive structure they once formed had ever been there, let alone testify to the bustle of life it once contained" (110).

Many other bits of Memphis's past turn up in the text—information about Boss Crump and the history of Memphis politics, remarks about W. C. Handy and Beale Street, the history of the Mississippi River.

This is a Memphis that Foote knows very well. The novel is set in that part of Memphis into which he moved from Greenville in the early fifties. The trio of white characters who come from Bristol rent a house on Arkansas Street, a house on the bluff overlooking the river and the three bridges spanning it. Arkansas Street "had been an all-Negro section . . . until three years ago [1954] a young writer moved into one side of the raw brick duplex, down the way" (25).

The "young writer" would have been very much like Shelby Foote. Arkansas Street was a cul-de-sac, and like his characters, Foote would have driven up Carolina and onto Riverside; downtown was "no more than a five-minute car ride" (25). Like them he could watch the sun set over the Arkansas mud flats across the river until he was forced away by urban renewal and the Great Society. A Holiday Inn was constructed on the site.

The three white characters from Bristol are Rufus Hutton, Podjo Harris, and Reeny Perdew. Podjo had known Rufus slightly when they were in prison in Mississippi, and perhaps that was the reason Rufus chose to draw Podjo aside in the Bristol poolhall to explain his kidnapping scheme. Inspired by the Bobby Greenlease kidnapping, Rufus planned to kidnap the son of a wealthy black family, depending on the fear inherent in the racial conflict building in Arkansas for the safety of his scheme. Podjo thought the plan, toned down considerably from Rufus's grandiose imaginings, might work, and so he agreed. Rufus brought his girlfriend, Reeny, along to help with whatever domestic chores developed. Rufus and Reeny made a preliminary excursion to Memphis where, for the month of September, they subleased the house on the bluff. Rufus told the owner, who had been sent away to school by his employer, that he and Reeny needed a quiet place for their son to recover from the eye surgery he was to have at the hands of a Memphis specialist.

Their victim, the eight-year-old grandson of Theo G. Wiggins, a well-to-do black entrepreneur in Memphis, was Teddy Kinship. Teddy's parents, Eben and Martha Wiggins Kinship, also had a daughter whom everyone except Theo called Sister Baby. Theo called her Lucinda, and Teddy was "young Theo." In the midst of the racial tensions surrounding the integration of Central High School in Little Rock, Rufus, Podjo, and Reeny kidnapped Teddy as he and Sister Baby made their way home from Leath School. Reeny gave Sister Baby a note that Rufus had written, in which he tried to make the kidnappers appear to be poorly educated whites, people who would have little concern for the welfare of blacks. Rufus also pointed out in the note, and in subsequent letters to the Kinships, that the white police in Memphis would share this lack of concern. *"They,"* Rufus wrote in one letter, *"don't care for a split minute what happens to some little nigger if losing him can get them us"* (217). Theo agreed with Rufus. "It's been a longtime rule of mine to stay clear of the law whenever and wherever the two colors are involved," he told Eben. "You got to remember the law is first of all the white man's law" (146), and Eben deferred to his father-in-law who then provided the sixty thousand dollars in the ten- and twenty-dollar denominations that Rufus and Podjo demanded. Sixty thousand, Podjo had reasoned, was a sum Wiggins could raise and one that was not large enough to drive him incautiously to the police or the F.B.I. On Sunday morning, 29 September, Eben placed the cash in a trash can behind the O.K. Sundry on Pontotoc Street. Just after sunset the following day, Monday, Sister Baby looked out the front window to see Teddy coming through the front gate. Reeny and Podjo had released him at almost the same spot they had grabbed him.

Throughout the month Podjo had watched the television news and had read the Memphis papers. The news media form a unifying thread through the text of the novel; Eben and Martha watch Douglas Edwards's newscasts and so do Podjo, Rufus, and Reeny. Headlines from the papers create the effect of a chorus, a backdrop, against which the events of the kidnapping develop.

Podjo Harris, a professional gambler had gone to Bristol following his release from the Mississippi penitentiary at Parchman. Podjo's father was a logger in southern Missouri; his Sicilian-Catholic mother, from Tonti Town in Arkansas, had wanted him to grow up to be a priest. For a time Podjo had lived in the southern part of Jordan County, where he had once known Reeny, or at least known who she was. In the foxholes of World War II, Podjo says, he became one of the many atheists of Patton's Third Army. After the war he served five years in prison for manslaughter, having killed a Buick dealer who found Podjo in bed with his wife, or, more accurately, found him "banging her bass-ackwards over the foot of a nearly waist-high bed" (49). The Buick dealer tried to kill Podjo with a kitchen knife but was killed instead. With his half of Theo Wiggins's ransom money, Podjo planned a three-day stand in Las Vegas at ten-thousand a day.

Reeny Perdew was the daughter of Brother Jimson, the preacher who saved, or thought he had saved, Eustis in *Follow Me Down*. "Foot washing Baptist, Total Immersun, True Vine Pentecostal; lots of things"—so Reeny describes his denomination. She lost her first husband, Len Perdew, in World War II. After two more husbands and two affairs, she found Rufus in Bristol and fell in love with his youth and with his need for her. Thus, Reeny came to ride with Rufus and Podjo to Memphis in the Ford that her last lover—before Rufus—had left her.

Rufus Hutton was born and raised in Bristol; the grandson of Mr. Cilley who worked in Lawrence Tilden's bank along with Harley Drew in *Love in a Dry Season*. Rufus, the youngest of the three white characters, developed the general idea of kidnapping the son of a wealthy black, and it is he who dies in the end, a victim of his own brashness, youth, and lack of self-control. Rufus's mother, Eva, was one of two daughters of Mr. Cilley. After his father had deserted the family and Mr. Cilley had been brought home from the bank paralyzed by a stroke, Rufus and Eva moved in with his Aunt Edna, her husband Pat, and his grandfather. Rufus tended his grandfather; several months before he died, old Mr. Cilley warned Rufus not to trust those who had the power and means. Where, Mr. Cilly asked, had honesty profited him? Rufus took the advice to heart. First he was expelled from Ole Miss for "pilfering," then given a dishonorable discharge from the Marines for theft. Later his Uncle Pat cashed in some political-favors-due to have him released from Parchman where he was serving a sentence for burglary. Then he met Reeny and his need for the means to live well became overwhelming. Any resolve to live within the bounds of the law melted away when exposed to her experienced passion.

Eben Kinship, father of the kidnapped boy, also traced his roots to Bristol. His sister, Julia Kinship, had helped bring Duff Conway to ruin in "Ride Out." She was the girl over whom Duff fought Chance Jackson, and she was, at one point, involved with one of Rufus's friends. Now Julia lived in Chicago; at their last meeting she had taunted Eben: "Sho don't want to be living yo kind [of life], no matter who gets hurt; including me" (22). Eben's parents ran a small cafe that Rufus remembered visiting while his friend visited Julia. After serving in World War II, he finished a degree at Tougaloo College in Jackson and soon moved to Memphis looking for work. Theo G. Wiggins hired him as a bookkeeper in September 1947.

Eben might have known he should have been suspicious of the motives of the well-to-do black entrepreneur, but he needed the work. Theo's purposes became clearer when, in October, Miss Lucy, who had been Theo's secretary for twenty years and had been inside his house on Vance Street only once during the twenty years, told Eben that Theo wanted him to come to dinner the following Sunday. Eben's future became clear to him on that Sunday, for that was when he met Martha Wiggins, Theo's daughter. He had become part of Theo's plan; four months later Eben and Martha were married.

If Theo's plan swept Eben along, it was certainly no more rigid for Eben than it had been for Theo himself. Theo had always been a man of purpose since he arrived in Memphis in 1909 from Moscow, Tennessee, where he had been born. Unschooled but ambitious, he denied himself, studying mathematics, investing all he could, and giving more than his share to both political parties, particularly to Mr. Crump's campaign. Crump, without public acknowledgment, returned the favor. By 1920 the Theo G. Wiggins Development Corporation had its office on Beale Street, and Theo could return to Moscow for the woman who would be his wife, Lucinda, and for "his lame niece Dolly," who would keep house for them on Vance Street. In 1922 their only child, Martha, was born, and grew up to be a female replication of her dark-skinned father.

Theo sent Martha to finishing school in St. Louis—"Miss Endicott's Finishing School for Young Ladies of Color"—and he bought her expensive clothes in Chicago. "Most everything I was, and am, came from getting my daddy's looks and not my mamma's," she mused at one point. "If I'd been born willowy like her, high-nosed and light of skin, instead of squat and froggy, dark like him, I wouldn't have had to spend so much time rising above my appearance" (150). Her first engagement had ended in disaster when her fiance, Lydel Partridge, discovered that she was seeing a poolhall bum, Snooker Martin. Theo had Snooker moved to Detroit, but that did not save the engagement. Then came Eben, light-skinned and available for purchase.

Characters in *September September* take on allegorical qualities in that personal fulfillment becomes a metaphor for historical change of much broader significance. Dean Fowler, reviewing the novel for the *Hudson Review,* remarked that the "new novel has something more than a pervading historical consciousness." It has, Fowler says, "a concept of character as unwitting witness and prime source for the history of his time."[3] It is not simply the current events, however, that affect character; Foote's characters bring a considerable portion of their own various pasts to these events so that the past adds shape and perspective to the present. The action of the novel pits the two sets of characters, one black and one white, against each other as they move in opposite directions. The black characters gain insight into themselves and discover, if not a sense of complete fulfillment, at least the possibility for satisfaction. The whites quite literally gain nothing except the experience of having lost what they had hoped to gain. The contrasting motion, the rise and fall of character, assumes suggestive historical dimension.

In both age and sex, the two sets of characters parallel each other. Both are basically sets of three—a younger couple and an older man. Reeny and Rufus, Martha and Eben are the younger couples; Theo G. and Podjo are the older men. The sets match thematically and structurally with the three-part form that Foote developed for *September September*. The general plot evolves from the conflict between the two sets because of the kidnapping. More significant, however, in the thematic development of the novel are the conflicts within the two sets themselves; the main action of the plot forces new and unusual pressures upon the internal relationships within the two sets of three. Inevitably the pressures alter the relationships; the white trio is led to dissolution and death and the other to a new sense of self, of communion and understanding within the group. Eben and Martha, in particular, discover a rich communion that they did not know they could experience. Without looking for it, unexpectedly, they discover the thing that Rufus spent his life vainly trying to steal from others. Rufus, at the end of *September September*, drives his new Ford Thunderbird, the symbol of mechanical and inhuman qualities, to his death.

The white trio forms under Rufus's initiative. The plan to kidnap the child of wealthy black parents is his, as is the choice of Memphis and, finally, of Teddy Kinship as the victim, but Rufus's instability, his "Dionysian" impulsiveness,[4] is a fatal weakness of the trio.

From the beginning Podjo realizes that Rufus, ingenious and creative as he may be, needs a calm, reasonable controlling hand. When Rufus took him aside in the poolhall in Bristol and explained the plan, Podjo was momentarily puzzled, but almost instantly he knew the answer to his question, "Why me?" "It was because the other [Rufus] mistrusted himself as much as Podjo did: as if he knew that if he tried it unassisted—unled—

he would be likely to fail in much the same way he had just failed at pool and had failed at so much else in his life, Ole Miss, the Marine Corps, and more recently, crime, which had landed him in Parchman" (31). Fascinated as he was with Rufus's plan, Podjo realized that it had to be scaled back to what an upper-middle-class family might be able to pay in ransom. "The plan was his," Podjo explains, giving Rufus ample credit for his inventiveness; "he dreamed it up; all I did was scale it down to workable proportions" (45). Nevertheless, Podjo knows his vigil must be constant, particularly after Rufus violates the agreement by bringing along a pistol. "I knew I had more to fret about than I'd lulled myself into thinking because of the ache I had for those thirty-thousand dollars," Podjo thinks. "I got to watch this fellow" (46).

Rufus proves to be more of a problem than even the watchful Podjo had imagined. Rufus's exuberance, after they have successfully secreted Teddy away in the attic of the house on the bluff, leads him to a recklessness that might clearly have endangered the plan. "I had that klansman voice down pat—if not patter," Rufus exults to Reeny and Podjo. Reeny realizes that the remarks Podjo makes to Rufus are an effort to calm him: "He's really enjoying this, she thought; enjoying it too much to let anything interfere" (116). Moments after the kidnapping at a restaurant, Rufus is even more incautious. There he tells the waitress to congratulate Reeny and him: "We just adopted ourselves a little boy. A dark one, cute as a button." Reeny was "frightened to think what Podjo might do if he was there" (119).

In the end, after they have collected the sixty-thousand-dollar ransom, Podjo completely loses control of the situation and holds himself responsible. Rufus has taken some of his share of the ransom and bought a new Ford Thunderbird, which is sure to attract the attention of the police if the bills that Podjo assumed were marked had not attracted them first. "My trouble was I got distracted, he thought" (267).

Rufus's more basic problem was that he had created a make-believe life for himself, a life based not simply on impulsiveness, but on exaggeration and falsehood. Asking around, Podjo learned that people in Bristol had a pretty clear notion of who Rufus actually was; it was only Rufus who was fooled. Podjo learned about Rufus's short career at Ole Miss and the dishonorable discharge. Nevertheless, Rufus bragged. Rufus made his grandfather, who had been a bookkeeper, into a banker; at Ole Miss he had played football. "And now there was this, up in Memphis, and me with him," Podjo explains, "and all the time all these lies about where he'd been, what-all he'd done; Ole Miss, football, Korea, big-time crime; all that. None of it was easy to put up with, coming at you steady as it did. There's worse things than a liar, by far, but Rufus had gone beyond lying to become the things he told. He wasn't just a liar. He was a lie" (45). Later Podjo still complains: "Instead of making a life for himself, he made one up" (252).

Reeny succeeds far better than Rufus at self-control, but sex is, as Podjo feared from the beginning, the trap. Self-discipline works for Podjo until his sexual drive overpowers it. Reeny's maternal inclination toward Teddy might have proven dangerous to the white trio, but Reeny manages to control it, and thus prevent disruption. Although her growing irritation at Rufus makes her more protective of Teddy, she avoids fighting with Rufus about it (133). But Rufus's drinking does bring on a fight, and the conflict that is the trio's undoing erupts over Reeny herself.

Even Rufus can see the potential for disaster should Reeny become the center of a lovers' triangle, so he offers Reeny to Podjo, on loan, so to speak. "I'll give her the word, if you want, on condition you don't try to steal her," Rufus bargains, trying to make the offer more attractive than it already appears. "It's really something; I'm not kidding. She'll make you think a whole covey of quail came whirring up out of your crotch" (34). Podjo turns down the offer because of his belief that he can manage for himself, but he is concerned: "What worried me was I might start wanting her for *her* sake" (50).

Sex is the most effective means Reeny has of controlling Rufus, calming him down. The crisis in their relationship comes when Teddy, who is usually drugged and sleeping on his cot in the attic, finds his way downstairs and interrupts their lovemaking. Both Reeny and Rufus are "left hanging." Rufus, who almost never drinks whiskey, responds to the interruption by finding one of Podjo's bottles of bourbon, and that, in turn, leads to a fight when Reeny returns from putting Teddy back in the attic. Reeny slaps Rufus; that brings out Rufus's worst. "What made it so strange," Reeny thinks, "is I'd come back down to get on with what we'd been interrupted in, both for his sake and for my own, and here he was trying to maul me—rip my head off, as he said" (172).

Podjo interrupts the struggle in time to prevent Rufus from hurting Reeny seriously, but she suffers an ugly bruise on her forehead. Reeny, whom Rufus has left not only bruised but "hanging," turns to Podjo and finds him more than ready for her. While Rufus snores, passed out in the bedroom, Reeny goes to Podjo on his couch in the living room. He was a far different Podjo from the one she had expected; the first time was a mad rush. "He barely made it in before he was half done," Reeny says with understanding, "all that time he'd been up here alone, with Rufus and me having at it" (175). Afterward they settled in for a more relaxed and prolonged coupling. Reeny had "had better," but she knew Podjo would improve: "And I could tell it would get better, later on. Lots better: I could tell" (177).

Podjo is caught much against his better judgment. "What he wanted was more, not only then but later as well, when he found that desire was no less compelling because its edge had been dulled." After three days Podjo is even more certain. "I'll just sweat it out, he told himself, incurably optimistic even in what, after three days of abstinence, he had come to see would surely be defeat. What he wanted, maybe most in all the world, was a little touch of Reeny in the night" (208). The problem is Rufus: "It's not like we are dealing with any part of a whole man," he says to Reeny. Rufus should not know, but of course he does. The first clue comes when Reeny slips and says, "Goodness, Rufus, you were about as bad off as Podjo" (211).

In spite of his growing awareness of Reeny's distance from him, Rufus wants to keep her. Their life together is after all, what had driven Rufus to devise his plan in the first place. Podjo's concern, Rufus feels, is gambling, Las Vegas, but for Rufus there is a far different concern: "Mine" he tells us, "was fucking, in one form or another, and for me that meant Reeny, wherever we went." Reeny has become a "trophy" for Rufus, "an outsized demijohn of jism, filled to overflowing with the viscid, pearly essence of myself, my very seed" (225–26).

Podjo, his and Reeny's means of controlling Rufus compromised, knows that an explosion is inevitable, and he fears that the success of their "job" is in serious jeopardy. Podjo tries to ease the strain but the danger, after Rufus has learned that Reeny is leaving him, is magnified.

> I knew him well enough to know he might explode under that kind of pressure, blow the whole job to hell-and-gone before we wound it up. Nothing is as dangerous as a coward when he's crossed and cornered; that is if he's got some angle he can work to get back at you, never mind what's likely to come down on his own head afterward; especially when he's keyed-up as Rufus was all through that time. The calming-down job Reeny did on

him two nights ago, while I was gone to Jim's for ribs, barely lasted out the evening. There's no top to that ladder for men like him, built around their privates, with a brain that ticks like a time bomb in the shape of a clenched-up cunt. If it was big enough, and you could smoke in there, theyd live in it. [252]

Podjo's concern proves to be well-justified, for a desperate Rufus, now altogether beyond control, spends part of his money on the new, glittering Ford Thunderbird that is almost certain to attract attention. At the point of the pistol that Podjo told him not to bring along in the first place, he claims Podjo's share of the ransom also—except for two packages of tens, one thousand dollars in all. Podjo can only chide himself that he was distracted.

Rufus's end is appropriate to his character. There had been a robbery and police had set up a blockade on the Mississippi River bridge. Thinking his new Thunderbird powerful and fast enough to drive past the police, Rufus drives to his death against the girders of the bridge. Before the car catches fire, the police recover the Kinship's cash, almost all of it, from the front seat of the car.

Control, self-discipline, is also an issue with the black trio. Just as Podjo loses control over Rufus and thus over the outcome of the "caper," Theo loses control over Eben. The result, however, is that Eben gains not only independence and self-esteem but a much fuller sense of selfhood and a much closer relationship with Martha. Eben gains much of what Rufus loses.

Eben's father-in-law had mastered the "system," the unwritten codes and traditions that governed race relations. By manipulating the system when it was possible and by working within it when it was not, Theo created a comfortable life for his family. Theo developed a lifelong "admiration" for Booker T. Washington, whose advice about hard work and sobriety he greatly admired; he also quietly supported the white political machine, Mr. Crump's machine, and had little use for the sporting life on Memphis's Beale Street. In his view W. C. Handy, the famous Beale Street musician, "was some kind of clown, performing at people's beck and call, for very little cash, and no credit whatsoever" (57). He was all business; in Eben's eyes he resembled a poker player who never let anyone guess what he was thinking.

Over the years Theo has developed a routine that provides for self-discipline, and both the routine and discipline create a mask behind which he can obscure his feelings. This is required by the system if one is not to be hurt. Eben feels that he has never understood Theo, but he has become a part of the routine that altered only once—the day Teddy was born. "You could have set your watch by all three of us," Eben observes.

Eben rebels against Theo's control and against the system, but in doing so Eben gains a life for himself. Theo has made his money in real estate, buying and renting houses and businesses, making deals quietly and profitably. Martha, Eben, Sister Baby, and Teddy live in a house that Eben rents from his father-in-law, and he pays the rent from the salary his father-in-law provides. Little wonder that he feels caged even though at first he agrees with Theo's views. "The thing to do," Eben says in response to the news from Little Rock before his son is kidnapped, "and everybody knows it, is hump hard inside the system." He has little respect for "that preacher's son, King." According to Eben, King should not care "which end of the bus he rides on, just so it gets him there" (18). King and the other integrationists are "fixing to fix it so we won't be able to do business even with men like Mr. Crump, men right here who know us and respect us enough to give us a chance to get what's coming to us under our own steam" (19). Martha observes that Eben sounds "just like Daddy would sound if he'd talk about it" (18).

Under the pressure of the kidnapping, though, Eben begins to change. His first response to the kidnapping is to take issue with Theo, though Martha recognizes clearly enough that his restiveness is not rebellion, not yet. Rufus's notes and phone call warn them against reporting the crime to the police, but Eben favors doing so because the kidnappers seem to fear the police. Theo is against it. "It's been a longtime rule of mine to stay clear of the law whenever and wherever the two colors are involved," Theo says. "You got to remember, the law is first of all the white man's law" (146). Eben argues that it ought not be that way, taking issue with Theo for the first time to Martha's knowledge. "He'd only acted ugly out of stubbornness," Martha concludes, "out of knowing he was in the wrong and not being willing to admit it, especially there in his own house, or anyhow the house he was paying rent on, even if it was to Daddy and with money that had been Daddy's in the first place" (146–47).

Eben's dependence on Theo to supply the ransom is obvious, but that does not prevent his growing anger at the system that provided Theo with his money. It is the same system that prevents Eben's reporting the crime to the police, and he realizes that he has long hated the system that his father-in-law and he himself have accommodated. The hate "had been with him as far back as he could remember" (217). "He was part of a system which asked certain things of him—things he gave, if not gladly then anyhow willingly; taxes, for one, and close to four years in the army for another—yet which turned out to be unavailable when he got around to needing something in return; in this case, assistance in the recovery of his son. There was no refusal, not even the occasion for refusal, since, knowing as he did that almost nothing worse could happen than for him to be granted that assistance, he did not ask it" (217).

The result of this recognition is Eben's determination to change the system. Theo's money and the system have, in effect, emasculated him. If he can earn self-respect, then he might make conditions more tolerable for Teddy. First, Eben faces his impotence and frustration. He has no choice, because the law will not be enforced to benefit him. "Even before, though," Eben realizes, "while I was holding it down out of sight by talking and even believing that Tom talk, I knew that, deep down underneath— and maybe not all that deep—it was because I didn't want to face up to being a man" (240). Booker T. Washington's solution, as far as Eben is concerned, is no solution at all. "'Let down your buckets where you are,' old Booker T. advised, and I believed him . . . until I let my bucket down, the way he said, and found it had no bottom" (241). This time Eben declares that the system ought not to be as it is, certainly not for Teddy, and he says it with such conviction that Martha and later even Theo believe him. After Teddy's safe return Eben asks for and receives a house for his family ("so we can be paying taxes instead of rent") and a substantial raise (fifty dollars a week). But that is not what Eben is ultimately after; he needs a more basic change. "'It's a system that's been good to me,' Theo admits, 'I used it against itself, and beat it'" (288). Theo knows, however, that his way will not do for Eben: "I decided you were right about a lot you told me, yesterday and last week, under all that pressure. Right for you, I mean, not me."

For the white trio the action of the novel ends in death and dissolution. Rufus is dead in the front seat of his Thunderbird. Podjo and Reeny are off to Las Vegas, where Podjo quickly loses the thousand dollars that Rufus did not take. The black trio, however, gains much. Eben has earned self-respect and Theo's respect, and he has also developed a much closer sexual relationship with Martha. The thematic emphasis on sexual relationships in both trios suggests that the significance of the social change that Eben desires has its basis in matters much too universal and fundamental to human nature to be limited by race. It also suggests that Foote has not lost the modernist vision that informed his earlier fiction and *The Civil War*. Western culture, particularly that dominated by Europeans, is a waste land. As a narrow white culture, it is a failure. Foote seems here to suggest that, if our civilization has a future, the future will be in the hands of men like Eben and women like Martha Kinship, who, jarred from their complacency by a collision with rigid plans and systems, fall into rhythm with the impulses that lie behind and inform Mozart's music.

Martha and Reeny both recognize the powerful, emotional, animalistic thrill of sex, something hard to control if controllable at all. Rufus, in the throes of cunnilingus, reminds Reeny of an animal: "The moans and slurps and growls were like the sound of some animal feeding—some wild animal" (169). Snooker Martin introduced Martha to something that "lurked inside [her], locked in [her] blood till something beckoned and it came raging out like some wild animal, all teeth and claws and snarling" (156). Martha links her reaction to her African past. "All my raising went by the board: Miss Endicott's, Mamma, Daddy, everything I'd been taught since my Sunday School days at Beale Street Baptist. In my shame I decided what I felt went back to Africa, jungle doings, and we really were animals, wild animals, the way some people said of those who did the things that got them lynched—wild animals deserving of being cut and blow-torched, not only for what we did, but for what we were, deep down in the blood brought here from Africa two hundred years ago" (157).

Rufus finds animal imagery, a "covey of quail," an apt description of sex with Reeny, but sex is more than pleasure for Rufus. Through the sexual experience he seeks a dimension of self, an inner self. Reeny and Podjo know that Rufus seeks more than gratification. It might be a celebration of one's ties to humanity or to the human past, the jungle, the lurking beast; whatever it is, after he undertakes his kidnapping, Rufus fails to find it. "What he wanted," Podjo tells us, "was manhood—wholeness—on his own terms; that is by sacrificing nothing to achieve it. And he not only knew he'd never have it, he also knew he'd never stop trying to get it, *his* way, till he died" (50). Reeny is, of course, much more closely involved, and more articulate about Rufus's problem: "He couldn't get outside himself" (140), she explains about his sexual involvement with her in Memphis. "It wasn't so much *me* he was after as it was something inside him that wanted out but couldnt make it" (141).

Before the kidnapping, sex for Reeny and Rufus had been truly exuberant, transporting them beyond physical release and pleasure. They had found a deep joy in each other. Rufus had undertaken the crime to support the two of them, but under the building pressure in Memphis, his means of release and fulfillment failed. Their first meeting in Bristol had led to as thrilling an encounter as Rufus had experienced, but, as he tells us, there was more to it than just the sex. "It was also that she liked me, really liked me for myself," he explains (72). Reeny, later, also recalls those early days in Bristol, but it is with the recognition that a change has taken place. "What mattered was what was between us, and what was between us now had changed," she explains after the drunken Rufus has hit her. "None of it, such as it was, was really for me, no matter how much I wanted or enjoyed it. It was all for him, a kind of wrestling, a struggle to get outside himself by catching his excitement from mine; *feeding* on me" (174).

For Eben and Martha the opposite pattern emerges; from routine, almost meaningless gratification, they develop a less restrained, more exuberant shared experience that is emblematic of Eben's achieved manhood, his escaping the system and the self that unwittingly had supported it. Because of her brief encounter with Snooker Martin and the discovery of her capacity for passion, Martha imposes a rigid self-control on her life with Eben. She undresses for bed, but "all without showing so much as an inch of flesh" (21). "I took care to see that what Snooker Martin had shown was in me, caged in my blood, did not come raging out. And it didnt; I didnt let it," Martha tells us (158). Then under the pressures of having Teddy taken from them, a change occurs, signaled for them as for Reeny and Rufus by a blow, an openhanded slap. Anger for Eben and Martha leads to a reconciliation and more when they go to bed.

"Everything was as before, up to that point, and then it changed. It changed even more tonight than it had done on any of the three preceding nights since the change began. Perhaps the urgency, so evident on both their parts, grew out of the fight they had just patched up between them. In any case the connection was sudden, almost without preamble. She even hitched up her nightgown herself, while he threw the bedclothes back, and in no time at all they were joined in a strain of mutual need. 'Do it! Oh, do it!' she cried, churning her hips and raising both feet in their fuzzy socks to pound the backs of his thighs with her heels" [190–91].

In the narrator's first description of Eben and Martha's nighttime ritual, before Teddy was taken, Eben, lying across the bed from an inert Martha—she more a mummy than a woman, and he holding his breath "to get rid of what remained of the erection" (22)—had complained aloud of his flabbiness. Again, on the night of Teddy's return, he makes the same observation, but this time it is to a different Martha.

> They lay there in the faint moonlight, on their backs. Presently Eben groaned and said fretfully, "I ought to get some of this fat off."
> "I'll help you," Martha told him.
> "How?" He looked over at her.
> "Youll find out," she said.
> They laughed, both at once, and turned and put their arms around each other, and it's likely there were no two happier people in all of Memphis on this last night of that particular September. [284]

The religious connotations of the emphasis on sex are unavoidable. Once again in this novel, for Foote as for many of the modernists, the foundations of religious expression lie in sexuality. The dilemma faced by man in this modernist vision is that the traditions that gave rich substance to religious expression have eroded, leaving behind an emotion that is nonetheless intense for its ephemerality. In short, the thought and the feeling have once again, in the instance of the white trio, parted ways. With the blacks matters are different for, through their love, many things are possible. For the white trio, especially for Rufus, money becomes the end rather than the means. The religious metaphor is reflexive; it focuses back onto itself and does not lead to a fuller life, the wholeness that Rufus seeks—and the money is no adequate replacement.

The association Rufus makes between sex and Christianity may be unconscious, but the connection cannot be lost on the reader. Sex is the energy, obvious or subliminated, in the psyche which fuels religious intensity. For Rufus the associations are there, but the sense that would give cohesion to those traditions is not. For example, on the first night of their occupation of the house on the bluff, Podjo is treated to the chorus of Rufus and Reeny's passion.

> One voice was shrill, mostly an *ee* sound, high, prolonged, operatic. The other was somehow obstructed, submerged, like someone moaning under water or maybe oil, a gargled growling. Both continued, mounting in intensity, melded in a common need, an urgency only just short, if short at all, of unbearable. Then it stopped, not suddenly but on a dying fall, a double suspiration, followed not by applause, as might have been expected for so

virtuoso a performance, but by silence, also prolonged and profound. "Oo, good. *So* good," he heard Reeny murmur, and soon afterward Rufus said fervently, in a tone of prayerful gratitude: "Sweet Jesus." It was what he had been saying, or singing, all along—Jeeesus—only it sounded now as if a long-distance swimmer might have said it, just reaching the beach. [35]

Rufus almost always celebrates the joy of copulation "with something religious." Reeny notes that "Sweet Jesus" and "Holy Mother" were common expressions, but once the four gospels were the denouement of his climax—"Matthew, Mark, Luke and *John*" (142). In Memphis, however, sex becomes economic for Rufus. The mysterious force it may have represented earlier is lost to him. In fact his first response to the ransom is identical to his response to great sex: " 'Holy Mother', I said, looking too, like into a well or down a mine shaft, with something bright at the bottom, way way down. 'Holy Mother, Mother, Mother' " (225). His past with Reeny has become nothing more to him at this point than an "investment" (226).

In a world unravaged by ambition and greed, Reeny might have carried the symbolic religious burden of the Holy Mother or the Earth Mother for Rufus, and she might have provided Rufus with the means to escape himself, an escape in which, according to religious tradition, he would be able to find himself by losing himself. He might find the "wholeness" that Podjo knows he seeks. Both Reeny's name and her family background suggest such a role. Her father was Brother Jimson, the foot-washing Baptist preacher in *Follow Me Down*, who, in Reeny's words, believed in "lust and the Lord." She knew, too, that the women in his congregation "didnt mind sharing him any more than they minded sharing rain and sunlight" (135). Reeny's reference is to the procreative earth that we celebrate through the metaphor of the dying and rising deities, the analog of annual crops dependent upon "rain and sunshine." She was born "September sixth" and is thus a Virgo: "Virgo, that's me, the virgin," she explains to Rufus and Podjo. Furthermore, her name, Renée in French, means rebirth. She believed Brother Jimson named her this because her mother had died giving her birth, but she knows, as well, that the name "means reborn; born again, as they say in church" (135).

However much she may understand about the ancient analogies and primitive rites associated with her name, Reeny is completely modern. Her interpretation of rebirth is popping out of a cake naked, or almost so, at a bachelor party. Still even that has for her the hint of innocence. "I think it's

that the artist might supply what the modern priest is unable to provide. In *September September,* Rufus is Foote's failed artist, and it is significant that Foote draws upon his own background for developing Rufus's character.

At Ole Miss, Rufus studied literature and music; he had even encountered William Faulkner in Oxford. Like Stevenson in *Follow Me Down* and Amanda Barcroft in *Love in a Dry Season,* Rufus reads and knows a great deal about literary history. He mentions having read Elizabethan drama, particularly the *Duchess of Malfi,* and he compares a restaurant owner to "a character from Kafka" (119). Podjo gives Rufus credit for having imagination even though his imagination is so overworked that his life becomes a fabrication. Rufus takes pride in his artistry, such as it is. He believes that, in completing his scheme for kidnapping Teddy, he knows "how Shakespeare must have felt when he wrote *Flourish. Exeunt* at the bottom of the last sheet of *Macbeth,*" and thus he concludes: "I was an artist, sure enough" (72). He planned the ransom notes "with all the care youd take in writing a sonnet if you wrote sonnets" but found that "writing is hard work" (78), even if the artifact is a ransom note and not a sonnet. Early in the novel, even sex involves artistry for Rufus: "Babe, youre an artist" he congratulates Reeny, who returns the favor, "So are you, hon" (72).

Likewise, Rufus is something of a student of music. There is a notice of Sibelius's death in the newspaper, and that stirs Rufus's memory of his college days. "I thought of all the hours I spent over in the Music Department when I should have been in class—mostly math—listening to that crashing, spooky music he wrote, with the icy wastes of Finland in it and the loneliness of all men everywhere" (79). Just before his death on the bridge, his memories of Sibelius's music recur: "Braced like a racer for the take-off, he began hearing Sibelius, passages from symphonies he had long forgotten or thought he had: first the clarinet solo at the start of the E Minor, plaintive and forlorn, and then a sort of melding of the later ones, toward their climaxes: a rustling, eerie and crepitant, then a ponderous, frantic beating as of wings in preparation for flight" (276).

Often in his letters to Percy, Foote emphasizes the hard lonely work involved in writing, and, like Rufus, Foote devoted hours to music, even though in high school he had cut his math classes to read Joyce in the *Pica* office. Rufus also shares Foote's interest in history. It is he who has read about Memphis's past and takes rather obvious pride in showing the reader what he knows. "I knew, all this and more, because I looked it up in the library one day when I had nothing else to do," he tells us (68–69).

Not only do Rufus and Foote share certain interests, their pasts show certain commonalities. Both were raised by their mothers, aunts, and uncles—Foote because his father died; Rufus because his father deserted the family. Both worked for the U.S. Gypsum Company in Bristol or Greenville. The writer who lived on the bluff near the house Rufus rented surely must have been Shelby Foote. Rufus thinks that his real talent lies in invention, in telling lies, that he "should have been a writer" (76). Here, of course, Foote has the advantage over his creation. Rufus has succeeded in finding a "pattern to those last few years" but his is "a pattern of failure rushed to completion" (76).

Pattern has engaged Foote the artist from the beginning of his career, and *September September* is no exception. Form is central to his artistry here as it was in his earlier work. Any consideration of the artistic significance of the novel which does not take form into consideration is incomplete. The form for *September September* was derived once again largely from his interest in musical form. Though the seven parts of the novel do not correspond precisely to the seven parts of the Fourteenth String Quartet of Beethoven, it is nevertheless worth noting that both the quartet and the novel consist of the same number of sections. It is also worth noting that the English translation of Proust's *Remembrance of Things Past* is in seven volumes.

The novel is carefully planned so that each of the seven chapters divides into three almost equal parts, each set off by Foote's delta symbol in the text. The three parts of the form correspond with the two sets of three characters—the black trio and the white.

Table of Contents

A general narrator tells four of the seven chapters; 1, 3, 5, and 7; between these are three even-numbered chapters labeled "Voices." Each of the "Voices" has three monologues, carefully balanced so that Podjo narrates the first in Chapter 2 and the third in Chapter 6. Rufus is last in

Chapter 2, first in Chapter 6. Eben narrates a section between each of these in both chapters. Chapter 4 is made up of monologues by Reeny and Martha; Reeny's two frame Martha's central monologue, which thus occupies the same central position that the *Heiliger Dankgesang* occupies in Beethoven's Fifteenth Quartet. The form most nearly resembles that of *Follow Me Down,* in which Beulah occupies the center, the "keystone," of the novel. Thus, in *September September* the form gives Martha Kinship the central role, lending her more prominence than the dramatic events themselves give her. Form centers more attention to her and points up the contrast with Reeny.

The narrator in the four general chapters speaks of many matters. He will comment on the general action, explaining, for example, as he does in the opening paragraph, that this "was a bad time in many ways, some of them comprehensible, others not." He reports the necessary news: "On this hot clear Wednesday in early September, twenty years ago, the morning paper bulged with yesterday's news from Little Rock, where Orval Faubus had drawn the line at last" (3). He presents his characters and comments on them: "'A real crock,' Podjo said from the back seat, the *Commercial Appeal* spread along his thighs like an out-of-season lap robe. He was talking about Faubus, not the Edsel, though later he would see how well the phrase applied in that direction too" (3). And he has his opinions: it was a bad time "twenty years ago" perhaps because "we had a great big kewpie doll in the White House, commander-in-chief of all the cold-war warriors on our side, and the Russians were up to something they would fling skyward from the dusty steppes of Kazakhstan just one month later" (3). Upon occasion, as the narrators of Foote's earlier novels did, he will tell us what the community thinks, as in his synopsis of Eben Kinship's role in Memphis: "Women marveled at his fidelity to his wife, and it was true that he was faithful to her, both for her sake and his own, thereby linking principle and desire. They also said he knew which side his bread was buttered on, and that was true as well" (13). If the narrator seems somewhat unsympathetic to Eben at this point early in the novel, then that will change just as the reader's sympathies change when Eben takes charge of his life.

The three sections of monologues move the action forward but not as markedly as the general sections. In these sections of "Voices," the characters reflect on their roles in the action, on their views of themselves, on their feelings for the other characters, and on the events in their lives that have brought them to this September in Memphis. They think about the past, about childhood, youth, family—the lives they have led. They tell us how they feel, what they know about themselves, and what they have learned about the other characters.

Rufus's failure is largely a failure of form. He is not the artist he would like to be because he cannot find the appropriate form for his artistry. Sex and crime are his media although he is also conversant with the arts. He cannot write sonnets; ransom notes are his best work. He could not even control his bladder under the stress of being arrested for the crime that sent him to Parchman. If his plan for the Wiggins-Kinship kidnapping is imaginative, then it is also much too grandiose at first to be of much use. Podjo's control is necessary to its success, and the plan fails when Podjo loses that control. Even Rufus recognizes, in his calmer moments, that Podjo's control is essential. Rufus recognizes a "pattern" in his behavior, but it is "a pattern of failure rushed to completion as soon as [he] saw failure looming" (76).

Martha, too, finds a "pattern" in events, but it is far different from Rufus's. Under the stress of events, she is able, as she tells us, to discover things in the pattern she had not seen before. "At times like that, with everything still and empty-feeling all around you, you see things you never saw before: the way sunlight falls on a rug, say, and shows you colors you didnt know were in it till then. So it is with people, sometimes, in the lives they lead. What you have been makes you what you are, and in times of strain you see things in the pattern you never saw before" (150).

What Martha sees is the inadequacy of her response to events and the opportunities she has had. She sees that, after her encounter with Snooker Martin, she has intentionally "kept a tight rein on [her]self, and on Eben, too." Theo, both she and Eben know, is in charge of their lives for he has the money. "Eben has the prick but Daddy pumps it," Martha says (159). In the stress of the events, though, both Eben and Martha change. Eben acquires assertiveness and claims his manhood, and Martha begins to venture from the cage she has made for herself. On the Tuesday night after the Monday kidnapping, they "went to bed right after the news, worried sick, and did it again. Twice," Martha tells us, but she thinks she knows why. "I told myself it was some kind of nervous affliction" (159). But she knows, or at least learns, that it is much more than that. It is the fulfillment of the primitive and continuous role of woman freed, at least somewhat, from shame and puritan guilt. It is the celebration of the earth and the life that earth, sunlight, rain, and air make possible. It is the role that, in the end, is no longer available to Reeny.

Although the black trio tells less of the novel than the white characters, they nevertheless occupy the crucial and central place in its form, implying that they are what holds the civilization they represent together. Eben narrates the sections between those of Podjo and Rufus, and Martha narrates a single central section between Reeny's two. Even though Eben and Martha, and by extension all blacks in the South, represent what is central to the culture, they are also caught, caged as it were, between the white interests. It is from this trap that they emerge, particularly in the final section of the general narration. They emerge to claim their due in a civilization that has denied them and, in so doing, failed in its human potential.

September September is a rich, mature novel that is the result of years of diligence. Foote invested considerable time and careful planning to create an appropriate form, and his achievement is that of an artist for whom artistry means almost everything.

Recapitulation

Shelby Foote, at this writing, is by no means at the end of his career as an artist, but as the proprietor of a wasteland whose landscapes are as littered as Faulkner's with figures of the failed artist—Bart, Florence, Hector, Rufus—it is appropriate to assert tentatively some conclusions about the quality of his artistry.

Writing to Percy in 1963, Foote repeated his conviction that "writing is the search for answers, and the answer is in the form, the method of telling, the exploration of self, which is our only clew to reality (13Aug63)." It might seem from these words that he is asserting self-reliance with a romantic, Emersonian texture, or perhaps he is admitting that he wants to write a Whitmaneseque "Song of Myself." To a limited extent, that may be the case, but in light of what Foote has published, it would seem more likely that, following Proust and James, Foote's "reality" lies in the past, in history rather than in the broadly romantic world spirit or "oversoul." In the historical perspective, form is seen as something growing from human experience over time, as humans attempt to give shape to their understanding of experience. We are not dealing here with Thoreau's "maker of this earth" who "patented a leaf." Approaching the novel as an instrument for conducting a search, Foote concludes that the answer lies in the discovery of form, not a new form but a form that has evolved over time and is a composite human invention. Form enables one to discover the past and to understand one's self in relation to the discovery of a "reality" that goes beyond the chain of everyday events and incorporates the human spirit as it has evolved.

The problem that Foote has faced aesthetically lies in presenting the discovered form to the reader and making it available for the reader to experience and appreciate. Herein the form of his work becomes problematic, for it is not a form discovered in the process of a search, which characters like Binx Boling in Percy's *The Moviegoer* conduct, as much as a form filled with experience of the characters which are presented to the reader. The result is that readers, having developed expectations from reading other modern texts, may feel a diminished imaginative involvement when reading Foote's novels. We may feel the diminution of what Henry James, in "The Art of Fiction," identified as "intensity." When the demands of form weigh too heavily, the novel loses its "freedom to feel and say." James feels that the "tracing of a line to be followed, of a tone to be taken, of a form to be filled out, is a limitation of that freedom and a suppression of the very thing that we are most curious about." The reader is removed further from the events narrated so that he becomes not so much a participant in the artistic process as an observer, a watcher of a skilled artist demonstrating his talent, unveiling his wares. Louis D. Rubin, Jr., has recognised this distance as a limitation in Foote's first novel, which, Rubin feels, offers something of a "pat solution to the complexities of human beings in time, place, and history." The "solution" is one that seems to be "implanted upon the novel . . . rather than organically infused throughout the narration."[5]

The impression that readers of Foote's fiction are likely to bring away with them is that the novel exists only after the narrator's search has concluded. We have an artist/narrator who, in considering aforehand the events related in the novel, has discovered the form in which answers, posed by the problems that led to the search in the first place, may be found. He is presenting the form after the fact. This impression is intensified by the diagrams and discussions of plot in Foote's letters and in his *Mississippi Quarterly* essay. In his fiction we do not have artists in search of a vocation who are facing the anxiety of failure or the joy of discovery. The readers of Foote's fiction do not feel themselves encouraged to participate imaginatively in shaping the form; it is, rather, presented as a finished product for readers to observe.

This is not to say that Foote's novels are not superb artistic creations. "It is not that *Tournament* doesn't 'work' as a novel," Rubin says, "on the contrary, as fiction it works . . . very nicely indeed." Rubin continues by pointing out that "the development" of Foote's fiction "has been toward more dramatic 'objective' fiction, in which the experience, instead of being drawn relatively straightforwardly out of 'real life' . . . has been transformed into characters and situations that furnish their own dynamics and set up their own relationships." Character and situation work within form, but given the interest that Foote has had in history from the beginning of his writing career, his aesthetic decisions seem appropriate for they give the shape of the work a larger symbolic function. Form focuses the reader's responsive involvement on the shape of a completed action rather than on the unfolding of events. We are offered, in the narrative texture, patterns that the characters miss and by which their failures as human beings can be weighed. These patterns are missed because the characters had no artist, no Shelby Foote, to point them out. It is an aesthetic that works particularly well for history, perhaps better than for fiction, because we approach history with different expectations. We do not anticipate the degree of reader involvement in the lives of historical figures that we expect with characters in fiction.

Foote's fictional world and his vision of history might seem to give the impression that powerful historical forces exercise absolute control over human destiny, but this is not the case. These forces are not rigid laws that impose themselves on human action; they are what make life possible not what denies it. They are the expression of what is most fully human so that, when we feel their rhythms and harmonize with them, we find rich rewards through intuitive if not intellectual understanding. These patterns are human patterns. Furthermore, it is within human possibility to effect change and contribute to the shape of history, which is, after all, what our fellow human beings have made. Lincoln and Lee did that, and so did Eben Kinship, whose case presents a fine example of Foote's basic optimism. The first short story that Foote published in *The Carolina Magazine* was about a black character who successfully made his peace with the modern wasteland. Eben Kinship, in *September September,* manages to understand the restrictions that the artificial patterns of racism impose, and there is hope that, by confronting the system, Eben can help change it.

Hugh Bart was separated from the forces that had made him successful and as the separation grew so did his corpulence. Eben, with Martha's help, may clear away the fat, the isolation, and the loneliness of the enclosure that the fat represents.

Foote's history is one of the great literary achievements of his generation. It will continue to be read, as much for finding out what Americans did with their words and what they felt about themselves in the third quarter of the twentieth century, as for a record of what happened in the middle of the nineteenth. The novels will also continue to be read because, in them, Foote subsumed a great deal of the art of his time into his own and gave this art the imprint of his imagination.

Notes

Chapter I: The Wilds of the English Language

1. Helen White and Redding Sugg, "A Colloquium with Shelby Foote," *Southern Humanities Review* 15 (Fall 1981): 282; reprinted in *Conversations with Shelby Foote*, ed. William C. Carter (Jackson and London: University Press of Mississippi, 1989), p. 198.

2. Evans Harrington, "Interview with Shelby Foote," *Mississippi Quarterly* 24 (Fall 1971): 372–73; *Conversations*, p. 98.

3. John Griffin Jones, "Shelby Foote," in *Mississippi Writers Talking*, Vol. I (Jackson: University Press of Mississippi, 1982), p. 38; *Conversations*, pp. 151–52.

4. "Deep Delta" in *A Climate for Genius*, ed. Robert L. Phillips, Jr. (Jackson: Mississippi Library Commission, 1976), p. 18.

5. Jones, "Shelby Foote," p. 42; *Conversations*, p. 155.

6. Jones, "Shelby Foote," pp. 42–43; *Conversations*, pp. 155–56.

7. Unpublished letter to Walker Percy, Shelby Foote Papers, Southern Historical Collection, University of North Carolina at Chapel Hill. Foote usually dated his correspondence in the form given here. Before 1952 most letters were written in Greenville, and after 1952 most of his correspondence with Walker Percy was written in Memphis. The dates of letters are given in parentheses in the text; all have been standardized to fit Foote's preferred form.

8. White and Sugg, "Colloquium," pp. 289–90; *Conversations*, p. 206.

9. Lewis Baker, *The Percys of Mississippi: Politics and Literature in the New South* (Baton Rouge: Louisiana State University Press, 1983), pp. 162–63.

10. Ibid., passim.

11. White and Sugg, "Colloquium," pp. 290; *Conversations*, pp. 206–7.

12. John Griffin Jones, "Walker Percy," *Mississippi Writers Talking*, Vol. II (Jackson: University Press of Mississippi, 1983), p. 16.

13. Jones, "Shelby Foote," pp. 43–44; *Conversations*, p. 156.

14. Jones, "Shelby Foote," p. 44; *Conversations*, pp. 156–57.

15. Unpublished lecture, Memphis State University, 9 January 1967.

16. Jones, "Shelby Foote," p. 44; *Conversations,* p. 157.

17. Harrington, "Interview," p. 352; *Conversations,* p. 80.

18. "Child by Fever," *Jordan County,* reprinted in *Three Novels* (New York: Dial Press, 1964), p. 117.

19. Jones, "Shelby Foote," p. 47; *Conversations,* p. 159.

20. Jones, "Shelby Foote," p. 43; *Conversations,* p. 156.

21. Jones, "Shelby Foote," p. 59–60; *Conversations,* p. 169.

22. Jones, "Shelby Foote," p. 60; *Conversations,* p. 169.

23. White and Sugg, "Colloquium," p. 283; *Conversations,* p. 198.

24. Harrington, "Interview," p. 373; *Conversations,* p. 99.

25. White and Sugg, "Colloquium," p. 283; *Conversations,* p. 198.

26. White and Sugg, "Colloquium," p. 283; *Conversations,* p. 198. Foote usually writes the dates of the beginning and the ending of work on a book manuscript or typescript. All of his books are written by hand in a carefully drawn calligraphy.

27. James E. Kibler, Jr., "Shelby Foote: A Bibliography," *Mississippi Quarterly* 24 (Fall 1971): 437–65; Kibler's bibliography includes excerpts from a lengthy correspondence with Foote.

28. This letter to Percy is dated simply "Thursday"; Percy apparently wrote in 1950.

29. Harrington, "Interview," p. 373; *Conversations,* pp. 98–99.

30. White and Sugg, "Colloquium," p. 288; *Conversations,* p. 204.

31. Harrington, "Interview," p. 354; *Conversations,* pp. 81–82.

32. White and Sugg, "Colloquium," p. 288; *Conversations,* p. 204.

33. Unpublished lecture, 3 March 1967, Memphis State University.

34. Ibid., 9 March 1967.

35. White and Sugg, "Colloquium," p. 289; *Conversations,* p. 205.

36. Jones, "Shelby Foote," p. 57; *Conversations,* p. 167.

37. Foote recounts the incident in "Faulkner's Depiction of the Planter Aristocracy," in *The South and Faulkner's Yoknapatawpha: The Actual and the Apocryphal,* ed. Evans Harrington and Ann Abadie (Jackson: University Press of Mississippi, 1977), pp. 52–53.

38. Ibid., p. 44.

39. There is one bibliographical curiosity from these years. In November 1955 *Nugget Magazine* published a story titled "A Marriage Portion." The title is identical to that of the story in *Jordan County* but the *Nugget* story that George Garrett reprinted in *The Girl in the Black Raincoat* (New York: Duell, Sloan and Pearce, 1966), pp. 303–7, differs entirely; it differs from the story in *Jordan County* and is based on a joke Foote heard. A worn-out Delta belle turned prostitute narrates the story of her first marriage in the *Jordan County* version. The *Nugget* story features a Bristol housewife who covets a black raincoat that costs fifty dollars (a peach-colored negligee in the *Nugget* version) and an automobile sales-

man who covets the wife. The salesman borrows fifty dollars from the husband, telling him that he will leave repayment at the husband's home that afternoon. The husband sees the salesman leaving and is delighted that his loan has been repaid. Later, Foote was somewhat surprised to learn how closely his tale follows one of Chaucer's.

40. White and Sugg, "Colloquium," p. 286; *Conversations*, p. 201.

41. Jones, "Shelby Foote," pp. 60–61; *Conversations*, p. 170.

42. White and Sugg, "Colloquium," p. 286; *Conversations*, p. 201.

43. Jones, "Shelby Foote," p. 61; *Conversations*, p. 170.

44. Kibler, "Shelby Foote," p. 449.

45. Unpublished lecture, 20 February 1967, Memphis State University.

46. Jones, "Shelby Foote," p. 75; *Conversations*, p. 181.

47. Unpublished lecture, 20 February 1967, Memphis State University.

48. Jones, "Shelby Foote," pp. 75–76; *Conversations*, pp. 181–82.

49. Shelby Foote, "The Novelist's View of History," *Mississippi Quarterly* 17 (Fall 1964): 219–25.

50. Harrington, "Interview," p. 365–66; *Conversations*, p. 92.

51. Jones, "Shelby Foote," p. 68; *Conversations*, p. 176.

52. Foote, "The Novelist's View of History," pp. 219–20.

53. Foote, "The Novelist's View of History," pp. 224–25.

54. Foote, "The Novelist's View of History," p. 223.

55. White and Sugg, "Colloquium," p. 288–89; *Conversations*, pp. 204–5.

56. Harrington, "Interview," p. 354; *Conversations*, p. 81.

Chapter II: *Tournament* and *Shiloh*

1. John Griffin Jones, "Shelby Foote," in *Mississippi Writers Talking*, Vol. I (Jackson: University Press of Mississippi, 1983), p. 15.

2. Jones, "Shelby Foote," p. 50.

3. The *Pica* is in the library of the Greenville High School; a transcription of Foote's poems has been deposited in the William Alexander Percy Library in Greenville, and a microfilm copy of the *Pica* is in the Mississippi Department of Archives and History.

4. *The Carolina Magazine* 66 (Mar. 1937): 7.

5. Evans Harrington, "Interview with Shelby Foote," *Mississippi Quarterly* 24 (Fall 1971): 357; reprinted in *Conversations with Shelby Foote*, ed. William C. Carter (Jackson and London: University Press of Mississippi, 1989), p. 84.

6. Harrington, "Interview," p. 371; *Conversations*, p. 97.

7. *The Carolina Magazine* 66 (Nov. 1936): 29–30.

8. Harrington, "Interview," p. 357; *Conversations*, p. 84.

9. *The Carolina Magazine* 65 (Nov. 1935): 5–7, 32.

10. Ibid., 66 (Dec. 1936): 26–28.

11. Ibid., 65 (Apr. 1936): 9–11.

12. Ibid., 65 (Feb. 1936): 6–9, 29–30, 32.

13. Ibid., 66 (Dec. 1936): 25.

14. Ibid., 66 (Apr. 1937): 10–15.

15. Ibid., 65 (Dec. 1935): 19–20.

16. Ibid., 66 (Jan. 1936): 6–9.

17. Ibid., 66 (Feb. 1937): 5–11.

18. Unpublished lecture, 9 March 1967, Memphis State University.

19. Helen White and Redding Sugg, "A Colloquium with Shelby Foote," *Southern Humanities Review* 15 (Fall 1981): 284; *Conversations,* p. 199.

20. White and Sugg, "Colloquium," p. 282; *Conversations,* p. 197.

21. Shelby Foote, "Faulkner's Depiction of the Planter Aristocracy," in *The South and Faulkner's Yoknapatawpha: The Actual and the Apocryphal,* ed. Evans Harrington and Ann Abadie (Jackson: University Press of Mississippi, 1977), p. 49.

22. Foote has repeated these details in several interviews. See particularly Jones, "Shelby Foote," pp. 38–41; *Conversations,* pp. 153–56; and White and Sugg, "Colloquium," p. 286–87; *Conversations,* p. 197.

23. Jones, "Shelby Foote," 40; *Conversations,* p. 153.

24. White and Sugg, "Colloquium," 282; *Conversations,* p. 197.

25. Shelby Foote, *Follow Me Down,* in *Three Novels* (New York: Dial Press, 1964), p. 233.

26. Allen Tate, *Essays of Four Decades* (reprint; Chicago: Swallow Press, 1968), pp. 547–57; quotations are from pages 551, 555, and 556.

27. Shelby Foote, *Tournament* (New York: Dial Press, 1949). All references included in parenthesis in the text are to the first edition. Foote omits apostrophes where possible.

28. Unpublished lecture, 3 March 1967, Memphis State University.

29. Miller Williams, *The Poetry of John Crowe Ransom* (New Brunswick, N.J.: Rutgers University Press, 1972), p. 29.

30. Shelby Foote, *Tournament* (Birmingham, Ala.: Summa Publications, 1987), n. p.

31. Marcel Proust, *The Past Recaptured,* Vol. II of *Remembrance of Things Past,* trans. Frederick A. Blossom (New York: Random House, 1927), p. 1013.

32. Malcolm Franklin, *Bitterweeds: Life with William Faulkner at Rowan Oak* (Irving, Tex.: The Society for the Study of Traditional Culture, 1977), pp. 59.

33. White and Sugg, "Colloquium," p. 285; *Conversations,* pp. 200–201.

34. Shelby Foote, *Shiloh* (New York: Dial Press, 1952); reprinted (New York: Random House, n.d.); all references given in parentheses within the text are to the Random House Reprint.

35. Allen Shepherd, "Technique and Theme in Shelby Foote's *Shiloh,*" *Notes on*

Mississippi Writers 5 (Spring 1976): 3–10; page numbers of citations are given in parentheses.

36. Marcel Proust, *The Past Recaptured,* p. 1001.

Chapter III: A Jordan County Trilogy

1. Shelby Foote, *Follow Me Down* (New York: Dial Press, 1950). Reprinted in *Three Novels* (New York: Dial Press, 1964). Quotations are from *Three Novels.*

2. Coverage in the Greenville, Mississippi, *Delta Democrat Times* began on 21 June 1940. Stories of the events of the trial ran daily from 20 July to the sentencing, which was reported in the Sunday, 26 July 1941, issue.

3. Unpublished letter, Foote to James E. Kibler.

4. James E. Kibler, Jr., "Shelby Foote: A Bibliography," *Mississippi Quarterly* 24 (Fall 1971): 441n; Kibler includes quotations from this letter.

5. Simone Vauthier, "The Symmetrical Design: The Structural Patterns of *Love in a Dry Season,*" *Mississippi Quarterly* 24 (Fall 1971): 379–99.

6. Allen Tate, *Essays of Four Decades* (reprint; Chicago: Swallow Press, Inc., 1968), pp. 3–16.

7. Reprinted in *Selected Essays of John Crowe Ransom,* ed. Thomas Daniel Young and John Hindle (Baton Rouge: Louisiana State University Press, 1984), pp. 59–73.

8. Shelby Foote, *Love in a Dry Season* (New York: Dial Press, 1951). Reprinted in *Three Novels.* Quotations are from *Three Novels.*

9. Vauthier, "The Symmetrical Design," pp. 394–95.

10. Quotations are from *Three Novels.* In the 1964 edition, the subtitle "A Landscape in Narrative" is omitted.

11. John Carr, "It's Worth a Grown Man's Time: Shelby Foote," *Kite-Flying and Other Irrational Acts: Conversations with Twelve Southern Writers,* ed. John Carr (Baton Rouge: Louisiana State University Press, 1972), p. 19; reprinted in *Conversations with Shelby Foote,* ed. William C. Carter (Jackson and London: University Press of Mississippi, 1989), p. 35.

12. Evans Harrington, "Interview with Shelby Foote," *Mississipvi Quarterly* 24 (Fall 1971): 374–75; *Conversations,* p. 100.

13. Harrington, "Interview," p. 366; *Conversations,* p. 92.

14. *Pica,* 22 February 1933. For the history of Greenville and Washington County, see Bern Keating, *A History of Washington County, Mississippi* ([Greenville, Miss.:] Greenville Junior Auxiliary, 1976).

15. Allen Tate, *Stonewall Jackson: The Good Soldier* (New York: Menton, Balch & Company, 1928), p. 12.

16. Kibler, p. 447.

17. Harrington, "Interview," p. 366; *Conversations*, p. 92.

18. Keating, *History of Washington County*, p. 22.

Chapter IV: Form and *The Civil War: A Narrative*

1. Helen White and Redding Sugg, "A Colloquium with Shelby Foote," *Southern Humanities Review* 15 (Fall 1981): 286; reprinted in *Conversations with Shelby Foote*, ed. William C. Carter (Jackson and London: University Press of Mississippi, 1989), p. 201.

2. Shelby Foote, "The Novelist's View of History," *Mississippi Quarterly*, 17 (Fall 1964), 219–25. Subsequent references are given in parentheses.

3. See "Bibliographical Note," *The Civil War: A Narrative, Vol. III, Red River to Appomattox* (New York: Random House, 1974), 1064. All citations to *The Civil War* are given in parentheses; roman numerals identify the volume. *The Civil War: A Narrative, Vol. I, Fort Sumter to Perryville* (New York: Random House, 1958); *The Civil War: A Narrative, Vol. II, Fredericksburg to Meridian* (New York: Random House, 1963).

4. Unpublished lecture, 20 Feb. 1967, Memphis State University.

5. Reprinted in *Selected Essays of John Crowe Ransom*, ed. Thomas Daniel Young and John Hindle (Baton Rouge: Louisiana State University Press, 1984), pp. 59–73.

6. Louis D. Rubin, Jr., "Foreword: Asa Bart's Way," *Tournament* (Birmingham, Ala.: Summa Publications, 1987), n.p.

7. Foote quoted from an English edition, later published in the United States, of Marcel Proust's *The Past Recaptured*, trans. Andreas Mayor (New York: Random House, 1970).

8. William C. Carter, "Seeking the Truth in Narrative: An Interview with Shelby Foote," *Georgia Review* 41 (Spring 1987): 158; *Conversations*, p. 255.

9. Evans Harrington, "Interview with Shelby Foote," *Mississippi Quarterly* 24 (Fall 1971): 376; *Conversations*, p. 102.

10. John Carr, "It's Worth a Grown Man's Time: Shelby Foote," *Kite-Flying and Other Irrational Acts: Conversations with Twelve Southern Writers* (Baton Rouge: Louisiana State University Press, 1972, p. 8; *Conversations*, p. 24.

11. Unpublished lecture, 9 January 1967, Memphis State University.

12. Calvin Brown, *Music and Literature: A Comparison of the Arts* (Athens: University of Georgia Press, 1948), p. 215.

13. Simone Vauthier, "The Symmetrical Design: The Structured Patterns of *Love in a Dry Season*" *Mississippi Quarterly* 24 (Fall 1971), 379–403.

14. Shelby Foote, *Three Novels: Follow Me Down, Jordan County, Love in a Dry Season* (New York: Dial Press, 1964).

15. See pp. 136–38ff. above.

16. Helen White and Redding Sugg, *Shelby Foote* (Boston: Twayne Publishers, 1982), pp. 84 ff., note, for example, John Cournos's comments in *Commonweal* that the "shoemaker should stick to his last, the novelist to his fiction." Their survey of the critical reception of *The Civil War* also includes the more positive commentary following the publication of the third volume. C. Vann Woodward, for example, had high praise for Foote.

17. Carter, "Seeking the Truth in Narrative," p. 157; *Conversations*, p. 254. Helen White and Redding Sugg have discussed briefly the influence of the *Iliad* on *The Civil War* (*Shelby Foote*, p. 100).

18. White and Sugg argue that Foote's humor contributes to the southern quality of *The Civil War* (*Shelby Foote*, pp. 104–7).

19. James Cox, "Shelby Foote's Civil War," *Southern Review* n.s. 21 (April 1985): 329–50.

20. It is not difficult to hear, in Foote's prose here and throughout the three volumes, the reverberations of Lattimore's *Iliad*. "[W]atched him ride among them" is a phrase describing Achilles among the Achaieans. There are also many reflections of Foote's reading of Shakespeare. Lincoln's music, for example, "crept past them" like Ariel's song in *The Tempest*.

21. Proust, *The Past Recaptured*, trans. Mayor, p. 156.

Chapter V: September September

1. Now in the Southern Historical Collection, Wilson Memorial Library, University of North Carolina at Chapel Hill.

2. Shelby Foote, *September September* (New York: Random House, 1977).

3. Dean Fowler, review, *Hudson Review* 31 (Summer 1978): 347.

4. Monroe K. Spears, *Dionysius and the City: Modernism in Twentieth-Century Poetry* (London, Oxford, New York: Oxford University Press, 1970). Rufus is akin to the Dionysian character Spears identifies in modern poetry.

5. Louis D. Rubin, Jr., "Foreword: Asa Bart's Way," *Tournament* (Birmingham, Ala.: Summa Publications, 1987), n. p.

Selected Bibliography

Primary Sources

Books

The Civil War: A Narrative, Volume I: *Fort Sumter to Perryville.* New York: Random House, 1958.

The Civil War: A Narrative, Volume II: *Fredericksburg to Meridian.* New York: Random House, 1963.

The Civil War: A Narrative, Volume III: *Red River to Appomattox.* New York: Random House, 1974.

Follow Me Down. New York: Dial Press, 1950.

Jordan County: A Landscape in Narrative. New York: Dial Press, 1954.

Love in a Dry Season. New York: Dial Press, 1951.

The Merchant of Bristol. Greenville, Miss.: Levee Press, 1947.

The Night before Chancellorsville. Edited by Shelby Foote. New York: New American Library, 1957.

The Novelist's View of History. Winston-Salem, N.C.: Palaemon Press Limited, 1981. (Reprint of article)

September September. New York: Random House, 1977.

Shiloh. New York: Dial Press, 1952.

Three Novels: Follow Me Down, Jordan County, Love in a Dry Season. New York: Dial Press, 1964.

Tournament. New York: Dial Press, 1949.

Short Stories

"All Right about That." *The Carolina Magazine* 66 (Dec. 1936): 25.

"and the Gay and the Blue." *The Carolina Magazine* 66 (Apr. 1937): 10–15.

"Bristol's Gargoyle." *The Carolina Magazine* 66 (Feb. 1937): 5–8, 10–11.

"Child by Fever." *New World Writing: Fourth Mentor Selection.* New York: New American Library, 1953; pp. 194–223.

"Day of Battle: Private Luther Dade Rifleman, 6th Mississippi." *New World Writing: First Mentor Selection.* New York: New American Library, 1952; pp. 86–96.

"Flood Burial." *The Saturday Evening Post* 209 (7 Sept. 1946): 16–17, 159–163.

"The Good Pilgrim: A Fury Calmed." *The Carolina Magazine* 65 (Nov. 1935): 5–7, 22.

"A Marriage Portion." *Nugget Magazine* (Nov. 1955). Reprinted with editorial revisions in *The Girl in the Black Raincoat: Variations on a Theme.* George Garrett, ed. New York: Duell, Sloan and Pearce, 1966; pp. 303–7.

"The Old Man Who Sold Peanuts in New Orleans." *The Carolina Magazine* 65 (Jan. 1936): 6–9.

"Pillar of Fire." *The Night Before Chancellorsville and Other Civil War Stories,* edited by Shelby Foote, New York: New American Library, 1957; 125–58.

"Ride Out." *New Short Novels.* Mary Louise Aswell, ed. New York: 1954; pp. 1–52.

"Sad Hiatus: A Short Story." *The Carolina Magazine* 65 (Dec. 1935): 19–20.

"Shiloh." *Esquire.* 39 (Feb 1953): 75–94, 96. This is a condensation of the novel.

"Shiloh." *Blue Book Magazine* 89 (June 1949): 106–44.

"A Tale Untitled." *The Carolina Magazine* 66 (Dec. 1936): 26–28.

"Tell Them Good-by." *The Saturday Evening Post* 209 (15 Feb. 1947): 20–21, 43, 45, 47, 50, 53–54, 56, 58, 60, 62–64.

"This Primrose Hill." *The Carolina Magazine* 65 (April 1936): 9–11.

"The Village Killers: A Story." *The Carolina Magazine* 65 (Feb. 1936): 6–9, 29–30, 32.

Articles and Essays

"Faulkner and Race." With Darwin T. Turner and Evans Harrington. In *The South and Faulkner's Yoknapatawpha: The Actual and the Apocryphal,* edited by Evans Harrington and Ann Abadie, pp. 86–103. Jackson: University Press of Mississippi, 1977.

"Faulkner and War." In *The South and Faulkner's Yoknapatawpha,* pp. 152–67.

"Faulkner's Depiction of the Planter Aristocracy." In *The South and Faulkner's Yoknapatawpha,* pp. 40–61.

"The Literature of Fury." *The Carolina Magazine* 66 (Nov. 1936): 29–30.

"The Novelist's View of History." *Mississippi Quarterly* 17 (Fall 1964): 219–25.

"Preface to the Second Edition." *Tournament.* Birmingham, Ala.: Summa Publications, 1987.

Interviews

Breit, Harvey. "Talk with Shelby Foote," *New York Times Book Review* 27 April 1952, p. 16. Reprinted in *Conversations with Shelby Foote*, edited by William C. Carter, pp. 5–7. Jackson and London: University Press of Mississippi, 1989.

Carter, William C. "Seeking the Truth in Narrative: An Interview with Shelby Foote." *Georgia Review* 41 (Spring 1987): 144–72. Reprinted in *Conversations*, pp. 241–269.

Carr, John. "It's Worth a Grown Man's Time: Shelby Foote." *Kite-Flying and Other Irrational Acts: Conversations with Twelve Southern Writers*, edited by John Carr, pp. 3–33. Baton Rouge: Louisiana State University Press, 1972. Reprinted in *Conversations*, pp. 21–55.

Cavett, Dick. "Interview with Shelby Foote: Dick Cavett/1979." *Conversations*, pp. 137–50.

Covington, Jimmie. "Writer's Home Has Windows on Past, Present." Memphis *Commercial Appeal*, 21 August 1966, p. 5. Reprinted in *Conversations*, pp. 15–17.

Graham, John. "Talking with Shelby Foote: June 1970." Transcribed by George Garrett. *Mississippi Quarterly* 24 (Fall 1971): 405–427. Reprinted in *Conversations*, pp. 56–76.

Harrington, Evans. "Interview with Shelby Foote." *Mississippi Quarterly* 24 (Fall 1971), 349–77. Reprinted in *Conversations*, pp. 77–102.

Howard, Edwin. "Foote-Note on Faulkner." *Delta Review* 3 (July-Aug. 1965): 37, 80. Reprinted in *Conversations*, pp. 12–14.

Jones, John Griffin. "Shelby Foote." In *Mississippi Writers Talking*, Vol I., edited by John Jones, pp. 36–92. Jackson: University Press of Mississippi, 1982. Reprinted in *Conversations*, pp. 151–95.

Mottley, Bob. "Writer Critical of 'Tokenism' in South." *Roanoke World-News*, 18 April 1968, p. 56. Reprinted in *Conversations*, pp. 18–20.

Newcomb, James. "WKNO Presents a Conversation with Shelby Foote." Transcribed by William C. Carter. *Conversations*, pp. 112–30.

Phillips, Robert L., Jr. "Deep Delta." Transcripts of *A Climate for Genius: A Television Series*, pp. 17–33. Jackson: Mississippi Library Commission, 1976. (Foote appeared with Louis D. Rubin, Jr., Lewis P. Simpson, Thomas Daniel Young, Ellen Douglas, and Hodding Carter III.)

Richards, Robert. "Shelby Foote Hopes to Put Flesh and Blood of Memphis on Paper." Memphis *Press-Scimitar*, 22 March 1954, 2nd sec., p. 15. Reprinted in *Conversations*, pp. 8–11.

Rubin, Louis D., Jr. "Growing Up in the Deep South: A Conversation with Eudora Welty, Shelby Foote, and Louis D. Rubin, Jr." *The American South: Portrait of a Culture*, edited by Louis D. Rubin, Jr., pp. 59–85. Baton Rouge: Louisiana State University Press, 1980.

Sides, W. Hamkpton. "Shelby Foote." *Memphis* 10 (Jan. 1986): 38, 40–44, 49, 51–53. Reprinted in *Conversations,* pp. 230–40.

Thomas, William. "Appomattox for Shelby Foote," Memphis *Commercial Appeal/Mid-South Magazine,* 19 March 1978, pp. 22–25. Reprinted in *Conversations,* pp. 131–36.

———. "Shelby Foote's Love Affair with Civil War Began in '54." Memphis *Commercial Appeal,* 15 July 1973, sec. 2, p. 8. Reprinted in *Conversations,* pp. 103–11.

Tillinghast, Richard. "An Interview with Shelby Foote." *Ploughshares* 9 (2–3, 1983): 118–31. Reprinted in *Conversations,* pp. 218–29.

Vincent, Edwin. "Shelby Foote, Greenville Author, Says Writing Is His Hardest Job." Greenville, Miss. *Delta Democrat-Times,* 25 June 1950, pp. 1–2. Reprinted in *Conversations,* pp. 3–4.

White, Helen, and Redding Sugg. "A Colloquium with Shelby Foote." *Southern Humanities Review* 15 (Fall 1981): 281–99. Reprinted in *Conversations,* pp. 196–217.

Papers and Collections

The Shelby Foote Papers. Southern Historical Collection. University of North Carolina at Chapel Hill. John Inscoe, "Inventory." Sept. 1983.

Memphis State University Lectures. Audio tapes of the lectures Foote presented at Memphis State University, 1966–67, are housed in the Special Collections of the Memphis State Library.

The *Pica.* James E. Kibler, "Shelby Foote: A Bibliography," lists poems from the Pica, the high school newspaper that Foote edited during the 1934–35 school year. Microfilm of the *Pica* is in the Mitchell Memorial Library, Mississippi State University, and the Mississippi Department of Archives and History, Jackson, Miss.

Secondary

Bibliography and Biography

Bruccoli, Matthew J., and C. E. Frazer Clark, Jr., eds. *First Printing of American Authors, Contributing toward Descriptive Checklists.* Vol. II, pp. 165–66. Detroit: Gale Research, 1978.

Kibler, James E., Jr. "Shelby Foote." *Dictionary of Literary Biography.* Vol. II, pp. 148–54. Detroit: Gale Research, 1978.

———. "Shelby Foote: A Bibliography." *Mississippi Quarterly* 24 (Fall 1971): 437–65.

_____. *Shelby Foote: Novelist and Historian: An Exhibition of His Works at the McKissick Library, the University of South Carolina, 28 April–17 May 1970.* Pamphlet.

Phillips, Robert L., Jr. "Shelby Foote." In *Fifty Southern Writers after 1900: A Bio-Bibliographical Sourcebook*, edited by Joseph M. Flora and Robert Bain, pp. 188–95. New York, Westport, London: Greenwood Press, 1987.

Critical Studies

Carmignani, Paul. "Shelby Foote, Romancer du sud." Ph.D. dissertation, Université Paul Valery à Montpellier, 1983.

_____. "Derive à partir de *Pillar of Fire*." *Delta* 4 (1977): 135–58.

_____. "Jordan County: Going Back to the Roots." *Journal of the Short Story in English* 11 (Autumn 1988): 93–100.

_____. "L'ile et le tertre: Essai de topologie littéraire." *Revue Française Études Americaines* 36 (April 1988): 292–301.

Caldwell, Brenda Vaughn. "Character and Incident and the Exposure of Stereotype in the Works of Shelby Foote." Ph.D. dissertation, Bowling Green State University, 1986.

Carter, William C. "Introduction." *Conversations with Shelby Foote.* Jackson and London: University Press of Mississippi, 1989; pp. vii–xiii.

Cox, James M. "Shelby Foote's Civil War." *Southern Review*, n.s. 21 (Apr. 1985): 329–50. Reprinted in *Recovering Literature's Lost Ground: Essays in American Autobiography.* Baton Rouge and London: Louisiana State University Press, 1989; pp. 191–214.

Fleurdorge, Claude. "*A Marriage Portion* ou comment l'esprit vient aux filles." *Delta* 4 (Apr. 1977): 83–127.

Gale, Robert. "Shelby Foote Repeats Himself, a Review Article." *Journal of Mississippi History* 17 (Jan. 1955): 56–60.

Gallet, R. "Tragique et témoignage dans *Jordan County*." *Delta* 4 (April 1977): 45–53.

Garrett, George. "Foote's *The Civil War*: The Version for Posterity?" *Mississippi Quarterly* 28 (Winter 1974–75): 83–92.

Gresset, Michel. "L'Aval du texte: Propositions pour un commentaire du Tertre Sacre." *Delta* 4 (April 1977): 177–181.

Howell, Elmo. "The Greenville Writers and the Mississippi Country People." *Louisiana Studies* 86 (Winter 1969): 348–60.

Jaworski, Philippe. "Terre promise, terre conquise, terre vaine." *Delta* 4 (April 1977): 25–27.

Landess, Thomas H. "Southern History and Manhood: Major Themes in the Works of Shelby Foote." *Mississippi Quarterly* 24 (Fall 1971): 321–47.

Laroque, François. "*A Marriage Portion:* A la recherche d'un objet perdu, ou du recit comme bouche-trou." *Delta* 4 (April 1977): 129–134.

Phillips, Robert. *Shelby Foote.* Jackson: Mississippi Library Commission, 1977. (Pamphlet)

———. "Shelby Foote's Bristol in 'Child by Fever.'" *Southern Quarterly* 19 (Fall 1980): 172–83. Reprinted in *Order and Image in the American Small Town,* edited by Michael W. Fazio and Peggy Whitman Prenshaw, pp. 172–83. Jackson: University Press of Mississippi, 1981.

Richard, Claude. "Dux yeux au plat ou les jeux du recit et du discours dans *Rain Down Home.*" *Delta* 4 (April 1977): 55–70.

Rubin, Louis D., Jr. "Foreword: Asa Bart's Way." *Tournament.* Birmingham, Ala.: Summa Publications. 1987.

———. "Shelby Foote's Civil War." *Prospects* 1 (1974): 313–33.

Shepherd, Allen. "Technique and Theme in Shelby Foote's *Shiloh.*" *Notes on Mississippi Writers* 5 (Spring 1972): 3–10.

Skei, Hans. "History as Novel: Shelby Foote's *The Civil War: A Narrative.*" *Notes on Mississippi Writers* 13 (1981): 45–63.

Vauthier, Simone. "Fiction and Fictions in Shelby Foote's 'Rain Down Home.'" *Notes on Mississippi Writers* 8 (Fall 1975): 35–50.

———. "'Pillar of Fire': The Civil War of Narratives." *Delta* 4 (May 1977): 71–81.

———. "The Symmetrical Design: The Structural Patterns of *Love in a Dry Season.*" *Mississippi Quarterly* 24 (Fall 1971): 379–403.

Vitoux, Pierre. "*A Marriage Portion:* Etude du recit." *Delta* 4 (Apr. 1977): 71–82.

White, Helen. "Shelby Foote." In *Literature of Tennessee,* edited by Ray Willbanks, pp. 163–81. Macon, Ga.: Mercer University Press, 1984.

———, and Redding Sugg. *Shelby Foote.* Boston: Twayne Publishers, 1982.

———. "Shelby Foote's *Iliad.*" *Virginia Quarterly Review* 55 (Spring 1979): 234–50.

Williams, Wirt. "Shelby Foote's *Civil War:* The Novelist as Humanistic Historian." *Mississippi Quarterly* 24 (Fall 1971): 429–36.

Index